Essentials of Social Research

11. 2009

Essentials of Social Research

Linda Kalof, Amy Dan and Thomas Dietz

 Open University Press

Open University Press
McGraw-Hill Education
McGraw-Hill House
Shoppenhangers Road
Maidenhead, Berkshire
England SL6 2QL

email: enquiries@openup.co.uk
world wide web: www.openup.co.uk

and Two Penn Plaza, New York, NY 1012–2289
USA

First published 2008

A catalogue record of this book is available from the British Library

ISBN 13: 978-0-335-21782-3 (pb)   978-0-335-21783-0 (hb)
ISBN 10: 0-335-21782-6 (pb)   0-335-21783-4 (hb)

Library of Congress Cataloging-in-Publication Data
CIP data has been applied for

Cover Photograph by Linda Kalof

Typeset by BookEns Ltd, Royston, Herts.
Printed and bound in the UK by
Bell and Bain Ltd, Glasgow

The McGraw·Hill Companies

Contents

List of Figures, Tables and Boxes

Introduction

Essentials of Social Research is a short basic primer on social research methodology that will provide straightforward, clear answers to the key questions in research methods, such as: What are the components of scientific analysis? What is grounded theory? What constitutes a causal explanation? How believable are particular research findings? As an introductory primer, the book covers types of research, reasoning and data, basic logic of quantitative and qualitative inquiry, major data collection strategies, and identification of research limitations. *Essentials of Social Research* is different from other research primers in that it 1) offers ongoing exercises to illustrate the text material; 2) covers basic critical thinking skills; 3) emphasizes the complementary contributions of quantitative and qualitative methods; and 4) provides examples of research from the published literature that students can use to strengthen their methodological skills.

We use a common set of examples across all chapters. Some of the topics are used as examples in the text of the chapter, and those not covered in a particular chapter are included in an 'Applications' section at the end of each chapter. In this way, the examples will become 'old friends'. Here are the topics we consider throughout the book:

1 time use among adolescents;
2 the experiences of older adults with dementia (and their families and health care providers);
3 the death penalty as a deterrent to crime;
4 ecological modernization theory (the relationship between a country's affluence and its environmental impact);
5 gender differences in mathematics, science and language performance;
6 work and family balance issues/opportunity costs theory;
7 sexual and contraceptive behaviour and the threat of HIV/AIDS.

1 Foundations

Introduction

Most social science students are required to take at least one course in research methods. Why is such a course required in nearly every programme? It's because research methods are the tools we use to juxtapose theories with data. We hope theories offer insights into the world, but we have to check the theories against data to ensure that they really do describe the world. This is what is called the '**scientific method**' – we test assertions about the world with data, dismissing assertions that don't match the data, or modifying them so they are better descriptions. In this book we will cover the most important issues that emerge when we try to use data to develop and improve theory. The concepts, approaches and tools we discuss have emerged over more than a century of social science research. But there is still more to be done. The improvement of existing methods and the development of new approaches remains one of the most active areas of contemporary research.

As we move forward, you will learn the fundamentals of research methods. These ideas will help you understand and critically evaluate research in your field. You will find that the logic we develop is also helpful in evaluating claims made in everyday discussions about life, where we are always encountering assertions about how the world works and where evidence is offered that is supposed to support those assertions. The logic of research methods can help you become a better informed citizen and member of your community.

We think you will find research methods interesting for two reasons. First, it appeals to the part of all of us that enjoys solving puzzles and having 'aha' understandings. Methods are themselves a set of tools that help you think critically. They give us ways to solve the puzzles that occur in social research and get to those 'aha' insights. Second, methods can be applied to any set of research questions that interest you. While we use a number of examples throughout the book, the tools of methods can be applied to any problem in social research. We encourage you to apply the ideas we are developing to the questions that you are most curious about.

What is science?

The definitions of **science** in the *Oxford English Dictionary* occupy more than 60 lines. But we all have a commonsense understanding that science is *a way of learning about the world*, and that science is what scientists do. However, there is a tendency to think of science as an individual pursuit – something a person in a laboratory does alone or with a few colleagues or students. As social scientists we know that science is actually a social activity, undertaken not just by individuals but by communities of people interested in the same aspect of the world. These communities organize themselves into scientific disciplines, like physics (for those who are concerned with matter, energy, time and space), biology (for people interested in living things), and sociology (for people interested in people and societies). Disciplines then structure academic departments, degree programmes, professional societies and scientific journals. So, from a social science perspective, science is the activity of these communities.

The communities are held together by the conversations they have about how the world works. These conversations have rules. One of the strongest rules is that you have to share your understanding of the world with others, otherwise it's not science. This wasn't always true. The great scientist Isaac Newton was reluctant to share his results with anyone, apparently because he hated debating his work. But in modern science, secrecy is against the rules. If you want fellow scientists to believe and respect your work you have to share with them not just your conclusions but also enough information about how you came to those conclusions that they can follow your steps and see if they agree.[1]

In these discussions about the world, scientists propose theories. A theory is just an idea about how some part of the world works. They often take the form of causal statements: 'If this happens, then that will happen.' We will talk more about such statements later in the chapter. In the conversation of science, such theoretical statements are supposed to be judged by both their logic and by how well they describe what we observe in the world. If the theory makes sense and if it does a good job of explaining what is observed then the community of scientists will begin to believe the theory. But if the logic is found to be weak or is not a good fit to what is observed, the theory is modified or discarded. This kind of discussion, over years and decades, is the process of science.

If theories are just statements about what happens that are evaluated on their logic and their fit to the world, where do methods fit in? Methods are rules that the scientific community has agreed upon to figure out how well theories fit observations. The rules are very important to how science works. Scientists are like anyone else. They want to succeed, they have their favourite ideas and the ideas they don't like, they have friends and people with whom they are less than friendly. There is a politics to science just as there is to any other human activity. But science has strong, explicit rules about what should lead to an idea – a theory – being accepted or rejected. Personalities and politics can get in the way of this, and slow down or speed up the acceptance or rejection of a theory. But over time, the two rules – that theories must be logically consistent and that they must provide a good description of the world – tend to push out incorrect theories in favour of more correct theories. This is where methods become important – methods are the rules that help us judge how well a theory matches the data and thus help pick the better theories over the less useful ones.

---

[1]   Of course, since at least World War II, the military in most industrial nations funds a great deal of science, and they like to keep that science secret. Since 9/11 there have been arguments that research that might be used by terrorists should be kept secret as well. Secrecy in the name of national security violates a fundamental norm of science and the push for secrecy has produced ongoing debates both within the scientific community and between the community and the military and political systems. In addition, corporations like to keep research that they can use for profit secret as well. This too has led to conflicts, especially when private, for-profit corporations fund research at universities (see Krimsky, 2003, and McMillan *et al.*, 2006).

Science and social science

Many social scientists are a bit wary of being lumped together with scientists who study the physical and biological aspects of the world. Certainly there are important differences between doing sociology or political science and doing physics or molecular biology. But there are many similarities too. It will be helpful to examine both the differences and the similarities before we proceed further.

We can't (and shouldn't) change the world just to see what happens

Physical and biological scientists in many specialties can do experiments with the things they study. We don't object if a geologist breaks a rock to determine its strength or if a chemist dissolves a metal in acid to understand its properties. But social scientists study people, and that places two limits on our ability to do experiments. First, it is simply not practical to conduct many kinds of experiments. Second, even when we can conduct an experiment to see what happens, it may not be ethical to do so. Suppose we want to understand the effects of gender role socialization on ability in mathematics and science. We don't have power to have some children socialized into traditional gender roles and others into more gender-neutral roles to learn about the effects of gender socialization on mathematics and science ability. And even if we could, such an experiment would be beyond the pale of ethical practice. In the next chapter we will discuss research ethics in some detail. The important point now is that it can be hard to do social science research because much of what we want to understand we can't study via experiments where we make changes in the world.

Social scientists aren't alone in facing practical and ethical constraints on the kinds of experiments we can do. Astronomers and geologists can't change the things they study either. Like social scientists, they have to be very clever at collecting observations from the world as it is given to them. And biologists and medical scientists face many complex ethical issues in the use of humans and other animals in their research. So while people often divide the sciences into 'natural' and 'social' sciences, there are many ways in which that distinction doesn't make sense. There are lots of ways of dividing up the sciences, depending on what issues you are thinking about, and one way of making distinctions among the sciences is around the degree to which things can be changed just for the sake of doing research. In chemistry, physics and psychology, a lot of the scientific discussion is about experiments where we intentionally change the world to study it. In astronomy, geology, sociology and economics, experiments have a much smaller role in the discussion and most research is done by observing the world as it unfolds independent of the control of researchers.

So we could divide the sciences into experimental and non-experimental sciences and that division in many ways makes as much sense as a division into social and natural sciences.

Things change and are different in different contexts

A chemistry student can make a measurement and find out that an oxygen atom weighs about 16 times as much as a hydrogen atom.[2] Once the measurement is done, she is quite safe to assume that the ratio of the weight of oxygen to hydrogen was the same 5000 years ago, will be the same 5000 years in the future and will be the same if the measurement is done in London or in Kolkatta (Calcutta) or even in a different galaxy. Physical and biological scientists use 'invariance' principles in their discussion – they assume that many of the things they study don't change – are invariant – over time and across places.[3]

In contrast, differences over time and across groups are at the heart of what interests social scientists. We can't assume that the things that influenced the energy use of countries 250 years ago, when the industrial revolution was starting, will be the same things that matter today. We can't assume that gender role norms are the same in Germany as they are in Japan. In fact, these differences across societies and over time are among the most interesting subjects we study. But they do make our work harder. Once the oxygen/hydrogen ratio is measured, it becomes something that doesn't need much further work. In contrast, we must always re-measure as we look at social phenomena over time and across space.

We care about the situations we study

Most students of the social sciences, including us, were brought to the field by a mixture of curiosity and a concern with the state of the world. Most of us are motivated in part by curiosity – we want to be good scientists who help understand how the world works. Doing good science is awesome! But we also want to see our knowledge applied to make the world a better place. Social scientists are not alone in this. For instance, most chemists and biologists who work on environmental issues also have a strong interest in

---

[2]   Actually, the physicist would measure the masses of hydrogen and oxygen, and in this example we are ignoring the fact that there are isotopes of different weights.

[3]   It wasn't always so. Early geologists invoked Biblical floods as special explanations for such things as finding fossils of sea creatures on the top of mountains. One of the great advances in geology occurred when the community of geologists came to agree that geological theories had to assume that the processes going on thousands or millions of years ago are the same processes we see now. If we don't see global floods now then they shouldn't be invoked to explain things in the past.

protecting the environment. But the social science community is always wrestling with these issues in a way that we don't see as often in other sciences. Indeed, the community of social scientists called 'critical theorists' argues that good social science *must* examine not just how the world works but the problems with how it works. We don't disagree. We believe that the scientific approach we discuss in this book is one of the most effective ways to diagnose the problems of the world. Without accurate diagnosis, the chances of changes for the better are slim. So like the physical and biological scientists, we use the principles of science to guide us. But unlike many physical and biological scientists, the personal aspect of what we are studying is part of our discussion much of the time.

Science, theory and method

To explore the interplay between theory and methods in science, it will be helpful to have some examples. A few simple theories will give us something concrete to think about. Remember that these theories are proposed explanations; they aren't necessarily right. However, don't judge the worth of any of these theories by how we handle them here. Since we are just trying to make clear how methods are used to do research we tend to keep things a bit simpler (and we hope, clearer) than they would be in a debate about one of these theories in the social science literature.

Deterrence theory in criminology suggests that fear of being executed will prevent some people from committing homicide. If deterrence theory is right, we might expect that communities that have a death penalty should have lower homicide rates than communities where homicide is not punished with the death penalty.

Opportunity costs theory in demography suggests that people face a trade-off between having children on the one hand and pursuing education and a career on the other. If this is true, women with more education and/or who are pursuing careers will have fewer children than women with less education who are not pursuing careers.

Ecological modernization theory in sociology suggests that as countries become very affluent, their impact on the environment decreases. One of the largest environmental challenges of the twenty-first century is global climate change. The climate change we are worried about results largely from the emission of 'greenhouse gases' that cause more of the energy coming from the sun to stay in the atmosphere and less to be radiated into space. Carbon dioxide (CO_2) is probably the most important of these gases. It is created mostly by burning fossil fuels such as coal, gasoline and oil. So ecological modernization theory suggests that as countries become very affluent, they will generate smaller CO_2 emissions.

Role theory in sociology suggests that young boys and young girls quickly learn that there is a social expectation that boys should be good at mathematics and science and that girls should not. As a result, boys will feel good if they do well in those fields, but girls will hesitate to be perceived as 'geeks.'

Given the simplicity of these examples, it's easy to think of problems with them and ways to improve them. As we will see, methods and theory work together to help us develop more realistic statements about how the world works, and those statements tend to get a bit complicated because the world we are trying to describe is complicated. But as we start learning about methods, it is useful to have relatively simple examples even if they are a bit too simple to be realistic.

Do these theories pass the first criterion of good science? Do they make sense when we think carefully about them? For example, the deterrence theory example makes sense only if we assume that people think before committing homicide. If most homicides are the result of rage or impulse, then we might not expect to find much relationship between homicide rates and the death penalty. So we might elaborate the theory to indicate that it applies only to some kinds of homicide. The opportunity costs theory implies that women have some reasonable degree of control over both their fertility and the pursuit of education and careers. It makes sense when women have such control and opportunities for a career and education, but not in circumstances where women have few career or educational options or where they don't have the ability to control fertility. Again we could elaborate the theory to indicate the contexts where we think it applies and where we don't think it will work. Indeed, a sense of the scope of a theory – the contexts to which it should apply and the contexts not really covered – is an important element in the logic of any theory. But our purpose with these examples is to have some simple theories to help us think through the basic ideas of methods, not to reflect the subtlety of current social theory.

Many kinds of conversations judge the value of an argument based on its *logic and coherence* (in Chapter 6 we provide some standards for thinking critically not only about the claims of others but also our own reasoning). In everyday conversation, logic and coherence matter, and philosophers in particular rely on logic and coherence in trying to decide their debates. But as sociologist Jürgen Habermas (1984) points out, we also take account of the sincerity of a statement. And in many religions, while logic matters, there are people or texts whose authority is the final word on an issue.

In science, our additional criteria for the quality of an argument is *how well it describes the world*. In this way science differs from philosophy or religion, but is much like everyday experience. Thomas Huxley, the great defender of Darwin's theory of evolution and grandfather of novelist

Aldous Huxley once said: 'Science is organized common sense where many a beautiful theory was killed by an ugly fact'.[4] Most scientists are very creative, and we usually have more than one very eloquent and logical theory to describe the parts of the world that interest us. Gender differences in mathematics and science might be explained by genetic differences in ability, by teachers giving different encouragement to boys and girls, by general societal images that it is cool for a boy to be a 'geek' but unattractive for a girl to be a 'geek', or by a variety of other things. All of these are logically consistent, at least under a quick examination.

Let's consider arguments about gender and ability in science and mathematics in more detail. If we are working scientifically we would decide which explanations for gender differences are good and which are not so good by seeing how well each of these theories describe data we collect on gender and mathematics achievement. For example, we might expect, under role theory, that the difference in science and mathematics achievement between boys and girls would be strongest among boys and girls that have very stereotyped gender roles. If we measured gender stereotyping for a group of young boys and girls and sorted them into those who held very stereotyped views about gender and those that did not, role theory suggests that we should find more gender difference in mathematics and science scores among those holding stereotyped views than those holding more egalitarian views. We could compare this expectation with some data and see how well the theory matches the data. In the case of deterrence theory, we would expect, as a simple prediction, that communities with the death penalty would have lower homicide rates than communities without the death penalty.

An example: Deterrence theory

It is when we are working with theory and data together that methods come into play. Methods suggest things to watch out for when we make comparisons between theory and data. Suppose we looked up homicide rates for US states that have the death penalty and those that don't have the death penalty. If we examine the data for 2005, we would find the information given in Figure 1.1.

---

[4]   (http://www.worldofquotes.com/author/Thomas-Huxley/1/)

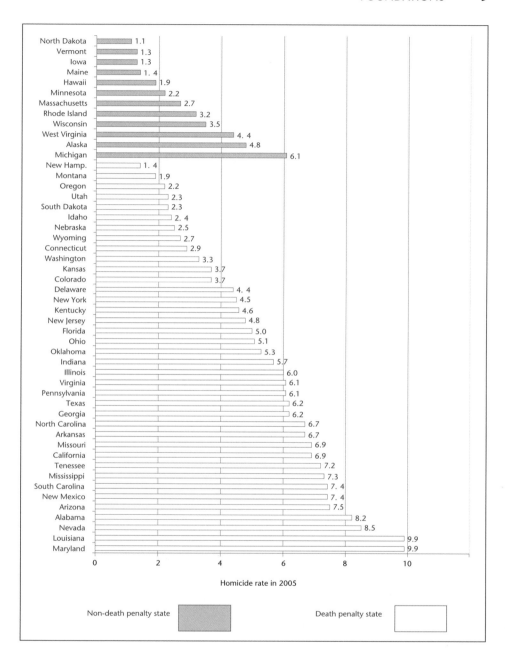

Figure 1.1   Homicide rates for US states with and without the death penalty, 2005

Source: Uniform Crime Reports (2006)

Box 1.1: How to read Figure 1.1

This kind of graph is called a bar graph because the bars show the value of the homicide rate for each state. The graph has a horizontal axis (often called the *x* axis) that indicates the homicide rate of each state. The name of the state is displayed on the vertical axis. The states without a death penalty are closest to the top followed by the states with a death penalty. Within each of these two groups, the states are in order from those with the lowest homicide rate (closest to the top) to those with higher homicide rates (closer to the bottom). To make the distinction between the death penalty and non-death penalty states, the bars are shaded differently. So to find the homicide rate of, say Vermont, you should skim down the list of states on the left hand side until you come to Vermont. Then look over to the right along the bar for Vermont's homicide rate until you reach the end. Then let your eye drop down to the scale at the bottom of the figure. You'll see that Vermont has a homicide rate just above 1 homicide per year per 100,000 people in the state. This is the per capita homicide rate. (In Latin, per capita means for each 'head.') It's the number of homicides in 2005 divided by the population of the state. It's important to use the per capita rate, not just the number of homicides because states differ greatly in their population. For example, states like California and Texas have populations more than 10 times the size of the population of Vermont, so we would expect them to have more homicides because of that alone. By dividing the number of homicides by the population and getting the per capita rate we can make comparisons that have factored out the difference in population size.

Graphs are very powerful ways of looking at data and can be of great help in making sense of them. But they have two important limits. First, they give up some of the accuracy that would be available if you had a table with the exact value of the homicide rate for each state. But since we could get such a table if we wanted it, this is a small cost. If we want exact values, we'd look at the table, if we want to see patterns we can look at the graph.

The second problem is that this kind of graph works well when there are a relatively small number of data points. If we had much more data to examine, the overall patterns could easily get lost in the complexity, and we would have to use other ways to look at them.

Just looking at the figure, it may be hard to know if the data are consistent with the theory. A lot of states with the death penalty are above the national average homicide rate, but so are two states (Michigan and Alaska) without the death penalty. A lot of states without the death penalty have low homicide rates, but so do some states with the death penalty. One way to think through this is to compare the average homicide rate for all states with the death penalty to the average for all states without it. Taking the average is one way to think about what is typical for a state with and without the death penalty. Table 1.1 does that.

Table 1.1 Average homicide rates for US states with and without the death penalty

	Average homicide rate	*Number of states*
States that have the death penalty	5.3	38
States that don't have the death penalty	2.8	12

Source: Uniform Crime Reports (2006)

Box 1.2: How to read Table 1.1

It can be hard to make sense of a graph like Figure 1.1 because there are so many individual data points. Even with 50 states it's a bit hard. You can imagine that if we were looking at data on a hundred or more countries or on hundreds or thousands of people, the bar graph won't be much help. We often use 'summary statistics' when we want to summarize data. The simplest of these, and the most commonly used, is the average. (In statistics it is called the arithmetic mean, but it's just what we call the average in everyday language.) Recall that you take the average of a group of numbers by adding them all up and dividing by how many you have. For Table 1.1, the homicide rates for the 38 states with death penalties are added together and divided by 38. Then the homicide rates for the 12 states without death penalties are added together and divided by 12. So the second column of the table (the first column with numbers in it) shows the average homicide rate for states with and without the death penalty. When showing data in tables, it's always a good idea to let the reader know how much data you used, so the second numeric column displays the number of states in each group. We can easily see that the average homicide rate is higher in the states with the death penalty than in those without the death penalty.

A caution: If you added up the homicide rates for all 50 states and divided by 50 you would get the average homicide for all states. But that would not be the average homicide rate for the US overall. Why not? Because if you take the average for the states, small states like Vermont with few people and few homicides count as much as big states like California and Texas that have lots of people and, unfortunately, lots of homicides. To calculate the homicide rate for the US we would add up all the homicides in the country

cont.

Box 1.2: How to read Table 1.1 cont.

and then divide by the population of the country. Instead we have taken the average homicide rate by adding up the homicide rates for the 12 states that don't have the death penalty then dividing by 12, and by adding up the homicide rates for the 38 states that have the death penalty and dividing by 38. We have not taken into account that some of these states have very large populations and some have very small populations. We would get different numbers if, for each of the two groups of states, we added up the number of homicides and divided by the total population of that group of states. Here we are trying to compare states, not find the homicide rate for the country as a whole. So we give each state an equal weight rather than weighting by the size of its population. This is because each state is a sort of an 'experiment' in the effects of the death penalty. In the language of research methods we would call the state the 'unit of analysis.' We will discuss units of analysis in more detail later.

The table tells us that the average across the 38 states with the death penalty was 5.3 homicides per 100,000 population. For the 12 states that didn't have the death penalty the average was 2.8 homicides per 100,000 population. Obviously, this table doesn't support deterrence theory. States with the death penalty have higher average homicide rates than states without the death penalty.

But advocates of deterrence theory would be quick to point out that there is more going on here. These states may differ in their homicide rates due to reasons other than the death penalty. One of the most important rules of research methods is to consider things that may influence the results other than the variable suggested by the theory. For example, the states with the death penalty may have more social inequality than those without the death penalty, and social inequality may promote homicide. So unless we take account of social inequality as a possible explanation of homicide rates, we cannot draw the conclusion that deterrence theory is wrong.

Criminology and other sciences proceed by discussions just like this. Someone offers a theory. Then evidence is offered that may seem consistent with the theory or may seem inconsistent with the theory. The quality of the evidence and the conclusions are discussed at professional meetings, in published papers, in classes and informally. The theory might be modified and further evidence offered. The discussion goes on with the theory changing until it is seen as being a good description of the world or until it is discarded. In our example, we might try to take account of factors that influence the homicide rate other than the death penalty by trying to compare states that are similar in many ways but differ in whether or not they have the death penalty. As we will see, in the social sciences this approach (called matching) isn't always a good way to deal with the problem of taking account of other factors, although it sometimes works well in other fields. But it's still interesting to do such a comparison. One simple way to do this is to compare neighbouring states. Figure 1.2 compares the homicide rate in four pairs of neighbouring states where one has the death penalty and the other does not. In every case the death penalty states have higher homicide rates, which is not consistent with deterrence theory.

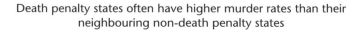

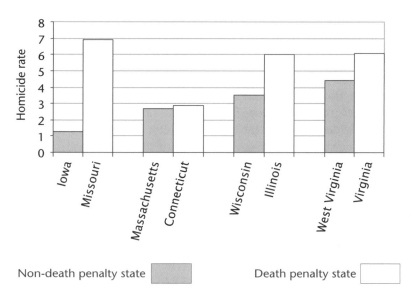

Figure 1.2 Comparison of homicide rate and death penalty in neighbouring states

Source: Uniform Crime Reports (2006)

Box 1.3: How to read Figure 1.2

This is another bar chart. But this time the homicide rate is on the vertical axis, rather than on the horizontal axis as it was in Figure 1.1. There is no strong reason to do it one way or the other, though some have argued that it is better to have the bars run across the page rather than up and down. Why? Because in English and other European languages we read from left to

cont.

Box 1.3: How to read Figure 1.2 cont.

right so our eyes are trained to look that way. In other cultures there might be a slight preference for doing it differently but as far as we know, no one has experimented with whether or not different cultural traditions of reading influence how easily people see graphs.

The states are all those in the US that meet two criteria. They share a border and one has the death penalty and the other doesn't. The state without the death penalty comes first, then the state with the death penalty. The height of the bar indicates the homicide rate, so the homicide rate for Iowa is a little more than one, and for Missouri it's just under seven. In every pair the non-death penalty state has a lower homicide rate than the death penalty state.

Again, the discussion wouldn't end here. Those who think deterrence theory is a good explanation would offer criticisms of this analysis. For example, even though the pairs of states are adjacent, they still differ in many ways that may influence the homicide rate and hide the relationship between homicide rate and the death penalty. Some states with the death penalty don't actually have many executions and the death penalty in the absence of executions may not be a deterrent. Many of the homicides in the data might be crimes of passion and rage not influenced by the deterrence effect of the death penalty. And so on. Science proceeds by this kind of discussion and continues until the evidence is pretty clear that a theory works, or that it doesn't, or in most cases, until the theory has been modified so that we have a good description of the world. Science differs from philosophy, theology, and many other fields because the arguments for and against a theory have to be based not only on whether or not they make sense logically but also on how well the theory fits the data.

Methods are the tools we use to help *juxtapose theory and data*. As we move through the book, we will learn about the questions we should always ask about a data analysis, about ways of collecting data and organizing information so we can see patterns clearly, and about ways to consider factors other than the ones emphasized by the theory under scrutiny.

Science and statistics

In the example above, we used numbers – the homicide rate. When we use numbers in science, we call it **quantification**. We call research that uses numbers **quantitative research**. Research that doesn't use numbers is

qualitative research. **Statistics** is the set of methods we use to make sense of the numbers we use in research.

Many social science students are apprehensive about dealing with numbers and having to learn statistics. Don't worry – this is not a statistics book. But because statistics are an important set of methods, we will often use numbers when talking about quantitative research. However, we think you will find the examples easy to follow. They rest entirely on ordinary logic rather than special statistical techniques.

Unfortunately, sometimes those who like to use numbers in their research, and those who feel that the only useful number is a telephone number, don't agree that both approaches are valuable. Some researchers have extreme positions, either arguing that 'if you can't quantify it you don't know what you're talking about' (a statement attributed to the physicist William Thomson, Lord Kelvin)[5] or that numbers can never adequately describe the social word. As is often the case, such extreme positions are not very logical and often reflect a misunderstanding of what others are actually doing. The use of numbers in social science can be very flexible and creative or it can be rather foolish. Research that doesn't use numbers can be rigorous and lead to general statements about how the world works, or it too can be rather foolish. The point of methods is to help researchers do good work, whether quantitative or qualitative. Almost any research problem can be addressed with either qualitative or quantitative methods. In fact, we usually feel a theory is strongest when both qualitative and quantitative research supports it. So we hope you will join us in avoiding stereotypes of any approach to research, and learn to think critically about all forms of inquiry.

Inductive and deductive reasoning

Up to this point we've talked about using data to see how well a theory describes the world and also about how the confrontation of theory with

---

[5]   The actual quote is: 'I often say that when you can measure what you are speaking about and express it in numbers you know something about it; but when you cannot measure it, when you cannot express it in numbers, your knowledge is of a meagre and unsatisfactory kind' (Thomson, 1891). Thomson's fame came from his work in thermodynamics and his many inventions. However, he considered his most important work to be his estimates of the age of the earth. Over the course of his career, these ranged from 400 million years old (the high end of his first estimate) to 24 million years old (his final estimate). We now know that the earth is about 4,550 million years old. We mention this not to make fun of an eminent scientist, but to emphasize that in science, prestige is less important than an accurate description of the world. Lord Kelvin's prestige while he was alive meant that people gave a lot of credibility to his estimate of the age of the earth, but over time the evidence was strong enough to convince everyone that he was wrong.

data leads to modification of a theory. But where do theories come from? Sometimes they come from our imagination, but sometimes they come from data. We can think of the research process as flowing in two directions, depending on how the **empirical** data and theory are linked. This is illustrated in Figure 1.3.

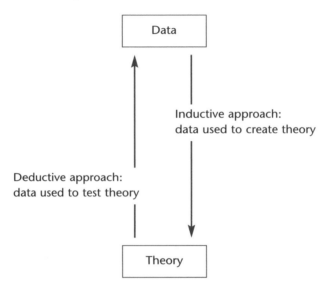

Figure 1.3 Inductive and deductive approaches to research

A **deductive** approach to research begins with a theoretical statement about how the world works. So far we have focused on this approach to research. The researcher then *tests the theory* in the form of a hypothesis. A **hypothesis** is a statement of what we expect to observe if the theory is true. We use the fancy term hypothesis because we want to emphasize that we don't know that the theory is true.[6] A hypothesis indicates what should occur if a particular condition exists. You can think of a hypothesis as an 'if, then' statement: if this happens, then that will take place. If a state has the

---

6   Unfortunately, in everyday language, the term theory can be rather confusing. Two of the best established understandings we have of the world, relativity theory and evolutionary theory, are described by the term theory. Yet to some the use of the term theory implies that we are not sure if they are right. In a sense we are never sure that any theory is completely correct. We are always open to new evidence. But usually well-established theories are not shown wrong but are replaced by a much more general way of describing the world. We expect the progress of science will lead to modifications. Newton's theory of gravity wasn't really proven 'wrong' by Einstein, rather Einstein showed that Newton's theory had some limits that the theory of relativity didn't. For the things Newton was trying to explain (the trajectory of a canon ball, the orbits of the planets) the difference between the Newtonian theory and the relativity theory are very minor, smaller than the limits of what could be measured in Newton's time.

death penalty, homicides will be lower than would otherwise be the case, according to deterrence theory. The theory and specific hypotheses suggest what information we should gather. Once data are collected and analysed, we can determine whether the hypotheses are supported or refuted – whether the data match the prediction. This approach is called deduction because hypotheses are deduced from theories – they are what the theory implies. This process is commonly thought of as moving from the general (theory) to the particular (data). Thus we deduce the pattern we expect to see in the data from the theory because the theory tells us what the data should look like. Of course the data may or may not match the predictions that come from the theory.

Suppose for a class project you are assigned to investigate predictors of life satisfaction. You begin with the general theoretical proposition that stress reduces well-being, including satisfaction with life. Previous research has established a strong link between traumatic events, such as the death of a loved one or experiencing a natural disaster, and lower personal well-being. You decide to see if more daily stressful events also have negative effects. You therefore make the following hypothesis: working many hours each week (let's say more than fifty hours) and having primary responsibility in the household for chores and childrearing, which together may increase levels of stress, reduce life satisfaction. Here is another way of stating this hypothesis: *if* an individual spends an extensive number of hours each week working, caring for children, and doing household tasks, *then* his or her satisfaction with life will be reduced. To test this hypothesis, you gather data from working-age individuals on how many hours each week they devote to work for which they are paid, to household responsibilities, and to care for children. You also measure their life satisfaction. You find that people who work for pay for more than fifty hours a week are less satisfied with their lives than those who work fewer hours, but that the number of hours spent on household tasks and caring for children do not affect life satisfaction. You conclude that your hypothesis is only partially supported. This is an example of deductive research. In the homicide example, we examined the hypothesis that if a state has the death penalty, it will have a lower homicide rate than if it does not, and found that, as far as we got in the analysis, the data aren't consistent with the hypothesis.

In other instances, researchers start with empirical data and develop larger generalizations and theoretical insights from the data. This is an **inductive** approach. There may be no established theory on which to draw and the research is trying to *develop theory*. This is sometimes called **exploratory research**, in contrast to deductive research, which is sometimes called **confirmatory** (because we are trying to *confirm* a theory). Some scientists conduct inductive research because they think preconceived ideas should not be imposed on data since they can limit and bias interpretations of the data. Instead, the theory is created from the data. The researcher analyzes empirical information and in the process identifies theoretical propositions. In contrast to deduction, induction proceeds from the particular (data) and moves toward the general (theory).

To illustrate an inductive approach to research, we can draw on the work of Hinton and Levkoff (1999). They were interested in how family caregivers of Alzheimer's patients create understandings of the nature and meaning of Alzheimer's disease and how perspectives vary by ethnicity. The research team conducted face-to-face, in-depth interviews with African-American, Irish-American, Chinese-American, and Latino-American caregivers. After transcribing the interviews, major themes, patterns and experiences were identified, from which they derived theoretical insights. Three different types of illness narratives were identified from the data: 1) some caregivers focused on how the disease was eroding the identity of their loved ones; 2) others emphasized how their families were managing the illness symptoms, which were viewed as natural processes of ageing; and 3) some described the disease within the context of loneliness, major losses and family responsibilities. Caregivers drew on both biomedical perspectives and their own cultural beliefs about ageing and families, which lead to differing narratives. This research used inductive reasoning – the interviewers collected data about the meaning of Alzheimer's among caregivers and from this information formed a theoretical framework about how individuals of different ethnic backgrounds craft an understanding of the disease.

While at any one moment we may be doing inductive or deductive research, the overall process of doing science always involves both. When we find that in a deductive analysis the theory doesn't match the data, we would modify the theory to see if we can get a better description of the world than we had at the start. This might involve looking at the data to see what patterns are there. So we start deductively, and having rejected the hypothesis suggested by the theory, we move to an inductive mode, trying to develop a theory that does fit the data. Or we might start with an inductive approach, and from the patterns we see form a theory – a generalization of what we saw in the data. Then we could develop hypotheses from the theory and test them. Of course, if we developed a theory based on the patterns in the data, we'd want to check the theory against other data – we would expect that the theory would match the data that was used to develop it!

Philosophy of science: Positivist and constructionist inquiry

It is common in discussions of social science methods to contrast positivist and constructionist approaches to social inquiry. Unfortunately these two terms, while commonly used, are a bit problematic. Both have their origins in philosophy of science but the discussions of philosophy of the social sciences have moved beyond this simple juxtaposition of these seemingly opposed views. And in addition, we think that neither position accurately describes social science (or physical or biological science) as actually practised.

Before we discuss these two approaches, it is important to distinguish two philosophical concepts: ontology and epistemology.[7] Here we keep these definitions simple, but we believe we convey what you need to know to understand the ideas that swirl around the discussion of constructionism and positivism. Ontology is the theory of what exists. There are two basic distinctions in ontology. One argues that there is a real world, independent of our observation and interpretation of it. This is called, not surprisingly, **realism**. The opposite view, often called **phenomenology**, suggests that it is not meaningful to speak of a 'real' world; our interpretations of it are all that matter. **Epistemology**, in contrast, is the theory of what we can know. Here too we can think of two polar positions. At one pole is the belief that we can conduct objective, unbiased observations and through them come to understand the world accurately. At the other pole is the view that all observations of the world are our own social constructions rather than images of an objective, external world. Needless to say, the view that we can understand the world objectively aligns with the realist notion that there is a world independent of our observations of it, while the view that all we can know is our social constructions aligns well with the phenomenological approach to ontology.

Positivism draws on ontological and epistemological realism.[8] In most social science discussions, this term refers to the view that there is an objective world independent of our observations and that science can lead us to an understanding of the world that is free of social, political and cultural influences. This view is contrasted with **constructionism**, which,

---

7   Our treatment is indebted to Eugene Rosa (1998) who provides a clear discussion of these issues.

8   In the social sciences, the term positivism is a shorthand for 'logical empiricism' or 'logical positivism' or 'neo-positivism', an approach to science mostly associated with a group of scholars commonly called the Vienna circle because they worked in Vienna in from 1924 to 1936. A useful overview of the Vienna circle can be found in Thomas Uebel (2006) Vienna Circle. The Stanford Encyclopedia of Philosophy. http://plato.stanford.edu/entries/vienna-circle/ (accessed 10 January 2008).

drawing on phenomenological or constructionist perspectives in ontology and epistemology, emphasizes the social construction of knowledge about the world. In this view, the best approach to understanding the world is to examine how people see and define it. In the social sciences constructionism has its most influential statement in Berger and Luckman (1966) but draws on a deep tradition of German and French social science and philosophy.

It is very common to view positivism and constructionism as opposite and antagonistic approaches to the social sciences. But by decoupling the ideas of ontology and epistemology, we can see that these extremes may not be the most fruitful way to think about the social sciences. In particular, one can be an ontological realist, believing that there is an external reality that exists independent of our perceptions of it, while embracing elements of a constructionist epistemology. That is, we can believe that there is a reality 'out there' but realize that our observations and interpretations are shaped by psychological biases and quirks, cultural lenses, power relations and a variety of other forces that comprise the social construction of reality.[9] If we are ontological realists but embrace the insights of constructionism we have to be very cautious, reflective and self-critical about how we do research, which is exactly what we are doing when we think about and improve our research methods.

How well we can apprehend a presumed reality will vary depending on what we study. Some things are easier to get at, more 'ostensible' than others. Many of the things of interest to the physical and biological scientists are the same wherever they are observed and are at least a few steps removed from political controversy that may shape our perceptions. This makes them more ostensible and easier to study using a 'positivist' sort of approach. Within the social sciences, the things we study will vary in the degree to which they are stable over time and space and across groups and the degree to which psychological biases, cultural lenses and political interests shape our observation and interpretation of them. So for some sorts of research problems, methods that assume there is a reality and that it is, with care, observable, are quite appropriate. But when we turn to people's understandings of their world and their place in it, and the dynamics by which those understandings are contested, supported and changed, we are in a domain where the things being studied, while very important, also can be turbulent and our observations subject to many influences. Then a constructionist view of epistemology seems more appropriate. And of course anything we wish to study in the social sciences is multifaceted and can benefit from approaches at various places along the

---

9   This approach has many versions and many names. Among those advocating an approach like this are Bhaskar (1975/97), Hayles (1995), Rosa (1998), and Shrader-Frechette (1991).

line running from the two extremes (we are tempted to say stereotypes) of strict positivism and strict constructionism.

In the social sciences, the constructionist approach is closely aligned with qualitative methods while a realist ontology and epistemology are more closely aligned with quantitative methods. So as we discuss these two basic methodological approaches, you will see how realist and constructionist orientations play out in shaping research practices.

Science and values

One of the oldest and most contentious debates in the social sciences is around whether or not science can be '**value-free**'. As with the debate about ontology and epistemology, we have to disentangle the terms commonly used in these discussions to understand the issues. In this case, we have to think about where values impinge on the process of doing science. We must do this to determine the degree to which science can or should evolve independently of the values of those who practise science and those who have power over scientists as workers (e.g. administrators, funders, politicians).

Few would disagree that values are important when scientists choose an area of research or topic for research. This choice always reflects a sense of what kind of topics the researcher sees as interesting and what kind of day to day research work seems exciting and satisfying. Often the choice of a field or topic reflects a view of what will be seen as important by the institutions of the field of research – the editors of journals, the committees that make decisions about hiring and promotion. At a somewhat larger scale, public and private investments of funds have a substantial influence on what kinds of research do and do not get done; funding agencies, including governments, typically set priorities for areas of research they think are important to be studied at particular times.[10]

In the social sciences, most of us have chosen fields and individual research topics because we care very deeply about the issues we study, such as inequality, injustice, environmental degradation, and the plight of other species. So our social values are very much engaged in the direction our research takes. A mentor to one of us, for instance, has said that most gerontologists are either afraid of ageing or had very positive experiences with older adults when they were young. These experiences or fears may help drive gerontologists' research. Of course, this example is simplistic since there are likely to be multiple different factors influencing a scholar's interest in ageing and other social science topics, but it does illustrate how personal interests influence what is studied.

---

10 Greenberg (2001, 2007) has written excellent accounts of how US science has been shaped by politics and the interests of the powerful.

There are many ways this ethical commitment around the issues we are studying can shape our research. One approach is **value-engaged** research in which the choice of the research problem is driven primarily by the needs of those whose interests the researcher hopes to support. One sophisticated view of this has been called 'the analytic deliberative process' (Stern and Fineberg, 1996). In such a process, researchers regularly engage with the public to define the research questions, shape methodology and evaluate results. This helps 'get the science right' by drawing on the insights and experiences of people 'on the ground,' while also helping to 'get the right science' by making sure that the questions asked in research and the way they are answered make sense in terms of the experiences of the people who will be interested in and affected by the results of the research.

An even more engaged position is **advocacy research** in which the researcher carries out studies specifically to lend support to a group they support and/or that is paying the researcher. Sometimes such research is carried out at the behest of social movements or communities. Sometimes it is in the form of expert testimony in support of one side of a legal dispute or another. Sometimes it takes the form of employment by a group advocating a particular position. In the political processes of most nations, those with political and economic power can easily hire scientific expertise as advocates for their positions, while those less powerful have far fewer scientific resources at their disposal. This can influence the way in which problems are defined and what views are considered legitimate and not legitimate in a policy debate. For example, one of us has conducted a study showing that those with the greatest ability to hire scientific expertise are most likely to define environmental policy conflicts as debates about facts, while those with fewer scientific resources are more likely to define the conflict in terms of who wins and who loses (Dietz *et al.*, 1989). In the US there have been serious concerns about the ways in which political power has been deployed to influence scientific conclusions about environmental issues, such as climate change (Mooney, 2007).

Critical theory, originating at the University of Frankfurt, is an example of a perspective that incorporates the role of personal values into its research (Geuss, 1971; McCarthy and Hoy, 1994; Wiggershaus, 1994). Critical theorists believe the goal of research is to expose social injustices, power differentials and other pathologies of society and work to change them. Their research tends to focus on the individuals and groups in a given society who are oppressed and bring their situations to light in the hopes of improving them. In a sense, it is rather like a diagnosis in medicine, where science is used to understand what is wrong and why it is happening so that one can find remedies.

It is very important to remember that our values can enter into scientific practice in ways that are more troubling and in ways that may not be obvious. Stephen Jay Gould (1981/1996) has carefully documented the history of research on human intelligence (we touch on Gould's work and the issue of researcher bias again in Chapter 6). Gould has shown that over centuries, researchers introduced into their measurements errors that reflected their gender, racial and class biases. Somehow, most white male researchers of Northern European descent, whatever methods they used, showed that Northern European white males were the most intelligent of all human groups considered! In some cases these errors were more or less fraud, or at least the biases are quite obvious. But in other cases the methods used seemed, at first examination, to be 'objective' in the sense that they did not seem to presume the conclusion. And in some cases the researchers were trying to be extremely meticulous in their methods, but biases emerged nonetheless. The lesson we take from this is that even though a method seems objective, it is always wise to be critical of how subtle biases may be introduced that skew the results to favour the interests of those who dominate the research process, either individual researchers or powerful groups in society. In the latter half of the twentieth century, feminist research developed, in part, in response to the general bias in science toward focusing on the experiences of white males. As an illustration, Calasanti (1996) pointed out that research on retirement was largely based on the experiences of white males. The 'retirement model' used for years was predicated on the assumption that retirement is a discrete event in which an individual works for a number of decades and then enters a non-work stage of life. Calasanti recognized that this model ignores the experiences of many women and non-white men, who often move in and out of the labour force and in and out of retirement. This bias extended beyond the social sciences – for years, the majority of medical research studied only samples of men.

Gould reminds us that 'science, since people must do it, is a socially-embedded activity' (1996, 53). Because science is a social process, it is not free from the cultural presumptions and power differentials in the larger society, nor is it free from the preconceived notions and biases of individual researchers. But at the same time discussion among multiple researchers working on the same issues, and especially making different assumptions and using different methods, can help us hone our understanding in ways that are not possible with a single approach by a single researcher. For example, the US National Research Council frequently convenes panels of scientists to assess the state of knowledge in areas important to public policy. One of the first discussions for such a panel is on 'bias'. The admonition is not to claim one doesn't have biases, but to be explicit about what one's biases are so everyone else on the panel is aware of them. The overall approach therefore is to acknowledge that every scientist has biases, so that a successful panel will include researchers representing all the important biases active in a field of research. That way the social process of discussing the state of knowledge in a field can take into consideration those biases.

Social scientists do not always deal with personal interests or biases in research in the same way. As we've said, some biases are so subtle that the scholars themselves do not recognize them as such. Some researchers believe it is important to be continually self reflective during all phases of the research process to identify ways their own views and prior experiences may be impacting what they are studying. For instance, if a researcher thinks that gender differences in children's mathematics and science skills result from socialization processes occurring in families and school, when he carries out a study where he observes children in classrooms he may focus more on those student–teacher interactions that suggest gender-stereotyped socialization, rather than on the full range of interactions. By being self-reflective, the researcher would recognize that the range of interactions isn't being documented and then would work to overcome that bias, resulting in a more honest and accurate representation of the interactions. In other instances, it is not really possible to 'overcome' personal biases, but rather researchers can only acknowledge the biases. For example, a black professional woman studying the impact of racism on promotions in the corporate world may have a different vantage point on the issue than a white professional man studying the same topic. This is not to say that both researchers would not be equally able to carry out a quality study on the topic but they may approach the topic very differently because of their differing positions in the social structure. And finally, there are some researchers who do not really emphasize the possible role of their own interests or biases in the research process, but rather believe that if a research study is designed rigorously using the scientific principles we outline in this book, personal biases are minimized. None of these positions regarding values is more correct than the others, but it is undoubtedly important to think about the role of values in all research.

Integrating the pieces

One of the most important ideas you can learn from this book is that there is a unity to research that spans methods and theory, induction and deduction and qualitative and quantitative research. Let's consider the example we've developed in the text using quantitative data.

In examining the death penalty and homicide rates, we found that our simple analysis was not consistent with the theory in that death penalty states seemed to have higher rather than lower homicide rates than non-death penalty states. This was a deductive, quantitative analysis. But it suggests both inductive and qualitative research might clarify what is going on. An inductive approach might indicate that we need other explanations for the death penalty that substitute for or complement deterrence theory. Since the death penalty states are consistently higher in homicide rates, two ideas come to mind. One is the culture of violence theory. Something in the history and current culture of some states leads to a greater occurrence of violence. This in turn might lead to a higher homicide rate and a feeling that it's appropriate for the government to use violence as a crime deterrent. Or it might be that some states, for reasons related to a culture of violence or other historical reasons, simply have higher homicide rates. That in turn leads them to take stronger measures to reduce homicide rates than other states, including invoking the death penalty. If the first idea is true, we can deduce that if we could find measures of the acceptability of violence in a state's culture, we might explain the homicide rate and perhaps identify which states have and don't have the death penalty. In fact Straus and his collaborators have elaborated such a theory and developed measures of the culture of violence (Baron and Straus, 1988). If the second idea is true, we might deduce that high homicide rate states will take many steps to reduce homicide, not just impose the death penalty. So we might look at police budgets, programmes to prevent recidivism among violent felons, and other measures of government effort. Alternatively, we might look at changes in homicide rates over time as states adopt or drop the death penalty.

Our example was quantitative but we can imagine ways of doing excellent qualitative work on deterrence theory. For example, we might interview violent felons to see what kinds of things they thought about before committing a violent crime. Are they aware of the penalties they may face? Do they think about the chances of getting caught and convicted? Of course there will be some difficulty in being sure we are getting accurate responses in these interviews. But again, no approach to research is perfect and if well designed, multiple approaches can complement each other. We could also examine the histories of the states and the arguments involved in invoking the death penalty to see what motivated its use.

We have used the traditional distinction between qualitative and quantitative approaches to research to organize the book. Most researchers tend to do most of their work preferring one of these orientations over the other. But we strongly believe the best way to study the social world is by triangulation. **Triangulation** is taking multiple approaches to study a particular topic. We can triangulate by using multiple strategies for collecting data, by using multiple sources of data (e.g. if studying gender differences in children's mathematics skills, different sources of information could be students, teachers and parents), by using different approaches to analysing data, or by considering a topic from a variety of theoretical orientations. So while we can learn a lot about how the death penalty may impact crime rates from state level data on homicide rates, we can gain a much better understanding of the issue by taking into account the other approaches we've just described. When we draw on only one theory, one source of data, or one technique for collecting data to understand something, our perspective is limited.

As you become introduced to research methods in this book, it may be helpful to think of the metaphor of a researcher as a bricoleur.[11] A **bricoleur** is a 'Jack of all trades or a kind of do-it-yourself person' (Lévi-Strauss, 1966: 17). While often discussed in the context of doing qualitative research, all students of the social sciences should think of themselves as bricoleurs. A bricoleur uses whatever strategies and methods are best suited to a particular situation. Some of us who like numbers will be more inclined towards using quantitative approaches to research, while those of us who don't like numbers but prefer stories and narratives will be drawn to the qualitative orientation. Some will like the idea of using surveys to collect data and others will prefer to do an experiment. Which methods of research and which scientific tools to use should not be set in advance but should depend on the issue of interest. A bricoleur is not rigid in their thinking about science. We hope you will keep an open mind to the various strategies we introduce in this book for thinking about social science topics, collecting data and analysing data. Remember that there is no single 'right' way to do research, just many different strategies.

Applications

We will use a common set of examples across all chapters. Some of the examples will be worked out within the text of the chapter. The examples not considered in the text will be included in an 'Applications' section at the end of the chapter. In this way, the examples will become 'old friends'. Understanding how an analysis makes sense of patterns in the data in one chapter will aid in understanding a different way of analysing the data in another chapter. Here is a brief introduction to the topics we will consider throughout the book. Many of these topics have been designed to be quite broad so they can be applied in several different ways throughout the book.

---

[11]   The French term *bricoleur* was introduced by Lévi-Strauss in 1966 as a metaphor for the social sciences.

1   Time use among adolescents

Adolescents vary in how they allocate their time. They divide their time among education, paid work, housework, leisure and sometimes childcare. Young people's patterns of time use are regulated by social norms and social constraints (e.g. some countries have laws about young people's education and employment), as well as by their families. How teenagers spend their time may relate to their future experiences and life course trajectories, including criminal activities, post-high school education, career pathways and decisions, and marriage and childbearing patterns.

2   The experiences of older adults with dementia (and their families and health care providers)

A significant number of older adults (especially those aged 85 and older) experience memory problems and cognitive impairment. Common symptoms of Alzheimer's disease and dementia include memory loss, disorientation, difficulty performing everyday tasks, problems with language and abstract thinking, and changes in mood and personality. These symptoms can be very frustrating to individuals and can affect their everyday functioning. At late stages of the disease, individuals experience major personality changes, need extensive assistance with daily activities, and may even be unresponsive to their environment.

Alzheimer's disease/dementia also significantly affects spouses, children and other loved ones. Family members must adapt to their loved ones' memory loss and consequent behavioural changes and increasing care needs. As the disease progresses, family members may have to take on the role of caregiver and make decisions about care. The unique needs of dementia patients also require special care by health care professionals.

While there are many interesting medical, psychological and social issues related to dementia, studying people with severe cognitive limitations presents some challenges. For instance, at what point is a person with cognitive limitations no longer able to consent to participate in research? How can a researcher achieve an accurate understanding of the experiences of those with dementia if they cannot directly obtain information from patients, particularly in late stages of the disease?

3   The death penalty as a deterrent to crime

Historically, the death penalty has been used to punish offenders who commit heinous criminal behaviours. The United States is the only Western industrialized democracy that permits capital punishment. Capital punishment has generated a heated debate over its practicality, use as a deterrent to criminal behaviour, and morality.

Many Americans support the use of the death penalty because they think it serves as a deterrent to crime and provides retributive justice. Those who are not in favour of the death penalty argue that it does not have a deterrent effect, it is immoral and inhumane, there is a possibility that an innocent person could be executed, and inequalities in the justice system may affect death penalty sentencing and outcomes. Research has not consistently found a relationship between the death penalty and crime rates (e.g. homicide). One proposed explanation for the death penalty not having a deterrent effect is that most killings are not rationally planned and carried out.

4   Ecological modernization theory

The environmental impacts of a nation or a household are partially a result of the amount of consumption that takes place, as well as of the technologies used to support that consumption. Generally speaking, as people or countries become more affluent, they emit more effluent. However, theorists in sociology, economics and political science have suggested that this process reaches a point where further affluence leads to reductions, rather than increases, in environmental impact. The sociological version of this theory is called 'ecological modernization'. The idea behind the theory is that as societies become sufficiently well off, they increasingly take account of the environment, and shift consumption patterns and especially laws that govern the use of the environment and the technologies used to produce what we consume to limit adverse effects on the environment.

5   Gender differences in mathematics, science and language performance

In many countries, differences have been found between male and female school-age children in mathematics, science and language performance. Researchers have wondered whether females and males generally differ in their aptitude for particular subjects or whether something else is leading to varying academic outcomes. Several factors hypothesized to affect academic performance in these subjects have been investigated, including self-esteem, intrinsic motivation to perform, learning styles and gender stereotypes. Cross-cultural research has documented some differences in the strength of relationship between gender and mathematics, science and language outcomes, suggesting the important influence of gender socialization practices in societies. This is a significant topic because academic performance and confidence in one's skills, abilities and knowledge affects the occupational pathways young people have available to them.

6   Work and family balance issues/opportunity costs theory

A popular topic of inquiry among social scientists and one that women and men of all ages confront is how to balance demands in the realms of both work and family. Women have historically been primarily responsible for the household and for childrearing. The increasing trend for women to do paid labour in many countries these past few decades has meant that women must make decisions, especially when they have children, about whether and how to maintain their careers and how to also take care of the house and children. These decisions are based on societal norms and structures (e.g. acceptability of, availability of, and institutional support for professional childcare), individual family situations (e.g. income, spousal viewpoints and careers), and personal preferences and opportunities. Work and family balance decisions affect the well-being of individuals and their family members.

Demographers have proposed opportunity costs theory to explain how people make these decisions. Opportunity costs theory argues that people must make trade-offs between pursuing education and a career or having children. For women in particular, it is more likely that those with higher levels of education and/or who are pursuing their careers will have fewer children than those who have lower levels of education who are not pursuing careers because the former group is giving up more to have children – the costs of the lost opportunities are higher. Opportunity costs theory also suggest that both men's and women's level of education and career aspirations and opportunities as well as the number of children in the household are likely to have an impact on the division of labour in households.

7   Sexual and contraceptive behaviours and the threat of HIV/AIDS

HIV/AIDS has become increasingly prevalent worldwide since the 1980s. A key to stopping the spread of HIV/AIDS is education about how the disease is transmitted. Consequently, it is important to understand what information people have about HIV/AIDS. It is reasonable to hypothesize that perceptions of AIDS risk and knowledge of the disease may affect people's sexual and contraceptive behaviours. Factors affecting HIV/AIDS education, perceived risks, sexual activities, and contraceptive behaviours include: education level, age, religious and cultural norms about family planning, partner preferences and exposure to media campaigns to increase HIV/AIDS information.

Researchers across the globe have studied this topic and have found many cultural differences in HIV/AIDS related knowledge and behaviours. Here are just two examples. In a study of adolescents and young adults in Ghana, 20% of urban and 30% of rural respondents did not know a girl could get pregnant the first time she has sexual intercourse (Agyei *et al.*, 2000). In a project implemented to understand women's sexual and reproductive lives in Zimbabwe (Feldman and Maposhere, 2003), condom use was believed to be inappropriate in marriage, and women's economic dependence on their spouses restricted the control they had over contraceptive use.

2 The Discourse of Science

- Science as a process
- Quantitative and qualitative queries
- Components of scientific analysis
- Types of data
- Unit of analysis: Who or what is being observed?
- Sampling
- Ethics
- Applications

Science as a process

Too often, science is perceived as absolute. A person posits a theory and it is right or wrong, implying a static, individualistic view of science. In fact, science is a process, a discourse among people that is guided by rules about how to make an argument. Scientists seek to understand what others are saying and accept some assertions as correct and others as incorrect, some as legitimate and others as not legitimate.

Consider arguments that might be made about why states in the US differ in their homicide rates. Some might suggest that poverty breeds violence, and therefore states with high levels of poverty will have high rates of homicide. Such a theory, stated in simple and absolute terms, would be something like: 'The more poverty in a state, the higher the homicide rate'. Figure 2.1 provides some evidence regarding that argument. It shows the relationship between the percentage of people in a state below the federal poverty line in 2004 and the homicide rate in 2005.

Instead of thinking of the theory that poverty causes homicide as either right or wrong, we can think of the theory as a process by which we learn about what drives homicide. In looking at Figure 2.1 someone might argue that these data seem consistent with the poverty/ homicide theory (see Box 2.1 for more information on how to read the **scatterplot**). States with more people in poverty tend to have higher homicide rates. But a key rule in the discourse of science is the need to entertain **alternative explanations** for research findings. Indeed some philosophers of science feel a proposed explanation must be falsifiable if it is to be considered a **scientific explanation**. In this view, an explanation is a scientific one only if we can think of ways it could be disproven. If we try to disprove it and fail, then that lends **credibility** to the explanation. If there is no way to disprove an explanation, then it doesn't fall within the realm of science.

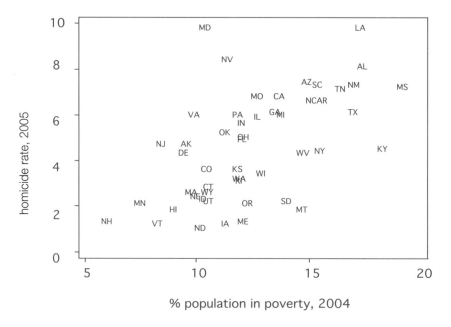

% population in poverty, 2004

Figure 2.1 Scatterplot of homicide rate versus poverty rate

Source: US Census Bureau

Box 2.1: How to read Figure 2.1

Figure 2.1 is called a scatterplot. A scatterplot shows the relationship between two variables. The variables that are plotted in a scatterplot have multiple categories or values, such as years of education, annual salary in dollars, or number of companion animals in a household. When we are interested in looking at variables that have two or a few categories (e.g. home ownership; responses of 'yes' and 'no'), we would use charts like the ones we used in Chapter 1 (e.g. bar charts). In Figure 2.1, we have used state abbreviations to indicate each state's poverty and homicide rates. Since there are only fifty states, it was possible to use abbreviations. (The state abbreviations are listed in Table 2.1 at the end of the chapter.)   *cont.*

Box 2.1: How to read Figure 2.1 cont.
When we have many cases though, circles or dots or some other small marker would need to be used to locate the cases on the graph.

In looking at Figure 2.1, we can see that the percentage of the population in poverty for each state is shown on what is called the horizontal or 'x' axis (we'll explain what the 'x' means in the next chapter). In this case, percent in poverty is graphed from 5% to 20% since the state with the lowest state poverty rate, New Hampshire (NH), is at 5.5% and the highest state poverty rate, Mississippi (MS), is at 18.7%. We could have selected another range for plotting poverty data, such as 0% to 100%, but this would leave a large portion of the graph empty since the highest poverty rate is 18.7%. The scatterplot is most useful for examining the overall relationship between two variables. If we are interested in finding out the exact poverty rate for a state, we would not want to rely on the scatterplot for this information since we cannot see the precise values.

The homicide rate is plotted on the vertical or 'y' axis. As you can see on the scatterplot, the range of homicide rates depicted is 0 to 10.0. If we want to know which state has the lowest homicide rate, we could look at which state on the scatterplot is closest to a homicide rate of 0. In this case, it appears that North Dakota (abbreviated as ND) has the lowest homicide rate, followed closely by Vermont (VT) and Iowa (IA). We have used the 2004 poverty rate and the 2005 homicide rate. Since causes occur before the effects, it is a common practice in social research to have the cause variable for an earlier point in time than the effect variable. We sometimes refer to a "lagged" value of the cause variable when we do this.

We made the graph so we could explore the relationship between poverty and homicide rates. To do this, we want to see if there is any pattern in the location of the data points. We can start by looking at states with low poverty rates. We see that many states with low poverty rates, like New Hampshire (NH), Minnesota (MN), Hawaii (HI), and Vermont (VT), tend to have low homicide rates. If we look at states with high poverty rates, such as Louisiana (LA), Alabama (AL), New Mexico (NM) and Mississippi (MS), we see they tend to have high homicide rates. This suggests that there may be a relationship between poverty and homicide rates. But the pattern isn't perfect. New Jersey (NJ), for instance, has a low poverty rate and a moderate homicide rate, and Kentucky (KY) has a high poverty rate and a moderate homicide rate. Scatterplots are discussed in more detail in Chapter 3.

There could be a number of problems with the argument that poverty causes homicide. That is, we can think of ways to falsify the theory. It may be that both poverty and homicide are concentrated in cities and so it is really urban life that drives homicide. It appears that many of the states with the highest levels of homicide are in the deep south, so it may be that there are historical or cultural factors driving both homicide and poverty. And many of the high homicide states are in hot climates, so perhaps climate has something to do with homicide. In the discourse of science, we would propose those explanations and find data to see if they provide a better explanation than the argument that poverty is what is driving homicide.

Science proceeds by proposing theories, comparing them to data, considering alternative explanations and trying to find ways to choose among the alternatives. Theories are abstractions from reality that can help us understand the world. The process by which that understanding emerges is one of dialogue with oneself and with others. Each theory is flawed, but a good theory is one whose flaws suggest further insight into how the world works. The scatterplot in Figure 2.1 gives some support to the idea that homicide and poverty are related. It is consistent with the argument that poverty causes homicide. But the scatterplot may also be consistent with the three other arguments we've suggested. Figuring out what is really going on involves a discourse in which both data and theory are invoked to assess the plausibility of arguments.

To examine these other three arguments, we would want data on urbanization of the states. We would want data on culture and history after we clarified what we mean by those concepts. And we would want data on climate. Science is a process in which we hold either an internal dialogue ('What else should I consider in this analysis?') or a public dialogue ('Your argument is incorrect because you didn't take account of the following factors ... ') and usually both.

Science always involves *simplifying the world*. The graph in Figure 2.1 tells us something about a pattern in the world. But to focus our attention on this pattern means we are ignoring other elements of the world. Science is no different than art in this regard. A skilled artist draws our attention to a part of the stream of reality and so does a skilled scientist. There are other traditions of human knowledge that are concerned with awareness of the whole, such as the meditative traditions of Taoism and Zen. But science, like art, is about producing a pleasing and useful focus.

Quantitative and qualitative queries

As we mentioned in Chapter 1, there are two major approaches to empirical research in the social sciences. One is labelled **quantitative** because it uses numbers to try to understand the social world. In this tradition, data are collected by conducting surveys in which everyone is asked the same set of questions, or by making use of the numbers collected by government or by other organizations, or by otherwise gathering information in a form that allows what is observed to be captured by numbers.

In contrast, **qualitative** research makes use of words and sometimes images rather than numbers. Researchers may do in-depth interviews where each respondent is asked questions as they are in a survey, but as the interview proceeds, questions are tailored to what the respondent has already said. Researchers may do **participant observation** where they 'hang out' in a setting of interest to them and take careful notes about what is going on. Documents, including texts, photographs, and sound recordings may also be examined.

At least since the 1970s, there has been some tension between 'quants' (those using numbers) and 'quals' (those not using numbers in their research). Until recently, most researchers were trained to use the tools of one approach but not the other. In extreme cases, a kind of intellectual xenophobia developed in which quals denied that quantitative research was valid, and quants denied the utility of qualitative research.

We find the quant/qual distinction fuzzy at best and the prejudices that accompany them a serious drawback in the progress of research. Contemporary research methods are breaking down the traditional barriers. For example, it is has been customary for qualitative researchers to use a convenience sample (interviewing whoever they can access easily) and quantitative researchers to use a probability sample (one in which everyone of the type of person being studied has a known chance of being interviewed). (We will discuss sampling in more detail later.) But now qualitative researchers often use a probability sample when possible.

One of us (Kalof, 1993) has shown how content analysis (described in Chapter 5) and statistical analysis can be joined to give a more thorough understanding of perceptions of media images than either approach alone could do. And one of our colleagues (McLaughlin, 1996) combines a detailed historical account of the development of co-ops with sophisticated statistical analysis of their foundings and failures.

Some questions more readily call for qualitative methods, some for quantitative. But most research areas benefit from a healthy mix of methods. We strongly advocate triangulation, as discussed in Chapter 5. Indeed, we would describe our view as **methodological pluralism**, a strong belief that both qualitative and quantitative methods have a great deal to contribute to our understanding of the social world. We urge you to be suspicious of claims that any one way of doing research is generally superior to others.

Components of scientific analysis

One can think of the research process as having four components: 1) the **hypothetical** in which one proposes a relationship between two or more variables; 2) the **empirical** in which one makes observations (or gathers data) on the variables of concern; 3) the **conceptual** in which descriptive categories are generated from the observations; and 4) the **theoretical** in which an overall explanatory theme is composed from the conceptual categories, a theme that either supports, modifies or refutes the original hypotheses. Figure 2.2 shows the analytic system as a feedback loop, and we can think of these as a process that can be started at any one of the four levels. For example if you were designing an inductive study, you would begin at the empirical level, making observations that would (hopefully) show patterns that eventually develop into theory. A deductive study would begin at the theoretical (or hypothetical) level of analysis.

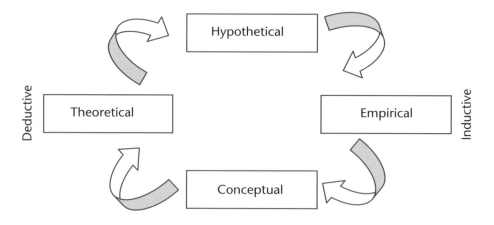

Figure 2.2 The four components of scientific analysis[1]

An example of a deductive approach: Durkheim's study of suicide

Working in the late nineteenth century, Emile Durkheim (1897/1951), a French sociologist, wanted to establish sociology as a scientific discipline that would have the same credibility as the psychological sciences of the time. His idea was that if he could show that a highly individualistic behaviour such as suicide could be traced to social rather than individual factors then sociology would gain what he considered well-deserved

---

[1]   Thanks to Sana Ho for this drawing of the four components of scientific analysis.

recognition as a science. We can use Durkheim's study of suicide to show how the four components of scientific analysis play out.

1 Hypothetical: make a guess about the relationship between variables

At the first level of analysis, Durkheim proposed that suicide resulted from social conditions. He considered key social institutions as essential to the healthy development of social individuals. For example, an individual thrives if she is a member of a religious group or has a family. The hypothesis can be specified as a mathematical statement, a common strategy in deductive work:

$$y = f(x)$$

In this case the y = suicide and the x = a social condition (here we will use family status) and the f means 'is a function of.' So Durkheim's theory is 'suicide is a function of participation in key social institutions, in this case, the family'. In this example we would call y (suicide) the **dependent variable** because it 'depends on' x (participation in family life), the **independent variable**.

It can sometimes be hard to understand what variables are independent (causes) and what variables are dependent (effects) when we are reading research or thinking about the implications of a theory. It can be very helpful to think about the time ordering of the variables. If one variable is describing things that occur before the things described by another variable happen, then the first variable can usually be taken as the independent variable and the second as the dependent variable. For instance, in thinking about the example of the deterrence effect of the death penalty, we can imagine a situation in which the death penalty is newly adopted in a state. If deterrence theory is correct we would expect that the homicide rate would decline in the years after the death penalty was imposed. So the death penalty is the independent variable and the homicide rate is the dependent variable.[2] We often structure studies so that we get data on the independent variables at a point in time before we get data on the dependent variable. In the analysis of homicide and poverty levels, we used the homicide rate for 2005 and the poverty rate for 2004, for example.

---

[2] High homicide rates may lead to political pressure to adopt the death penalty on the assumption that deterrence theory is correct. In that argument, we have the death penalty adoption coming after the homicide rate which makes the death penalty the dependent variable and the homicide rate the independent variable. In fact, many theories allow for variables to have causal effects on each other over time. This is called **reciprocal causation**. There are special research logics to handle this situation but they are a bit too complex for us to get into here.

2   Empirical: collect the data (make observations)

At the empirical level, Durkheim collected data on suicide rates from existing public records. He defined suicide as the number of deaths recorded as suicides in the official records. He also collected data on membership in social groups (religion, military, family), which he labelled 'social conditions' and which he had theorized would reduce the incidence of suicide.

3   Conceptual: look for patterns in the data

Durkheim found important patterns in the suicide data. For example, he discovered that men were more likely to commit suicide than women; single individuals were more likely than married individuals to take their own lives; and suicide varied by religious affiliation, with Protestants more likely to commit suicide than Catholics, who were more likely to take their own lives than Jewish individuals.

Durkheim named the patterns 'types of suicide', all of which (and there were numerous types) varied with the degree of social integration of an individual into certain social groups. Two types illustrate the patterns quite well:

> *Suicide type 1: Altruistic*. This pattern of suicide occurs when the importance of the individual is low but the social group to which she belongs is of great importance. For example, the men who hijacked the planes that crashed into the World Trade Center in New York City and the Pentagon in Washington, DC on September 11, 2001 would be considered altruistic suicides – their lives were sacrificed for the Al Qaeda social group.
> This can be diagrammed as:
>
> ↓ Individual worth   ↑ Social group worth
>
> *Suicide type 2: Egoistic*. When the importance of the individual is very high and she has minimal connection to a social group, the likelihood of an egoistic suicide increases. This is the altruistic suicide's opposite form. This can be diagrammed as:
>
> ↑ Individual worth   ↓ Social group worth

4   Theoretical: make a general explanatory statement about why the data fall into the patterns you found

Durkheim observed multiple patterns in the data, of which egoistic and altruistic suicide are examples. This allowed him to propose a general explanatory theory of suicide as a social phenomenon:

Suicide varies with the degree of integration into social groups.

Durkheim's theory not only explained the patterns he observed in the data but also helped to establish sociology as a science.

Types of data

Durkheim collected his data from government archives from major countries in Europe. This kind of data is called **secondary data** because someone else made the observations (the governmental unit), and he gathered the data from those existing records.

If the researcher collects her own data by making first-hand observations, the type of data is **primary**. For example, field researchers such as Jane Goodall spend long periods of time observing the behaviour of animals in their natural habitats, amassing huge archives of primary data.

And this introduces another distinction in types of data: longitudinal and cross-sectional data. Dr Goodall observed the behaviour of specific and special individual chimpanzees in her decades-long research in Gombe, Tanzania. The collection of data on what is affectionately called the 'F' family is a good example of **longitudinal data** on a specific primate family at the Gombe Stream Research Centre, with the same individuals observed over time.[3] Observations of Old Flo, the matriarch of the family, and Fifi, her daughter, created a large amount of data on family relations among Gombe chimps based on a close-knit and high-ranking chimpanzee family. While longitudinal data are certainly preferable in the attempt to discover patterns over time, many data collection efforts in the social sciences are **cross-sectional**. Observations are made at one period in time. Cross-sectional data are, obviously, easier to collect and can still reveal important patterns even though they lack the time depth of longitudinal data.

There is one more distinction that is important to make, although it is related to the scope of our research questions rather than the type of data collected. Some social science research is concerned with **macro-level** (large-scale) **phenomena**, meaning patterns that characterize a society or comparisons between societies or groups. The second orientation, **micro-level**, considers issues on a smaller scale, usually at the level of individuals. Studies with a micro orientation look at how individuals behave and how they interact with each another, while those with a macro orientation look

---

[3] Information on the 'F' Family is from The Jane Goodall Institute's website, http://www.janegoodall.org/chimp_central/chimpanzees/f_family/default.asp (accessed July 24, 2007).

at characteristics and interactions of larger **aggregates**, such as nations, cultures and institutions.

Unit of analysis: Who or what is being observed?

Some researchers focus on people, others study families, or family 'pets,' or communities, or organizations, or nations. A theory should be clear about the things to which it applies. In the language of science we call this the **unit of analysis**. For example, deterrence theory is trying to predict the behaviour of people and so is norm theory and opportunity cost theory. However, ecological modernization theory is trying to explain the environmental impact of nations, rather than individuals.

One way we examine the logical consistency of a theory is to think about what units of analysis it is describing, and whether the assumptions it makes about the behaviour of those units of analysis make sense. In ecological modernization theory, while it is reasonable to consider the energy consumption of nations, we would want to think about whether the actions the theory assumes will be taken by individuals, corporations, government and social movement organizations make sense.

Some theories apply at multiple levels. Both deterrence theory and opportunity cost theory can easily be applied to political and economic units such as states or nations. In the example we developed we assumed that individual behaviour would be influenced by state government policy on the punishment for homicide. This is a reasonable assumption in the sense that, whether or not it turns out to be true, it is plausible. In the next chapter we will compare the fertility levels and the educational opportunities for women of a group of countries. Again, this assumes that the country is the context in which women assess their opportunities.

There is a famous concept in research methods called the **ecological fallacy**. It is an important idea but a bad name. It would be better termed the 'aggregation fallacy' because it cautions us about making mistakes in using data on aggregate units (communities, organizations, nations) to draw conclusions about the behaviour of individuals. It has nothing to do with ecology in the modern sense of the term.

The problem was first pointed out by Ogburn and Goltra (1919) in a study of the first election in the state of Oregon in which women were allowed to vote. In most democracies, including Oregon in the early twentieth century, the actual votes of individuals are confidential. But the voting results are reported for voting districts, and in this case the researchers were able to find out the proportion of registered voters who were women. They wanted to see if women voted differently to men on 26 issues using the percentage of women in each precinct and the percentage supporting the issues in each precinct. Ogburn and Goltra noted that there was a problem with doing the analysis with the only data they had available – data on the aggregate unit of voting districts rather than on actual voters. They made conclusions about how women voted without actually having individual level data. But just because a high percentage supported a particular issue in a district that had a high percentage of women voters doesn't necessarily mean that women differed from men in their votes, only that the percentage of women in the district was related to the vote. While the details can get a bit complicated, it's possible to have a situation where women and men vote the same way but there is still a correlation between the percentage of women voting in a district and the support or opposition to a proposition on the ballot.

The ecological fallacy naively draws conclusions about individual behaviours from data on aggregate units such as voting districts. There is a long history of research on when you can and cannot draw such conclusions (King, 1997). For our purposes it is sufficient to note that in any analysis, we should be careful to check what the units of analysis for the theory are, what the units of analysis in the data are, and if they are not the same, be cautious about what conclusions can be drawn. In the example above about homicide rates, we are drawing conclusions about states, not about individuals, though deterrence theory has implications for both.

Sampling

When researchers design their studies, they are faced with how to ensure their work will accurately reflect the **population** in which they are interested. A population is a collection of people, objects, countries, etc., that share a common characteristic of interest. All residents of Switzerland today, countries in Africa in 1950, patients hospitalized in a particular hospital in 1999 and science textbooks currently used in the United Kingdom are populations. Often it is not feasible to study every member of a population, so researchers select a subgroup from the population, called a **sample**. If a researcher wants to examine the extent to which her fellow citizens in Japan think men and women possess different aptitudes for mathematics and language, it would be very time-consuming and expensive to collect data on the viewpoints of all citizens. It is also likely that many citizens would be difficult to locate or may not want to participate in her research. Instead she could select a subgroup of citizens, one that is representative of the population (i.e. Japanese citizens) and collect data from them.

Once a population is defined, a **sampling frame** can be created, which is the set of cases from which the sample will be chosen. The frame may consist of names from driver's license records or a telephone directory, subscribers to a magazine, school enrollees, and so on. In designing a sampling frame, researchers must consider how accurately it reflects the population. One way to ensure this is to define the population very specifically so that the definition describing the population reflects who is actually sampled.

Sampling frames are almost always inaccurate to some degree. A great deal of effort is spent on trying to get sampling frames to closely match the intended population and on learning what errors result from deviations between the sampling frame and the population. A telephone directory, for instance, does not contain unlisted households or individuals who do not have telephones. So if we are doing a sample for a phone interview survey we may make a special effort to create a sampling frame that includes unlisted numbers. We will discuss how to do this below.

Probability samples

Consider these two research questions: what percentage of people in a particular country believe investing in alternative energy sources should be a priority of the government? To what extent do men and women believe there is an unequal gendered division of labour in their society? The aim of these questions is to generate accurate statements about the population of the country in question. The researcher will want to build a list of people (the sampling frame) that closely approximates the population. Then she will use procedures based on sampling theory, a special branch of statistics, to actually draw the sample of people whose views will be assessed. Sampling theory allows us choose samples that are representative of the population we are studying and to understand how large the differences between the population and the sample are likely to be. How well the sample reflects the population of interest is called **generalizability** or **external validity** (Cook and Campbell, 1979), a topic we discuss in more detail in Chapter 6.

Random sampling. When every member of a population is given an equal chance of being included in the sample, this is a **random sample**. Putting everyone's name into a hat and pulling out names is one way of drawing a random sample. In large studies we use computer-based procedures to draw random samples. A random digit dialing procedure, which generates random lists of phone numbers, is commonly utilized for phone interviews. Even with random selection a sample can have error in it due to chance. For example we might draw a higher proportion of males for our sample than exists in the population simply by luck. Such error due to chance is called **sampling error**. We cannot make sampling error disappear but we can calculate how large it is likely to be in a particular study.

One way to ensure a particular group in a population is well represented in the sample is to divide the population into **strata**. Strata are groupings of the population, such as ethnicity, gender or income categories. Random samples are drawn within each strata. For example, the 2001 Canadian census indicated that about 4 percent of the Canadian population was of Chinese origin.[4] If we drew a sample of 500 Canadians without using strata, we would expect about 20 people of Chinese origin to be in our sample. This might not be enough people if we want to compare Canadians of Chinese origin with other Canadians, so we could take a sample with two strata, Canadians of Asian origin and other Canadians. We might select 200 people from the Asian Canadian strata and 300 from the other strata. This gives us enough people in each group to make comparisons. We use this kind of stratified sampling procedure when we want to be sure to get a substantial number of people from relatively small groups.

Systematic sampling. When every nth person is chosen from a list for inclusion in the sample. If we had a list of 1000 employees of a firm and wanted a sample of 100 we could choose every tenth name from the list until we had 100 people in the sample. With this approach, the starting point for selecting the sample is picked at random. It is important to realize that lists can be ordered in ways that may bias a systematic sample. Even an alphabetical list can have biases since some ethnic groups are clustered at different parts of the alphabet, and the systematic procedure may lead to their under-representation in the sample.

Cluster sampling. One method that can be used when it is difficult to obtain a complete listing of a population is cluster sampling. A researcher interested in teenagers' time use may identify all schools in a given area that teach 14–16-year-olds and select a random sample of the schools, and then choose a random classroom within each school and interview those students. In this example, the schools and the classrooms are clusters. Clustering has the advantage of concentrating all interviews in a few areas, a few classes in a few schools in this example. But cluster samples have to be done carefully or else they will not be representative of the population.

---

4   http://www12.statcan.ca/english/census01/products/highlight/ETO/Table1.cfm?
      Lang=E&T=501&GV=1&GID=0

Non-probability/non-random samples

It is not always feasible or necessary to use a random sample. Imagine these research scenarios: a study where one observes individuals who have late stage dementia; an experiment to see if exposing people to different types of capital punishment information affects their attitudes about the death penalty; and media portrayals of gender roles in the 1950s. It would be extremely time-consuming, costly and often unfeasible to observe a random sample of dementia patients, set up an experiment with a random sample of Americans, and analyse a probability sample of all media types from the 1950s. Traditional probability samples cannot be used to achieve some research aims, including investigating rare or unusual cases and exploring the experiences of groups that are difficult to locate. Some research is exploratory and a probability sample is not needed because we are interested in the existence of a phenomenon that is not generalizable to a larger population. With a non-random sample, we have no way of knowing the probability that a case will be selected for the sample. Thus, there is no way of knowing how representative the sample is. The most common types of non-probability samples are purposive, snowball, convenience, quota and extreme case samples. We will discuss each of these briefly.

Theoretical/purposive sampling. With theoretical or purposive sampling, the theory, research questions, and data collection and analysis processes determine the sample (Glaser and Strauss, 1967). Within this framework, the sample develops gradually as insights and questions emerge from information gathered from other cases. This technique can maximize the range of cases in the sample to ensure outlying and conceptually important cases are studied. If you are interested in the division of labour within two-adult households and you took a random sample of residents in the city you live in, you would not be likely to select many households in which the male is not in the labour force and is the primary caregiver of the children and the home. You could consider using a purposive sampling strategy and recruit households with different divisions of labour to make comparisons. You may decide on five household types: 1) the woman is not gainfully employed and is primarily responsible for the household/children while spouse is mainly responsible for paid labour; 2) man is not in workforce and is primarily responsible for the household/children while spouse is mainly responsible for paid labour; 3) both partners are in workforce and the woman is largely responsible for the home; 4) both partners are in workforce and the man is largely responsible for the home; and 5) both partners are in the labour force and are equally responsible for home and children. You would then seek to locate couples that fit into each of these categories. This differs from a **stratified sample**. In a stratified sample the selection of respondents in each group (strata) is random and representative; in theoretical or purposive sampling the researcher selects within categories but does not do so at random.

In constructing a theoretical sample, a researcher should not just choose those cases that support a particular argument or viewpoint, or the sample will be criticized as being biased and findings will not be viewed as meaningful. The researcher should rigorously look for cases that do not match with her ideas and explanations. For example, it can be helpful to use a grid to lay out a typology of different groupings to keep track of the types of cases that should be considered. The decision to stop adding to the sample occurs when all theoretically important types have been included and additional observations do not yield new insights (for more information see Mason, 1998). For instance, if for household type 1 above you interviewed eight couples and found that each additional interview did not yield any new information or insights, you would then stop sampling couples that fit that criteria.

Snowball sampling. This is when people in a group of interest inform the researcher about other individuals in that population who could also fit the criteria for inclusion in a study. Researchers form their sample by identifying a few individuals and then asking each person to give names of others they know. This approach is particularly useful for contacting difficult to reach groups. Suppose we are interested in learning about how the threat of AIDS may affect the contraceptive decisions of prostitutes. Since in many countries prostitution is illegal, no list of prostitutes exists from which to select a sample. Thus we may decide to locate a handful of prostitutes from city streets for participation and then ask each of them to give us some names of other prostitutes they know and perhaps even ask their help in recruiting them to be interviewed. If all members of the group we are seeking are connected via a social network, snowball sampling can be a form of network sampling.

Convenience sampling. A sample of convenience is comprised of readily available cases. A professor asking her students to complete a survey about views on the death penalty, interviewing the first 100 people encountered in a shopping plaza or observing students in a friend's classroom are examples of convenience samples. While these samples can save time and money, they are biased and not representative of the population. Convenience samples may however be useful for exploratory research or preliminary testing of survey questions.

Quota sampling. With quota sampling, the number of cases in the sample of particular categories is predetermined (e.g. we could designate 5 age categories and collect data from 50 individuals in each age group, for a total sample size of 250). Quota sampling differs from stratified sampling in that the individuals in each group are not randomly selected within categories. If the categories for quota sampling are based on theoretical criteria, then quota sampling is theoretical sampling. Otherwise, quota sampling is based on convenience, purposive or snowballing techniques.

Extreme case sampling. Extreme case sampling is the selection of unusual cases that fall outside general patterns. These extreme cases may be very interesting theoretically even though they are by definition not representative of the population.

Ethics

The ethics of research is an important topic because it defines what is and is not permissible to do when conducting research. Researchers have a professional and moral obligation to act ethically. Governments, professional organizations, universities and funding agencies have established ethical guidelines and codes of conduct for researchers to follow. A research project that is designed in an ethical manner maximizes benefits to both the scientists and study participants, respects participants' rights, and minimizes the risks to participants. Both biomedical and social scientists collect data on people. Sometimes we simply collect data by asking people questions or observing behaviours. In other studies we conduct experiments in which people are given 'treatments.' (We discuss experiments in more detail in Chapter 5.) In the social sciences, the treatments might involve watching a video, interacting with other people in a situation set up by the researcher, doing tasks on a computer or being involved in a special training programme. No matter what approach is used to collect data or how innocuous the topic we are interested in, we want to be sure we treat people (often called **subjects** or **research participants**) ethically.

Unfortunately many ethical guidelines we have today were established largely in response to serious abuses of human subjects. The Tuskegee Syphilis Study and the Nazi medical experiments are two of the most well-known studies that harmed research participants without their knowledge or consent about what was being done. In 1932, the US Public Health Service in Tuskegee, Alabama, initiated a study with around 400 poor black men diagnosed with syphilis. Another 200 men who did not have syphilis were enrolled as a comparison group. Telling the participants they were being treated for 'bad blood', for decades the men were never given any anti-syphilis drugs, not even penicillin, which became widely available during World War II and is quite effective for treating syphilis. The details of the study were not exposed until 1972, when the study was still being carried out and several subjects had already died of syphilis or syphilis-related complications (for more details see Gray, 2002 and MacDonald, 1974).

During World War II the fascist leader Adolph Hitler and his government conducted a series of 'experiments' on Jews, Gypsies and others being held prisoner that killed many and caused significant physical and psychological damage to many others. As just a few examples of the Nazi 'experiments', they sterilized many women by injecting them with a silver nitrate solution at their routine physical examinations, exposed men to sterilizing doses of radiation without their knowledge, and euthanized individuals they deemed 'unfit'. The Nuremberg trials after World War II exposed these criminal activities that were disguised as research (for more information see Freyhofer, 2004; Persico, 1995). Out of these trials came the Nuremburg Code, which is one of the first clearly articulated codes for the ethical treatment of human subjects.[5]

The Nuremburg Code included the necessity of conducting research only with those who give voluntary consent and ensuring research projects are designed to avoid all possible harm to participants. In 1964 the World Medical Association adopted the Declaration of Helsinki, which describes the rules for treating human subjects in medical research.[6] Social science ethical considerations developed from these sets of rules. Not only have ethical guidelines become standard amongst professional scientific organizations, but universities and funding agencies typically require that research protocols involving humans or animals be formally submitted for review by a human subjects committee to ensure participants' rights are protected and the risks of participation are minimal. These committees review research proposals before data collection commences to ensure there are no violations of ethical standards. Here we summarize key principles of human subjects research. Box 2.3 contains the code of ethics established by the International Sociological Association, which is similar to the guidelines of other organizations.

The first ethical principle is **informed consent**. Participation in research should be voluntary. Researchers must tell potential research participants what they are being asked to do so they can make an informed decision about whether or not to participate. The goals of the research, as well as any risks and benefits of participation, should be clearly conveyed,

---

[5]   The formal reference is: Trials of War Criminals before the Nuremberg Military Tribunals under Control Council Law No. 10. Nuremberg, October 1946–April 1949. Washington, D.C.: US G.P.O, 1949–1953. The text can be found on the web at: http://www.ushmm.org/research/doctors/Nuremberg_Code.htm

[6]   The formal title is Ethical Principles for Medical Research Involving Human Subjects. It can be found on the web at: http://www.wma.net/e/policy/b3.htm

although the goals can be stated generally so as to not bias the participants' responses during the study. Subjects should also be given the opportunity to withdraw from the study if and whenever they choose.

Some segments of the population cannot give informed consent, including children and individuals with cognitive impairments. Members of these populations can only partake in research if a legal guardian gives permission. In some situations it is difficult to know if people are able to give true voluntary consent. Can students or employees give voluntary consent if their professors or employers ask them to participate? How about prisoners? These groups may agree to take part in the research due to concerns about potential repercussions for not participating. A student, for instance, may wonder if her grade will be affected by the decision, and an employee may fear that not participating could hurt her future opportunities within the company. While it is reasonable to encourage others to participate in research projects, people in positions of authority cannot use their power to coerce participation.

Along with informed consent, a researcher's identity should be disclosed to study participants. Few studies of covert (concealed) observation and deception are acceptable today. There are some instances when a researcher would not be able to collect data if people knew she was doing research. In other situations revealing too much information about the study to participants could affect the study outcomes. Some experimental research is designed so that groups of subjects are given different types or levels of treatments. If there are multiple conditions in an experiment (e.g. in a drug trial one group may be given a specific drug regimen while a **control group** may be given a placebo) and if knowing which treatment condition one is in can affect results, the researcher can inform the subjects before consenting that they will not be told the group to which they will be assigned. In such cases, the subjects should be informed after data collection is completed. This is called **debriefing** and allows the subjects to leave the experience understanding the experiment and having had any questions that arise answered.

In some rare instances, the researcher must disguise her identity or the research scenario in order to obtain information. One can imagine a researcher needing to conceal her identity to observe behavior widely considered as deviant, for example. Such deception was a more common practice in the past than it is now. Generally, human subjects review protocols will not allow for studies in which subjects are misinformed by the researcher in significant ways. Researchers are expected to be honest about their research aims and procedures. Finally, there are instances when informed consent is impractical. If we are interested in conducting an observational study in a public setting, such as a park or a market, it would not be feasible to inform all people in those settings that they are being observed. In addition, such observations pose no risk (and likely no serious invasion of privacy since the settings are public) to those in the setting.

Most social science researchers who collect information directly from people promise confidentiality to their participants. **Confidentiality** means removing all identifying information about individuals from research records and reports. This encourages honest responses. However, in many countries there are limits to the ability of social scientists to keep such a pledge if the legal system becomes involved [see Box 2.2 for an example].

Box 2.2 Research ethics and confidentiality

As a graduate student, sociologist Rik Scarce spent time in jail. He was studying a radical environmental movement in the early 1990s as part of his dissertation research. The local prosecutor believed Scarce had interviewed people who had broken into a federally funded laboratory at Washington State University. He refused to divulge any information obtained as part of his research, arguing it was in violation of his First Amendment rights and his promise of confidentiality to respondents. (The First Amendment of the US Constitution establishes freedom of speech and of the press.) He was imprisoned for over five months until the judge decided Scarce was not going to talk. He chronicled his experiences in a book (Scarce, 2005). While instances like this are not common in the scientific community, they do happen and in most countries there are no laws to protect scientists from government demands to break confidentiality. An act was created in 1999 by a US Senator to protect data collected by journalists and researchers from being subpoenaed, but the legislation never made it to a vote.

With face-to-face interviews, only the researcher stands between the confidentiality of those studied and the legal system. It is common to have contact information for sample members, but this should be kept separate from data records. Frequently each study participant is assigned an identification number as a way of linking data to contact information. All information pertaining to a study should be kept in a secure location that only the research team can access. Summaries of the research should present aggregated findings. In some instances however, researchers use quotations from participants to illustrate points. Instead of stating that a comment was made by Louise, a 35-year-old woman with eight children who is living in Ottawa Canada, the researcher may modify the identity, maintaining only important details, such as 'A Canadian mother in her thirties'. Participants' identities in studies of unique groups (e.g. criminal gangs or cults), organizations, or towns are even more difficult to conceal but the researcher has an obligation to do as much as possible to protect confidentiality.

Compared to confidentiality, **anonymous research** means there is no link at all between individuals' data and their contact information. This is typically not practical, however, since researchers often need to know who participated so they can obtain follow-up information, re-contact those who don't initially respond or link different sets of data on the same individuals. While complete anonymity is often not possible, confidentiality of research participants should always be kept unless explicitly waived by individuals. A study should also be designed so privacy is protected. For example, if interviewing a person about a sensitive topic, the interview should not occur in a public setting where others could hear the discussion.

Box 2.3: Code of ethics of the International Sociological Association (ISA)

Approved by the ISA Executive Committee, Fall 2001

Introduction
The International Sociological Association's (ISA) Code of Ethics consists of a Preamble and four sets of specific Ethical Standards. Membership of the ISA commits members to adhere to it.
The Code of Ethics is not exhaustive, all-embracing and rigid. The fact that a particular conduct is not addressed specifically by the Code of Ethics does not mean the conduct is necessarily either ethical or unethical.

Preamble
Sociologists work to develop a reliable and valid body of scientific knowledge based on research and, thereby, to contribute to the improvement of the global human condition. The primary goals of the Code of Ethics, a symbol of the identity of the ISA, are (1) to protect the welfare of groups and individuals with whom and on whom sociologists work or who are involved in sociologists' research efforts and (2) to guide the behaviour and hence the expectations of ISA members, both between themselves and toward the society at large. Those who accept its principles are expected to interpret them in good faith, to respect them, to make sure they are respected and to make them widely known.

Each sociologist supplements the Code of Ethics in ways based on her/his own personal values, culture and experience. Each sociologist supplements, but does not violate, the standards outlined in this Code of Ethics. It is the individual responsibility of each sociologist to aspire to the highest standards of conduct.

cont.

Box 2.3: Code of ethics of the International Sociological Association cont.

The efficacy of a Code of Ethics relies principally upon the self-discipline and self-control of those to whom it applies.

1. *Sociology as a field of scientific study and practice*

1.1. As scientists, sociologists are expected to cooperate locally and transnationally on the basis of scientific correctness alone, without discrimination on the basis of scientifically irrelevant factors such as age, sex, sexual preference, ethnicity, language, religion or political affiliation.

1.2. Group work, cooperation and mutual exchanges among sociologists are necessary for sociology to achieve its ends. Sociologists are expected to take part in discussions on their own work, as well as on the work of other sociologists.

1.3. Sociologists should be aware of the fact that their assumptions may have an impact upon society. Hence their duty is, on the one hand, to keep an unbiased attitude as far as possible, while, on the other hand, to acknowledge the tentative and relative character of the results of their research and not to conceal their own ideological position(s). No sociological assumption should be presented as indisputable truth.

1.4. Sociologists should act with a view to mantaining the image and the integrity of their own discipline; this does not imply that they should abandon a critical approach toward its fundamental assumptions, its methods and its achievements.

1.5. The principles of openness, criticism and respect for all scientific perspectives should be followed by sociologists in their teaching and professional practices.

1.6. Sociologists are expected to protect the rights of their students and clients.

2. *Research procedures*

2.1. Sponsors

cont.

Box 2.3: Code of ethics of the International Sociological Association cont.

2.1.1. Research activities in sociology must often necessarily rely on private or public funding, and thus depend to a certain extent on sponsorship. Sponsors, be they private or public, may be interested in a specific outcome of research. Yet, sociologists should not accept research grants or contracts which specify conditions inconsistent with their scientific judgment of what are appropriate means of carrying out the research in question, or which permit the sponsors to veto or delay academic publication because they dislike the findings.

2.1.2. Sponsors should be clearly informed in advance of the basic guidelines of research projects, as well as of the methods which researchers are willing to adopt. Sponsors also should be advised of the risk that the result of an inquiry may not fit with their own expectations.

2.1.3. Sponsors, both private and public, may be particularly interested in funding sociological research for the sake of their own political aims. Whether or not they share such aims, sociologists should not become subordinate to them. They should also refrain from cooperating in the fulfillment of undemocratic aims or discriminatory goals.

2.1.4. The conditions agreed upon between researchers and sponsors should preferably be laid down in written agreements.

2.2. Costs and rewards

2.2.1. Funds provided for sociological research should be used for the agreed purpose.

2.2.2. In a situation where sociologists are bidding competitively on projects, they should not agree to carry on research projects which are not sufficiently funded or compete with other bidders by the use of further unfair tactics not consistent with appropriate scientific standards.

2.3. Data gathering

2.3.1. As scientists, sociologists should disclose the methods by which they proceed as well as the general sources of their data.

cont.

**Box 2.3: Code of ethics of the International Sociological
Association cont.**

2.3.2. The security, anonymity and privacy of research subjects and
informants should be respected rigorously, in both quantitative and
qualitative research. The sources of personal information obtained by
researchers should be kept confidential, unless the informants have asked or
agreed to be cited. Should informants be easily identifiable, researchers
should remind them explicitly of the consequences that may follow from the
publication of the research data and outcomes. Payment of informants,
though acceptable in principle, should be discouraged as far as possible and
subject to explicit conditions, with special regard to the reliability of the
information provided.

2.3.3. Sociologists who are being given access to records are expected to
respect the privacy conditions under which the data were collected. They
can, however, make use of data gathered in historical archives, both private
and public, under the legal conditions laid down in the country concerned
and usually accepted by the international scientific community, and subject
to the rules of the archive.

2.3.4. The consent of research subjects and informants should be obtained
in advance. Covert research should be avoided in principle, unless it is the
only method by which information can be gathered, and/or when access to
the usual sources of information is obstructed by those in power.

3. *Publication and communication of data*

3.1. Data gathered in sociological research activities and research work
constitute the intellectual property of the researchers, who are in principle
also entitled to copyright. Should copyright be vested in a sponsor or in an
employer, researchers should be entitled to fair compensation.

3.2. In principle, researchers have a right to submit their work for
publication, or to publish it at their own expense.

3.3. Researchers have the right to ensure that their results be not
manipulated or taken out of context by sponsors.

3.4. The contribution of scholars, sponsors, technicians or other collaborators who have made a substantial contribution in carrying out a research
project should be acknowledged explicitly in any subsequent publication.

cont.

Box 2.3: Code of ethics of the International Sociological Association cont.

3.5. Databases should not be regarded as being in the public domain, until the researchers who have assembled them have specified the sources of their data and the methods by which they were constructed. Information about sources and methods should be made available within reasonable time. Interim data sets should be available for inspection of their accuracy by other scholars.

[Note: Statement already adopted by the ISA Executive Council in its Colima Meeting, 26–27 November 1996]

3.6. Once published, information about a research project should be considered to be part of the common knowledge and background of the scientific community. Therefore, it is open to comments and criticism to which researchers should be allowed to react.

4. *Extra-scientific use of research results*

4.1. The results of sociological inquiries may be a matter of public interest. Their diffusion, which is an implication of the fundamental right of people to be informed, should not be hindered. Researchers, however, should be aware of the dangers connected with distortions, simplifications and manipulations of their own research material, which may occur in the process of communication through individual or mass media. Researchers should be able, and are entitled, to intervene to correct any kind of misinterpretation or misuse of their work.

4.2. Researchers should refrain from claiming expertise in fields where they do not have the necessary depth of research knowledge, especially when contributing to public discussion or policy debate.

Source: www.isa-sociology.org/about/isa_code_of_ethics.htm

Table 2.1 State names and abbreviations

Abbreviation	State	Abbreviation	State
AL	Alabama	MT	Montana
AK	Alaska	NE	Nebraska
AZ	Arizona	NV	Nevada
AR	Arkansas	NH	New Hampshire
CA	California	NJ	New Jersey
CO	Colorado	NM	New Mexico
CT	Connecticut	NY	New York
DE	Delaware	NC	North Carolina
FL	Florida	ND	North Dakota
GA	Georgia	OH	Ohio
HI	Hawaii	OK	Oklahoma
ID	Idaho	OR	Oregon
IL	Illinois	PA	Pennsylvania
IN	Indiana	RI	Rhode Island
IA	Iowa	SC	South Carolina
KS	Kansas	SD	South Dakota
KY	Kentucky	TN	Tennessee
LA	Louisiana	TX	Texas
ME	Maine	UT	Utah
MD	Maryland	VT	Vermont
MA	Massachusetts	VA	Virginia
MI	Michigan	WA	Washington
MN	Minnesota	WV	West Virginia
MS	Mississippi	WI	Wisconsin
MO	Missouri	WY	Wyoming

Applications

These exercises draw on the materials presented in both Chapters 1 and 2.

1   Time use among adolescents

a)   Imagine you are on a human subjects review committee and are asked
to review this proposal: Research suggests that teenagers who are
supervised after school (e.g. return home to a parent or other adult after
school, participate in formal activities after school like sports or clubs)
are less likely to commit crimes (e.g. theft) than are teenagers who are
unsupervised after school. To study this, we plan to locate 100 families
whose teenagers are currently supervised. For half of the families, we
will observe them for a one-year period in their present circumstances

(i.e. supervised group). For the other half of the sample, the teenagers' supervision will be removed, and they will be monitored for the same one-year period (i.e. unsupervised group). What, if any, ethical problems are there with this design? What other ethically-related questions would you ask the researchers (they may not be problems but issues you would want to know about)?

b) We want to learn how adolescents spend their time outside of school. Let's say we observe first hand a sample of adolescents over a period of three months to identify how they spend their time after school. What type of data have we collected – primary data or secondary data? Cross-sectional or longitudinal data? Macro or micro data?

2   The experiences of older adults with dementia

You are given a class assignment to investigate how being diagnosed with dementia impacts individuals and their families. You want to learn about patients' fears and how they think the diagnosis has affected how they live their daily lives.

a) Would you say this a qualitative or quantitative study? Why?
b) What is the unit of analysis in this project?
c) What sampling strategy would you recommend using to carry out this study? Why did you recommend this?
d) Would it be possible to collect this data using a random probability sample? Why or why not?
e) If your professor tells you to take an inductive approach to complete this assignment, what does she mean?

3   The death penalty as a deterrent to crime

a) In this chapter we described levels of scientific analysis. Return to the discussion about the relationship between state homicide rate and the death penalty in Chapter 1. State the hypothetical, empirical, conceptual and theoretical levels of analysis that were presented.
b) From the data presented in Chapter 1, can we draw the conclusion that individuals who live in a state where the death penalty is legal are more likely to commit homicide? If not, why?

4   Ecological modernization theory

According to ecological modernization theory, as countries become more affluent, they generate fewer CO_2 emissions and therefore have less of a negative impact on the environment. To preliminarily test this, we could obtain data that was collected by each country's government on CO_2

emissions and economic measures in the prior year. This would allow us to compare emission levels of more affluent and less affluent nations.
a) What type of data are involved in this design? Primary or secondary? Micro or macro? Cross-sectional or longitudinal?
b) Is this a qualitative or quantitative study? Why do you say this?
c) What is the unit of analysis in this project?

5 Gender differences in mathematics, science and language skills

Here's a research proposal. We are interested in whether or not reported differences in young girls' and boys' science, mathematics and language skills are due to their environment (e.g. school, family). We decide to conduct an experiment to test this. In one classroom, we give girls additional lessons in mathematics and science; the boys in this classroom are only given their regular lessons in mathematics and science. In a second classroom, we do not provide either the girls or boys with additional lessons in mathematics and science (no alterations are made to their learning). After a one-month period, we compare the boys' and girls' scores on mathematics and science aptitude tests in the two classrooms (they were also administered the same test before the experiment began).
a) What type of data are involved in this design? Primary or secondary? Micro or macro? Cross-sectional or longitudinal?
b) Is this a qualitative or quantitative study? Why do you say this?
c) Are there any ethical concerns with this project?
d) What is the unit of analysis in this study?
e) What sampling strategy would you recommend we use to conduct this experiment? Why did you recommend this?
f) If we find that the girls who received extra mathematics and science lessons, on average, scored higher on the test at the end of the one month than the boys in that same classroom, what is a potential alternative explanation for this finding?

6 Work and family balance issues/opportunity costs theory

We want to carry out a study with couples to learn how they divide responsibilities for work, children and the home and what predicts division of labour.
a) If the goal of the study is to describe the pattern of division of labour in a population in France, what would be the most appropriate sampling strategy to use? In other words, we want to report how common it is in a population for couples to have an equitable division of labour, for women to primarily take care of the home and children

and men to work (traditional division), and so forth. Explain why you selected this sampling strategy.

b) Is this type of sample feasible for this study aim? Why or why not?

c) Is this an example of a qualitative or quantitative study? Why do you say this?

d) If the goal of the research is to understand how couples negotiated their household division of labour, is this study more likely to use a qualitative or quantitative orientation and why do you say this?

e) Is there any sampling strategy (strategies) that would be best suited to address this topic (in d above)? Are there any types of sampling that would not be appropriate for this study?

f) When you begin interviewing couples, you become interested in learning about one particular form of division of labour. What sampling strategy(ies) would be the best choice for locating additional couples with that division of labour?

g) What is the unit of analysis in these studies?

7 Sexual and contraceptive behaviour and the threat of HIV/AIDS

a) Let's say we want to compare knowledge about how HIV/AIDS is transmitted in five different countries in the world. This would provide us with a cross-cultural comparison. We are particularly interested in whether or not people with different levels of education in these countries have the same level of knowledge about HIV/AIDS. To accomplish this goal, we plan to carry out surveys with citizens in each of the countries. Briefly discuss any advantages or disadvantages of the following sampling strategies and whether these strategies are feasible with our research design (assuming we have sufficient money to actually carry out research in all five countries)?

1) Convenience
2) Random
3) Quota
4) Stratified

b) If you are asked to take a deductive approach to study this topic, what does this mean?

3 Basic Logic of Quantitative Inquiry

- Causation
- Variance, multiple causes and random factors
- Causal language and diagrams
- Explanatory and extraneous variables
- Scatterplots
- Procedures of quantitative research: Moving from theory to data
- Applications

Causation

One way to think about inductive and deductive approaches to research is to ask whether we are looking for causal relationships in the data or simply trying to find and describe patterns in the data. When we state hypotheses, the 'if ... then' form implies that one thing causes another. If a state has the death penalty, then the homicide rate will be lower. If a woman faces high opportunity costs, then she will delay or forego having children. We are saying that the death penalty causes the homicide rate to be lower. We are saying that opportunity costs cause delayed or foregone childbearing. While philosophers debate the precise meaning of causation, for our purposes an everyday sense of the term is fine: if we change the cause then the effect changes too. (Technically, we have to assume that nothing else changes that might counteract the influence of the cause on the effect.)

We usually call the cause the **independent variable** and the effect the **dependent variable**. In the role theory example, gender norms are independent – they determine mathematics and science performance, the dependent variable.

One of the most common goals of a research project, and the one we have emphasized so far, is to see if proposed ideas about cause and effect – theories of what causes what – are consistent with data. If the data match the pattern predicted by the theory, we begin to have more confidence in the theory. If the data don't match the pattern, we have less confidence in the theory. But as we saw above in the death penalty and homicide rate example, no single analysis of data is ever sufficient to convince everyone that a theory is right or wrong. It is the accumulation of evidence over multiple studies that eventually convinces most researchers. This is the deductive approach that starts with a theory, produces an implication and sees if that implication is borne out in the data.

However, there are many research projects in which we are not trying to test theories but simply to find patterns in the data. Theory has guided us in that we have data on some variables we believe may be related to one another, but we may not have any 'if ... then' causal statements we are trying to test. Rather we are just trying to find general patterns in the data. This is an inductive approach that starts with the data and tries to find patterns in the data that can then be treated as theory. As we mentioned in the last chapter, the inductive approach is sometimes called exploratory analysis because we are 'exploring' the data, while the deductive approach is sometimes called 'confirmatory' analysis because we are trying to confirm (or disconfirm) a theory.

Variance, multiple causes and random factors

The social world we study is quite complicated and the things we study differ across cultures, across social groups of various kinds and over time. This means that our theories tend to be a bit more complicated than those used in other disciplines. The complexity of our theories requires us to take special care in drawing conclusions from data. A few of these complexities are worth noting here.

Variance

Variance simply means that things differ – they are *variable*. Social scientists are interested in why people, communities, organizations, nations and other social phenomena differ from one another. Why do some people commit crimes and others don't? Why do some countries use a lot of energy and produce a lot of greenhouse gas emissions and others don't? Why do some women have children early and others later or not at all? Our theories are attempts to explain the variability in one thing – crime or energy consumption or childbearing – in terms of other things – deterrence or ecological modernization or opportunity costs. So we often talk about independent variables explaining variance in dependent variables.

Multiple causes

Above we discussed the role of hypotheses and 'if – then' statements in making clear the implications of a theory. However, we never really expect only one factor to shape a person's behaviour, a country's social structure or anything else we study. Deterrence may influence criminal behaviour, but no one would say it's the only influence. Economic growth may influence energy consumption but so do many other things. Opportunities may influence fertility decisions, but it's certainly not the only factor.

This means that social scientists are often using the Latin phrase *ceteris paribus*, which means roughly, 'all other things being equal.'[1] An advocate of deterrence theory might argue that states with the death penalty will have lower homicide rates but will note that we will see that effect only after we take account of other factors that influence the homicide rate. This was the motivation for comparing neighbouring states in Chapter 1 – we were trying to make comparisons that kept other influences on the homicide rate the same. But of course the advocate of deterrence theory would argue that the comparison really didn't make the *ceteris* (all other things) *paribus* (equal); rather they would argue there were still important differences between the states compared that masked the effect of the death penalty.

A great deal of work in methods and statistics is concerned with how we take account of factors other than the one(s) on which we are focusing. One of the reasons statistical analysis has become so important in the social sciences is because it provides useful tools for taking account of, or **'controlling,'** the effect of some variables while looking at the effects of the variables that are the center of our attention. This is also why researchers in some fields of social science, especially psychology, like to do studies with experiments. As we will see in Chapter 5, in an experiment we can do a very good job of controlling for all the factors that might influence the effect we are interested in except the cause on which we are focusing.

Random factors

Even when we consider the effects of many variables on the thing we are studying – the variable whose variance we want to explain – we don't expect to understand that variance perfectly. People are idiosyncratic and while some of what they do is explicable, some of it is not. The same is true for communities, organizations and nations – we can develop good theories of why things differ but we never expect to explain things perfectly. Sometimes we can treat the variation that our theories can't explain as

---

[1]   Its literal meaning is *ceteris* – the other, *paribus* – equal.

random. By random we mean that it isn't related to any of the things we study and behaves rather like the toss of a coin or the draw of a numbered ball from a hopper. At least since Galileo scientists have expected that what we see in the world is a mixture of what we can explain with our theories and what is random. Of course, we are always challenged to develop better theories so that the amount of variance we can explain becomes larger and the part that seems random becomes smaller. But this is a goal we never expect to achieve perfectly. Statistics is particularly adept at helping us understand what variability we observe can be attributed to variables we are studying and what part is essentially random.

Causal language and diagrams

Since we often deal with causal statements, it is helpful to introduce some of the language used to describe causal relationships among variables. It is also helpful to consider some simple diagrams that are often used in sketching theories. Let's consider the opportunity costs example. The general theory says that opportunity costs influence important life decisions. So we might assert that the more educational opportunities women have the lower their fertility will be. In 'if ... then' language we would say, 'If women have good educational opportunities, then they will have fewer children than would otherwise be the case'. We are saying that differences in educational opportunities will cause a difference in fertility. Sociologists often use causal diagrams like Figure 3.1 to show such a relationship. The arrow pointing from educational opportunities to fertility indicate that in our hypothesis education is one of the factors that causes variation in fertility.

Figure 3.1 Hypothesized relationship between women's educational opportunities and fertility

Figure 3.2 shows us the relationship between one measure of educational opportunities and one measure of fertility for the countries in the Middle East and North Africa.[2] The 'total fertility rate' can be thought of as the

---

[2]   The data are from Roudi-Fahimi and Moghadam (2003).

average number of children women have. This is our dependent variable. The percentage of women in secondary school is the measure of educational opportunities for women.

These data seem consistent with the hypothesis. The countries with the lowest percentage of women in secondary school have the highest fertility. The countries with higher secondary school enrolment rates for women overall have lower fertility. Palestine is an exception with high secondary school enrolment but also high fertility. And once the school enrolment level gets above about 40 percent, there's not much further decline in fertility. So this raises two issues for further exploration. Why does Palestine deviate from the general pattern? And why don't we get further improvement with over 40 percent of women in school? Having confirmed the theory, at least at this simple level, we might use these additional patterns in the data in an inductive way to generate further theories about what influences fertility.

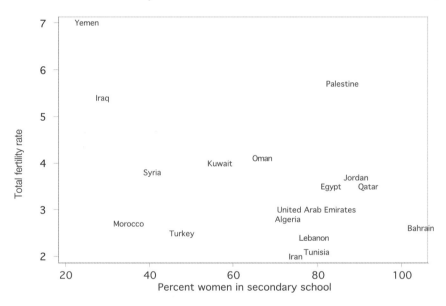

Figure 3.2 Scatterplot of women's education and fertility for countries in the Middle East and North Africa

Explanatory and extraneous variables

The term **explanatory** refers to the independent variables in a research problem. All of the many other variables that could possibly influence the dependent variable are called **extraneous**. For example, in a study of personal income level and parental educational level, the explanatory variables are parental educational level (the independent variable) and personal income level (the dependent variable). There are many other variables that could have an effect on variation in personal income, such as gender, race, type of job, length of time in job, and so on. These are all extraneous to the focus of the research.

Extraneous variables are of two types, controlled and uncontrolled. **Controlled variables** are held constant – not allowed to vary. Extraneous variables can be controlled in three ways. First, we can control by **randomization**. In an experiment, we can assign subjects (the people or other things we are studying) to groups by the flip of a coin or another random process. When we do this, we know that all variables (except those manipulated by the experiment) are going to be equivalent across the experimental and control groups. Any differences between the groups will be the result of a random process and that will limit the size of the effects of the extraneous variables. Not only does randomization limit the size of the differences between the two groups, but it also tells us how big those differences are likely to be. This is because statistics has given us a very good understanding of random processes, and we can use that understanding to assess the differences between groups that occur because of **random assignment**. We will discuss experiments in more detail in Chapter 5, but for now the important point is that randomization is a powerful tool for controlling for extraneous variables.

However, often we can't assign the things we are studying to experimental and control groups, so we must use one of the two other ways of controlling for extraneous variables. One is limiting the scope of our analysis by only looking at one group where we can assume the extraneous variables all have the same value. This is what the comparison of neighbouring states in Chapter 1 was intended to do, but of course in that example and in many other applications, it's hard to find situations where we have a set of cases in which the independent variable of interest varies but the extraneous variables can be assumed to all have the same values. Thus we often turn to the third strategy, where we control for extraneous variables by including them in a statistical analysis.

The most commonly used technique for statistically controlling for extraneous variables is **multiple regression** analysis. Multiple regression takes all variables as explanatory and uses statistical techniques to estimate the effects of each explanatory variable on the dependent variable, taking account of the effects of all the other explanatory variables. The way regression does this involves statistical analysis that is beyond the scope of this book, but the idea is straightforward. This approach has its limits too. In particular, we have to have data on all the extraneous variables we think might have an effect on the dependent variable. A lot of research proceeds by proposing new extraneous variables that, when controlled, change the effect of the estimated effect of an explanatory variable. But sometimes we can posit a variable that might have an effect, but we can't find reasonable data on that variable. For example, in understanding the effect of the death penalty on the crime rate, we have noted that some feel that a 'culture of violence', which varies across states, might legitimate both the death penalty and homicide. But official statistics don't include measures of 'culture of violence'. Baron and Straus (1988) have done considerable work in developing a measure of the culture of violence for US states. Without their efforts we could not explore this interesting idea about the causes of homicide.

Scatterplots

In our example of opportunity costs and fertility, one extraneous variable is obvious. Women won't be able to effectively control their fertility if they don't have access to effective contraception. Even if women have good education and good job opportunities, if they don't use modern contraceptive methods they will be likely to have substantially more children than they might if they were making a trade-off between opportunities and childbearing.[3] We can easily elaborate the **causal diagram** to include the possible effect of contraceptive use on fertility, as in Figure 3.3.

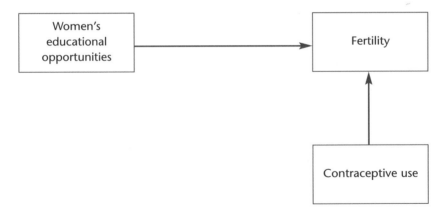

Figure 3.3 Hypothesized relationships between women's educational opportunities, contraceptive use and fertility

---

[3]   We work with data from The 2004 World Population Data of the Population Reference Bureau (http://www.prb.org/pdf04/04WorldDataSheet_Eng.pdf). They define modern contraceptives as: 'methods such as the pill, IUD, condom and sterilization'.

This diagram says that both women's educational opportunities and contra-ceptive access have a causal influence on fertility. Figure 3.4 shows a scatterplot of the relationship between fertility and modern contraceptive use.[4] A **scatterplot** is a visual tool used to show the relationship between two variables (see Box 3.1 for more information on designing and interpreting scatterplots).

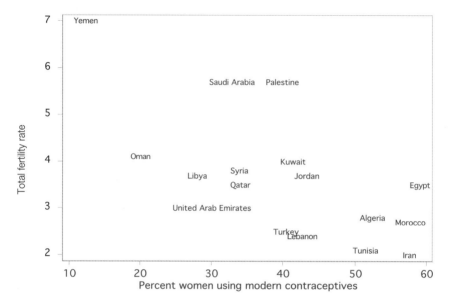

Figure 3.4 Scatterplot of women's contraceptive use and fertility for countries in the Middle East and North Africa

There is a strong relationship between contraceptive use and fertility, with countries with a large proportion of women using contraceptives having lower fertility than countries in which a smaller proportion of women use modern contraceptives. Of course, that is not surprising. Here we might think a little more carefully about the theory. If education provides women with opportunities that displace childbearing then those women might choose to use modern contraceptives to regulate their fertility. This might suggest a slightly different causal diagram, one that shows that education affects fertility but that it also affects the use of contraceptives. Figure 3.5 shows this.

---

[4]   If you have sharp eyes you will note that this diagram does not include either Iraq or Bahrain. Apparently data on use of modern contraceptives do not exist for these two countries. Missing data are a constant issue in research, and we will discuss this problem in more detail in Chapter 6.

Box 3.1: Creating and interpreting a scatterplot

Figure 3.2 is a scatterplot, a diagram of the relationship between two variables. This diagram is like the scatterplot in Figure 2.1, but with different variables. In Box 2.1 we described how to read a scatterplot, and here we show you how to draw one. The convention is that if we are making a distinction between independent and dependent variables we plot the independent variable on the horizontal axis. Often the horizontal axis is called the 'x-axis' because independent variables are often labeled x. We plot the dependent variable on the vertical axis, which is also called the y-axis because the symbol y is often used for dependent variables. Suppose we want to place the data for Turkey on the graph. The percentage of Turkey's school age women in secondary school is 48 percent so we would move along the horizontal axis until we were at 48. Turkey's total fertility rate is about 2.5, so we would now move up the vertical axis until we were at 2.5 and that's where we would put a symbol to indicate that there is a data point there. In this case we are using the name of the country, but we might use small dots, small circles or whatever makes for a graph that is easy to read. Using the name of the country as a marker works well when there are a small number of data points that are reasonably spread out, as is the case in this graph. But if we have a lot of data points or if they have values close together, the names can overlap and be hard to read and small symbols might work better.

We see that the countries with the lowest percentage of women in secondary school, Yemen and Iraq, have quite high fertility, with women on average having over 5 children. In contrast, countries with a high proportion of women in secondary school tend to have lower fertility. So the opportunity costs hypothesis is consistent with this data.

How can Bahrain have a percentage greater than 100? The ratio we are plotting is defined as the number of women in secondary school divided by the number of women in the age groups that normally attend secondary school. So if older women are attending secondary school, that can push the ratio above 100 percent.

In the language used to describe causal relationships, we would say that contraceptive use has a direct effect on fertility. We would also say that women's education has a direct effect on fertility but also an indirect effect because it influences contraceptive use which in turn influences fertility, according to the theory.

Figure 3.6 shows the relationship between secondary education enrolment and the use of modern contraceptives. The pattern here is less clear than we've seen in the other two scatterplots. Yemen has both the lowest percentage of women in secondary school and the lowest use of

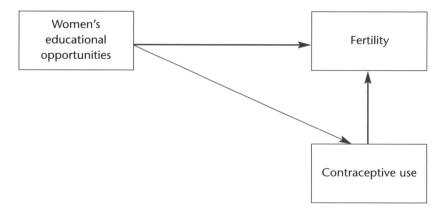

Figure 3.5 Revised hypothesized relationships between women's educational
opportunities, contraceptive use and fertility

contraceptives, but Morocco, with only a slightly higher level of enrolment,
has one of the highest levels of contraceptive use.

Overall we might interpret this graph as not very supportive of the
argument that education is related to contraceptive use. It suggests that
perhaps the arrow we drew from education to contraceptive use doesn't
belong there after all.

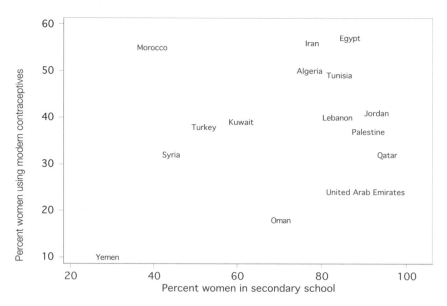

Figure 3.6 Scatterplot of women's education and contraceptive use in
countries in the Middle East and North Africa

Finally, we can try to look at the effect of education once we take into account the use of modern contraceptives. If the theory is correct, we would see a stronger relationship between education and fertility in countries with high levels of contraceptive use than in countries with low levels of contraceptive use. The scatterplots in Figures 3.7 and 3.8 break the countries into two groups, those in which less than 40 percent of women use modern contraceptives and those in which more than 40 percent of women use modern contraceptives. (We chose 40 percent as the cut point simply because it divides the group of countries roughly in half.)

We are now down to so few countries in each plot that we have to be cautious about interpreting the results. But for the countries with low use of contraceptives, there doesn't seem to be a link between fertility and education, except that Yemen is very high on fertility and low on education and thus sits by itself in the graph. In statistical jargon we call this an 'outlier.' Outliers are often worthy of further consideration as they suggest something interesting or unusual is taking place.

When we turn to the scatterplot for countries with higher use of contraceptives, our elaboration of the theory suggests we should see a strong relationship. But, as in the graph for countries with less use of contraceptives, we see no pattern save that Iraq has high levels of fertility and low levels of education compared to the other countries in the plot. This suggests that opportunity cost theory is not very consistent with these data.

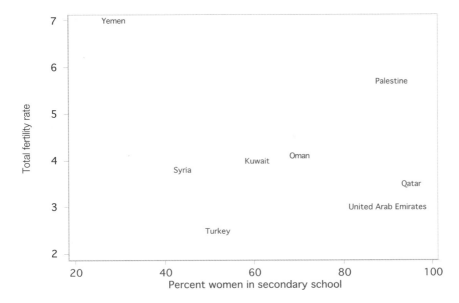

Figure 3.7 Scatterplot of women's education and fertility controlling for contraceptive use (countries with lower prevalence of modern contraception)

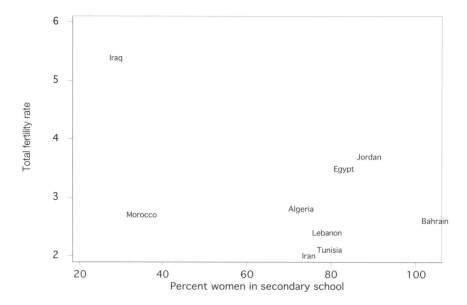

Figure 3.8 Scatterplot of women's education and fertility controlling for contraceptive use (countries with higher prevalence of modern contraception)

Of course, this use of scatterplots, while it shows us some patterns, would only be the beginning and not the end of a research project on this topic. We would want to use some statistical procedures, such as correlation and regression analysis, to get a better understanding of the links among these three variables. Such analysis is beyond what we are going to cover in this book, where we are using these examples to show ideas in research methods rather than draw strong conclusions. And of course, we could think of other variables that may influence fertility and examine their effects. We might also find other data sets to test the theory with the idea that the theory may work in some contexts and not in others.

Procedures of quantitative research: Moving from theory to data

In this concluding section of the chapter we will discuss the decisions that are made as we progress with a quantitative study. Each of these decisions has consequences for the believability of our conclusions and the degree to which we generalize from them to other contexts to which the theory might apply.

Choosing the basic approach: Deciding on context and units of analysis

The theory of opportunity costs suggests that the more opportunities available to women, the lower their fertility will be. We could think of multiple ways of testing this theory. A logical first step is to consider the context in which the theory might apply. Most work on the theory has been done in Western industrial nations or in South and East Asia or Latin America. We might think it useful to see if the theory applies in the Middle East and North Africa, where fertility is relatively high in some but not all nations. Can the variation in fertility in this region be explained by differences in opportunity costs? This seems like a reasonable challenge for the theory. So we have decided that the context of our study will be the Arab nations of the contemporary world. Proponents of the theory might argue that the theory doesn't apply in that context, but we see no reason why that should be the case; rather this seems like an interesting opportunity for the theory to show its ability to explain fertility.

We might do a qualitative analysis. However, that would almost certainly require that we travel to the region to make our observations (see Chapter 4) and that may be beyond the scope of what is feasible for this study (and wouldn't help us explicate how to do a quantitative analysis). We could collect survey data on individual women. Again, collecting that data ourselves would be expensive and time consuming. If we had funding for the study and a couple of years in which to complete it, such a survey would be a good way to proceed because we could measure exactly what we think is appropriate to test the theory. If we don't have the time or funding to do a survey ourselves, we might be able to find existing survey data on one or several countries in the region that measure the things we think are appropriate for testing the theory. This is called secondary data, and will be discussed in more detail in Chapter 5. There is a large data set called the World Fertility Survey (WFS) that collected data from samples in 62 countries in the 1970s and 1980s. About 350,000 women were interviewed. The data include a number of countries in the Middle East and North Africa. Using these data is certainly a possibility. The WFS collected comparable data in each country, and experts consider the data of high quality. The survey measures many things that we would need to test opportunity cost theory. However, the data are 20–30 years old. There is nothing in opportunity costs theory that suggests that the theory wouldn't apply then. Indeed there's a lot of value in testing the theory in different time periods. But we may choose not to use the WFS data either because we don't want to work with a large complicated survey data set (to do this with proper care takes a lot of diligent work to understand the data set and get it ready for our analysis) or because we don't like the way things were measured (always an issue when working with data collected by someone else) or because we want to take a more contemporary look at the theory.

We could try to look for other more recent survey data sets by checking data archives (discussed in more detail in Chapter 5).

But for the moment let's try a different approach, the one we have used for the example in this chapter; let's use cross-national data. We have seen that we can obtain data on a number of variables that seem relevant to the theory for nations in the Middle East and North Africa. By selecting data on nations we are working at an **aggregate** level, with nations rather than individual women or families as the units of analysis. As we have noted, working at the aggregate level is valid but a common error (the ecological fallacy) is to conclude, for example, that the results we have presented above show that well educated women in these countries have the same fertility as less educated women. What we have shown is that when we control for access to contraception in the nation on average, the national fertility rate is not closely related to the proportion of women in secondary school. It seems reasonable to conclude from this that education is not related to fertility for individual women, but the data show us what is true for the nations, not for the women. To be certain about the relationships among these variables for individual women, we would have to have data on the women – such as the survey data we have just discussed. In that case, the unit of analysis is individual women. If we use aggregate level cross-national data, the unit of analysis is the nation.

Operationalizing the variables

Given that we have chosen to use data on nations rather than individual women or households, we would now have to think about how to move from the general theoretical concepts of fertility and opportunity costs to measures that are available for this group of nations. Demographers have spent considerable time thinking about fertility and how to measure it. The total fertility rate is a well accepted measure for this purpose. Conceptually, it is the total number of children a woman would bear if her lifetime fertility matched the average for all women in the country in the year being studied. Thinking of it as an average family size is not far off the mark. So it seems quite appropriate for testing the predictions of opportunity costs theories, though of course there could be other measures of childbearing that would be appropriate, such as age at first birth.

Measuring the opportunity costs themselves is a bit trickier. Most discussion of opportunity costs invokes ideas of education and employment. So measures of women's educational attainment and employment in the labour market seem appropriate. There are a number of such measures available for the countries we are studying. For education we can find data on female adult literacy, primary school enrolment, secondary school enrolment and post-secondary school enrolment. In picking among these, we want to think about two things: 'How good are the data?' and 'How well do they match what is meant by opportunity costs?' Without getting into too much detail, suffice it to say that we have a sense that literacy data are less accurate than enrolment data – measuring literacy requires getting information on the whole adult population, while school enrolment data are counted routinely by most governments. So to get female enrolment rates, someone had to get the school enrolment data for women and divide it by the size of the female population in the appropriate age groups. While there are certainly some errors in these numbers, we think they are accurate enough for testing the theory. Employment data are harder to obtain because, again, each country has to conduct counts (usually via surveys) of employed women.

The data quality issue seems to give an edge to enrolment data. What variables most closely match the theory? We picked secondary school enrolment because it seemed more appropriate to the idea of opportunity costs for this group of countries than either primary or post-secondary enrolment. In less affluent nations than these, primary enrolment may be the stepping stone to opportunities for women; in more affluent nations substantial opportunities may require a college degree.

Of course, if we have data available on literacy and enrolment in other levels of education we could certainly analyse it, along with measures of employment. We could proceed in either of two ways. We could replicate the analysis above using these other measures of opportunity costs to see if the results are consistent across each operationalization of opportunity costs. If we find all the different measures of opportunity costs give the same result, then that gives us more confidence in our conclusion. If we find we get different results with some measures than we obtained with others, we need to think further about why those differences occurred. Perhaps it's because some of the variables are poorly measured. Perhaps it's because some opportunities matter and other don't. For example, we have posited that secondary enrolment is the appropriate measure of opportunity costs but we may be wrong, perhaps post-secondary education is what matters in these countries.

Alternatively, we could combine all the measures of education or all the measures of education and employment into a single number representing opportunity costs for a country. That process is called **scaling**. There is a very substantial literature in quantitative methods on how best to see if multiple measures belong together in a scale, to best combine them to make a good scale, and to take account of the error between what we have measured with the scale and the theoretical construct we hope to measure. For example, we could take the sum of primary, secondary and post-secondary school enrolment to get overall enrolment. The statistical methods that have been developed will give us an indication of whether or not this is a good idea – do these three things 'hang together?' They will also suggest how we might best give more weight to one or another in adding them together. And we can use statistical scaling procedures to see how well the resulting measure of opportunity costs predicts fertility and how much error there is in the measure compared to a hypothetical 'perfect' measure of opportunity costs. It's beyond the scope of this book to show you these tools in detail. Our point is that quantitative researchers think very carefully about how well they measure things and have developed some very powerful tools to help us understand measurement.

Analysing the data

We have used scatterplots to analyse the data because they are easy to interpret. However, one limitation of a scatterplot is that it is two dimensional and thus only allows us to look at two variables at a time. In Figures 3.7 and 3.8 we worked past this problem by comparing two scatterplots, each of which has a subset of countries. But as you can see, we quickly run out of data when we do this.

While each scatterplot only allows us to look at two variables and the strategy of developing scatterplots for subgroups of countries to control for other variables is limited by the amount of data we have, other quantitative procedures are not so limited. Indeed, one of the reasons we use quantitative methods is that they allow us to take account of multiple independent variables at once. In principle, it is quite easy to use statistical methods to look at the effects of dozens of independent variables on the dependent variable. The only limitation is that one typically needs at least 10 times as many cases as there are variables being considered. So with 17 countries, looking at two independent variables (opportunity costs and contraception) takes us to the limit. But if we expanded the context of the analysis to more countries, we could take account of more variables.

As we have noted, in quantitative research we often proceed in just this way. We might argue opportunity costs only matter in countries where women have political power. There are a number of ways we could test that assertion. For example, it's easy to obtain data on the proportion of national legislators who are women or of the year in which women were given the right to vote in national elections. These might be added to the analysis to control for women's political power. While we couldn't do this with scatterplots with so few countries in our data set, we could use other statistical techniques. Of course, there is only so much that we can learn with a quantitative analysis of this relatively small number of countries, so a logical next step would be to expand the data set. We might add more countries and change the focus of our analysis from just North Africa and the Middle East. Or we might be able to find data for the same countries for multiple years. Suppose we could find data for the 17 countries in our last analysis for circa 2000 but also for 1990 and 1995. We would then have 17*3=51 data points. If we expanded to all the larger (population greater than 1 million or so) nations in the world, we would have over 100 data points.

The tools used in quantitative analysis are very powerful and although they can also be rather complex, the basic logic is clear. We are usually trying to understand why something of interest, such as fertility, varies. We develop that understanding by looking at what factors (independent variables) are able to predict variations. By coupling these tools with theories about why the independent variables affect the dependent variables, we can test the ability of our theories to describe the world, and in the process hone our theories and thus our understanding of the world.

Applications

1   Time use among adolescents

In the first chapter, we introduced some of the ways adolescents spend their time outside of school and some of the outcomes these activities can impact (e.g. plans for higher education).

Drawing on that information or your own ideas about ways adolescents spend their time (e.g. video games) and potential outcomes, design a quantitative study using at least one independent and one dependent variable about teenagers' activities.
a)   Draw a diagram to depict the relationship(s) you propose.
b)   State what you hypothesize the relationship to be if we had data available to test it.
c)   What makes this a quantitative study?

2   The experiences of older adults with dementia

In the previous set of applications, we thought about patients with dementia. Having a loved one with dementia can be extremely challenging because as the disease progresses, most dementia patients cannot remember their loved ones and cannot take care of themselves. In this exercise, we focus on the primary caregiver of the dementia patient, whether it be a spouse, adult child, significant other, or other loved one.

a) Write out the relationship depicted in this causal model. In addition, determine the independent and dependent variables.

b) Write out the relationship depicted in this causal model. In addition, determine the independent and dependent variables. Name one possible uncontrolled extraneous variable.

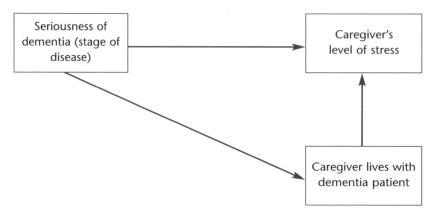

3 The death penalty as a deterrent to crime

We previously proposed that a relationship might exist between states having the death penalty as a punishment option and state homicide rates and between poverty and state homicide rates.

a) Draw a causal model that reflects the relationships we hypothesized in Chapter 1 (note: this is what we expected, not necessarily what we found with the data that were presented). Summarize the causal model; what are the hypothesized relationships?

b) What are the independent and dependent variables in this model?

4 Ecological modernization theory

a) Draw a causal model that reflects the relationship hypothesized in the ecological modernization theory.

b) What are the explanatory variables?

5   Gender differences in mathematics, science and language skills

Spencer and colleagues (1999) conducted an experiment related to gender differences in mathematics skills. They gave a mathematics test to a sample of men and women after half of the women were told that the test they would take previously showed gender differences in scores. The other half of the women were told that no gender differences were previously found on the mathematics test. Women who were told about the gender differences scored worse than the men. The women who were told there were no gender differences performed, on average, as well as the men did on the mathematics test. Interestingly, all the women in the sample were high mathematics achievers.
a)   What is the hypothesis in this study?
b)   What are the independent and dependent variables?
c)   Was the hypothesis supported or refuted by the data?

6   Work and family balance issues/opportunity costs theory

This has already been covered in detail in this chapter, so there will be no additional exercises.

7   Sexual and contraceptive behaviour and the threat of HIV/AIDS

As outlined in Chapter 1, it is hypothesized that countries will have a lower incidence of HIV/AIDS when their citizens have greater levels of HIV/AIDS education. Several factors contribute to the knowledge level citizens have about HIV/AIDS.
a)   Design a quantitative research question to investigate potential factors (at least two) that may lead to different levels of HIV/AIDS knowledge among individuals.
b)   What are the independent and dependent variables?
c)   What makes this a quantitative study?
d)   Identify at least one possible extraneous variable that was not included in your proposed research question.

4 Basic Logic of Qualitative Inquiry

- Introduction
- The nature of qualitative research
- Framing research: Inductive theoretical approaches
- Identifying a research topic and research questions
- Grounded theory
- The qualitative and quantitative divide
- Procedures of qualitative research: Moving from data to theory
- Applications

Introduction

The previous chapter described quantitative approaches to studying the social world. We can answer many questions with those techniques, such as do young girls and boys differ in their science and mathematics skills; to what extent do sexually active men and women utilize protection for the purpose of preventing sexually transmitted diseases; and how much time do working mothers spend with work, family and household activities? We can also use quantitative methods to answer questions such as what factors lead young girls and boys to have different levels of mathematics and science skills; how do sexually active individuals decide if and when to use protection; and how do opportunity structures influence women's fertility? However, the latter group of questions can also be examined using qualitative methods. And some questions are more easily answered with qualitative methods, such as: how do young boys and girls feel about mathematics and science; what do sexually active individuals think about when they make decisions about protection from AIDS; and how do women feel about their choices regarding education, career and childbearing? This chapter summarizes qualitative approaches, which constitute the other major form of scientific inquiry in the social sciences, and are better suited than quantitative methods to address these latter three research questions.

The goal of both qualitative and quantitative research is to achieve a better understanding about how the world works. But qualitative and quantitative methodologies achieve this goal differently, beginning with the conceptualization and design of the study and moving on to the sampling frame, data collection strategies, and how the data are analysed. Scholars select between qualitative and quantitative approaches depending on the nature of their research problem. Perhaps the simplest way of distinguishing qualitative and quantitative research is the following: quantitative research uses statistical tools to aid in the interpretation of data, while qualitative research investigates questions without statistical tools, relying instead on the ability of the researcher to observe patterns. Both approaches are increasingly making use of visual tools as well. Indeed, while there are strong and separate traditions of quantitative and qualitative research in the social sciences, the boundaries between the two approaches are becoming more blurred. It is useful when beginning to learn methods to think about quantitative and qualitative methods as different approaches, but it's equally important not to think that the distinction is too rigid.

Beginning students commonly assume that qualitative methods are 'easier' to use than are quantitative methods because they do not involve statistics – a topic many social science students view with apprehension. However, this perspective is not accurate. As we'll see in this chapter and in the remaining chapters, qualitative methods can be just as rigorous as quantitative methods, and also just as demanding of the researcher although in different ways.

The nature of qualitative research

Like quantitative research, qualitative research can be used to study almost anything you can imagine in the social world, including societal and cultural phenomena; individual behaviours; and decision-making and thought processes. However, the tradition of qualitative research tends to focus on the *meaning and motivations* that underlie cultural symbols (e.g. language), personal experiences, and phenomena and on detailed understandings of processes in the social world. As discussed in the last chapter, quantitative research methods are typically used to understand variation, test causal relationships and identify the prevalence or distribution of phenomena. The goals of qualitative research, on the other hand, are to understand processes, experiences and meanings people assign to things. Again, these are not absolute boundaries – a classic quantitative work is called *The Measurement of Meaning* (Osgood *et al.*, 1957) and many qualitative studies explore what causes what. But for the most part qualitative research focuses on *how* people make sense of their settings and experiences through symbols, social roles, identities, and other elements of culture and *why* people think and act as they do. The emphasis in qualitative research is on individuals' own interpretations of their experiences and studying what they say and do in detail. The data are observations of conversations and other forms of social interaction, the use of symbols, and increasingly images. Typically qualitative interpretation is in the form of text with little or no use of numbers.[1] In this section, we introduce the basic premises and uses of qualitative research.

Constructed nature of reality

While there are many theoretical strains that influence both qualitative and quantitative research, one line of theory, **social constructionism**, has been especially influential in shaping qualitative inquiry. The idea is that the social world is actively constructed by interactions, that those interactions usually invoke symbols that are important to those interacting (e.g. language, cultural symbols like a flag), and that a key goal of the social sciences is to understand how people construct and make sense of the world they live in and of the other people in it (Berger and Luckmann, 1966).[2] [An **interpretive approach** is also a common theoretical perspective that utilizes qualitative methods. An interpretive orientation to research aims to describe the lived experiences of individuals from their own viewpoints and to understand how people 'interpret' their experiences.]

  Thus the subject matter of most qualitative research is how people construct their understandings of the social world and how they view their lives. Reality is seen as subjective and variable across individuals, and a major goal is to understand how these views of reality differ. A central question is how people come to make sense of the world and carry out their everyday lives. To explore this, qualitative research focuses on behaviours, interactions, feelings and symbols to uncover the meaning embedded within them. In other words, one of the major uses of qualitative methods is to explore phenomena and experiences from the perspectives of individuals experiencing them. Data typically include rich descriptions of

---

1   One of our friends, Joseph Scimecca, who is a qualitative sociologist, likes to say that the only numbers he uses are page numbers.

2   We have simplified the definitions and uses of interpretism and social constructionism in this chapter since the intention is to give an overview of qualitative research. In addition, we recognize that several theoretical paradigms largely rely on qualitative methods for their inquiries, but we will not be describing all these paradigms in this book (e.g. postmodernism, feminism).

the experiences of those being studied. Qualitative studies usually make extensive use of the statements of the research subjects to illustrate how they are seeing and shaping the world.

In the last chapter, we presented country level data on the percentage of women using modern contraceptives, fertility rates, and the percentage of women in secondary school and examined hypotheses derived from opportunity cost theory using scatterplots. But it would also be useful to understand the significance of motherhood and education to the women in the countries we investigated and to know how women make decisions regarding their education, use of contraceptive devices and fertility. In what ways do cultural norms impact on women's decisions, and how do they view the role of women in their countries? Looking at these issues from the vantage point of the women themselves, rather than using national statistics, would be a qualitative approach to the theory of opportunity costs.

Let's consider another example of a constructionist orientation. Elective cosmetic surgery among women has been on the rise in some countries in recent years. One approach to understanding why this may be is to examine the meaning society places on the feminine body and norms regarding beauty and femininity. These normative prescriptions for the female body may impact how women view their bodies and the decisions they make regarding cosmetic surgery. To investigate the significance of the female body in a culture, we could examine cultural images, including body images of females who are highly regarded in a culture and body images of women commonly portrayed in the media. Or we could identify the predominant ways male and female citizens reference women's physical features (e.g. see Bourgois, 1989; 2000; Cohen *et al.*, 1988; Gimlin, 2000).

Insider's perspective and an in-depth orientation

As we have said, at the core of most qualitative research is understanding how people *interpret the social world*. To do so, it is necessary to study people in their **natural settings** (e.g. homes, workplaces, public settings). Quantitative research often uses experiments in research laboratories or uses survey information where individuals are given specific choices to select from to describe something. These data collection methods offer very limited ways to address interpretative questions that are at the heart of qualitative research. The methods of obtaining data in qualitative research utilize in-depth emic insights into individuals' lives. By **emic**, we mean the scientist seeks an insider's perspective on a particular subject matter. In the opportunity costs example, we would want to know how women think about their educational and job opportunities and about childbearing. To obtain emic insights, researchers often spend considerable time with the people they are studying and make extensive use of individuals' own words to summarize findings. And qualitative researchers also observe people as they go about their daily lives. Qualitative methods are often used to make comparisons between countries, institutions (e.g. justice systems) or groups or to study in detail a particular historical event or period of time using documents, official records, recordings, personal correspondence and other "traces" of what has happened or is happening. Thus there are a variety of data collection techniques for qualitative research, including document analysis (e.g. magazines, diaries, videos, historical papers), interviews and observations of behaviour. Qualitative studies often weave together extensive quotes, detailed descriptions and a researcher's observations of the subject matter to tell a story about an event, phenomenon or set of experiences or behaviours. We'll discuss data collection techniques in detail in the next chapter, but the important point is that quantitative and qualitative research each draw on the strengths of different data collection strategies to explore their research questions. In the case of qualitative research, the aim is often to study phenomena or individuals in-depth and in their natural settings.

Let's return to one of our research questions: what factors contribute to young girls and boys having different levels of mathematics and science skills? It is possible for us to study this using a quantitative perspective. We could develop and test the hypothesis that teachers' attitudes about mathematics and science skills may have a gender bias, which affects how they teach those subjects to boys and girls. We could administer a survey asking teachers their views about girls' and boys' aptitudes for mathematics and science. We could then compare that to the performance of children in those teachers' classes to see if their attitudes on gender differences in ability influence how well boys and girls do. Using a qualitative approach, on the other hand, we could observe several classrooms to document patterns of behaviour, such as whether teachers are more likely to call on girls or boys when teaching mathematics and how other students respond when girls give correct mathematics answers compared to when boys do. That is, we could look at how teachers and other students convey meaning to correct and incorrect answers to mathematics questions by boys and girls. We could also conduct in-depth interviews with both teachers and students to see how they view girls and boys who are highly skilled at and less skilled at mathematics to understand how children's identities are constructed around mathematics skills. We could then seek to better understand these findings in the context of theories about gender roles and socialization, among other theories.

As we just illustrated, both qualitative and quantitative methods can be used to study the same topic but from different vantage points. Both approaches have their strengths and weaknesses. If both were used in parallel, the results would be far more convincing than if either were used alone. Increasingly, studies are designed to allow qualitative and quantitative methods to complement each other.

Exploratory questions and difficult to access groups

Qualitative methods are particularly well suited for studying a substantive area about which little is known in order to describe phenomena in detail, and to explore topics that are difficult to study by other means. Imagine that you are interested in learning about the daily struggles of homeless people or drug addicts and their dealers. There is no formal list of homeless people or drug addicts and dealers from which to draw a sample, and it is not likely even if you can find these populations that they would readily sit down to answer a structured set of questions. In such circumstances, alternative methods may be necessary, such as participant observation, whereby a researcher would assume a role within a circle of drug addicts or homeless people and observe other drug addicts/dealers' behaviours by immersing him or herself into the drug culture (i.e. spend considerable time in areas where drug addicts congregate).[3] As we discussed in Chapter 2, the decision about when to carry out such covert research, where the researcher's role is unknown to those being observed, presents an ethical challenge. Ethical guidelines generally encourage overt research whenever possible so individuals are aware they are participating in a research project. However, there are exceptions to this, such as difficult to reach populations or when access to information is denied by those in power (see Box 2.3, item 2.3.4, page 53). When possible, the researcher should strive to carry out overt research, but when it is difficult to access a group or when quantitative data collection techniques are not appropriate for investigating a research question, qualitative methods may be a better approach. Of course, the qualitative approach cannot give us accurate information on how common homelessness or drug addiction is. Again, we find that qualitative and quantitative methods are each most powerful if they are complemented by the other.

Sometimes we study relatively unknown topics for which there are no or few prior theories or insights on which we can draw to create hypotheses. In such instances, more exploratory techniques are warranted. Qualitative studies can be done initially and the results can then be used to carry out a quantitative study. If we want to learn more about cosmetic surgery and

---

[3] We present this as an example of difficult to access groups and the challenges scholars face in studying them. This is not to say that no quantitative studies of these groups have been conducted (e.g. Rossi *et al.*, 1987; Koegel, *et al.*, 1996). Indeed, these studies reveal important information about homelessness and also about the care that must be taken in using quantitative methods in studies of hard to reach populations and the cautions that must accompany conclusions.

women's views of their bodies, we may begin by conducting a series of in-depth interviews with a number women who have had cosmetic surgery to better understand the major issues they considered in deciding to have surgery. This study would help identify the most relevant factors in cosmetic surgery decision-making. Then the researcher may carry out a larger study with a representative probability sample of women to understand the extent these factors influence women's decisions in a particular culture (or to make comparisons between cultures). It is becoming very common to conduct a qualitative analysis as a way to inform a subsequent survey that will be analysed by quantitative methods.

Qualitative methods are also sometimes used at the start of research on interventions to solve social problems. Some researchers, for instance, have proposed that one way to improve the mathematics and science skills of young girls is to have single gender classrooms. The premise is that through gender role socialization girls and boys are taught that boys have a stronger aptitude for mathematics and science and girls for language. Their test performances then reflect this socialization. Without the presence of boys, girls may feel more comfortable learning and participating in mathematics and science programmes and would not be competing with boys, which would help them improve their knowledge, confidence and skills. A school district may consider instituting same-gender classrooms to reduce the gender inequities in test scores. Before undertaking a district-wide restructuring of classrooms and curriculum, the district may test the same-gender programme in one or two classrooms first to see if the intervention is effective in improving test scores. A research team may observe the students in the classrooms before and after the intervention to see if the girls participate more in mathematics and science lessons in the same-gender classroom. Or they may conduct some in-depth interviews with the girls to see how they view the same-gender classrooms. This information would be used to gauge whether or not it would be beneficial to alter the classrooms district-wide.

Unusual and extreme events

It is not uncommon for qualitative researchers to study a single case in-depth, whether it is an historical event, a culture, a subgroup or an individual person. This is one of the particular advantages of qualitative methods. Quantitative analysis seeks to identify patterns and general tendencies. We saw this in the last chapter; we used scatterplots to identify patterns in how two variables were related and used evidence from the pattern of the majority of cases to describe the relationships. But we saw that there were some cases that diverged considerably from the majority. These are identified as outliers. Becker (1998) has emphasized that these outlying cases can often be the most informative and interesting ones and should be studied to better understand them. Because there are typically only a few such cases (and usually we are not sure why they are outliers), qualitative methods can be an ideal way of studying them. Investigating outliers can help us not only learn about those cases but also about the general pattern by identifying what differentiates the outliers from the typical cases. As we saw in the scatterplot between the percentage of women in secondary school and fertility rate in the previous chapter (Figure 3.2), Palestine was an 'unusual' or deviating case. It had a high percentage of women in secondary education and a high fertility rate. A qualitative researcher would ask why this country differs from the pattern in neighbouring countries and use in-depth interviews with women or perhaps analyze textual materials in Palestinian media to understand the situation better. Again we see that qualitative and quantitative methods are complementary.

Framing research: Inductive theoretical approaches

Qualitative research typically follows an inductive process, while quantitative research usually follows a deductive approach. With an inductive approach, data are collected and theoretical insights are *derived from the data*. In other words, the theory is 'induced' from the data rather than having conclusions about what the data should look like if the theory is true.

While there is a clear distinction between inductive and deductive research, as Berg aptly (1998) points out, both definitions portray the research process as being linear. In other words, induction implies that we first collect data and proceed to develop theory from the data (so data generates theory). With deductive approaches, as depicted in Figure 4.1, we test a theory and determine whether our data support or refute the theory (so theory drives the generation of data). In reality research pathways are seldom so simple. Typically a research question becomes better defined as one reads prior literature and begins collecting data. In addition, theoretical insights are uncovered throughout an inductive research project, not just at the end, becoming defined and refined over the course of the project as the data are collected and analysed. As a result, the theory 'in formation' will shape the kind of data being sought as more data are collected.

Figure 4.1 Overview of quantitative research process

Berg (1998) has described the qualitative research process as having a spiral rather than linear progression, with theory generation and data collection and analysis being interwoven. Since the goals of qualitative research are often to understand underlying meanings or describe experiences or phenomena in-depth, data collection, sampling, analysis and interpretation are typically done simultaneously. Once initial information is obtained and interpreted, this may lead the researcher in search of other data, including modifying the interview questions, or even altering the sampling frame (e.g. looking for specific types of cases that seem especially interesting in light of the emerging theory). Each piece of information builds on the others, evolving into an understanding of the research question at hand. Therefore, especially with qualitative research, the relationship between data collection and theoretical development is more reciprocal than strictly linear. We depict this iterative, reciprocal process of gathering and analysing data and generating theory in Figure 4.2.

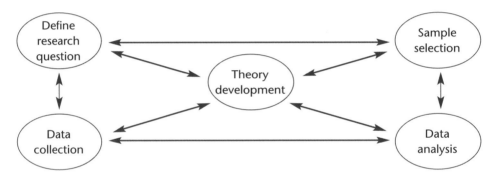

Figure 4.2 Overview of qualitative research process

What are the benefits of following an inductive approach to a topic? Some research topics do not have an existing theory on which to draw. Data can help generate theoretical insights in such cases. In other instances though, the decision to use qualitative methods is based on the epistemological orientation of the scholar. Some social scientists believe that allowing the theory to emerge from the data yields a more accurate view of reality than emerges from refining theories in the light of data. They argue that theories can be biased and limited. In other words, looking at a research question from a particular theoretical lens can cause the researcher to have tunnel vision. It's possible the researcher would miss some important insights by not being open to possibilities beyond the existing theory. To see the value of an inductive approach, we can use our previous example of making observations in a classroom to better understand gender inequities in mathematics, science and language test performance. If we go into the classroom with the theory that teachers' gender-biased approaches to student learning are impacting student performance, we may be so focused on teaching styles that other important factors are completely missed. An inductive approach would be open to influences outside the classroom and within the classroom aside from the teacher's role (e.g. how students interact). Of course, if we thought of these other factors in advance, they could be incorporated into a deductive approach. The advantage of the inductive approach is that factors we didn't think about before we began the study would be considered, as long as we are open to noticing them. For example, we may observe how the teacher behaves, how students react when girls perform well on mathematics questions or boys perform well on language tests, how girls respond when they do not perform as well as boys do on mathematics and science tests, and so forth. Some of these factors may be important but may not have been anticipated before observations in the classroom began. By keeping an open mind and not being tied down to a specific theory, we could obtain a more well-rounded understanding of what may be contributing to the gender differences. Remember that the influence of theoretical assumptions can have a powerful influence on what we observe as we saw in our discussion of the measurement of presumed racial differences in intelligence in Chapter 2.

In some circumstances, we are interested in elaborating on a theory using qualitative methods. We could begin our research project with a general theoretical framework and from there expand on and identify new theoretical contributions when analysing data. Thus, not all qualitative research begins without any theoretical framework. But qualitative work develops and refines theories during the course of data collection and analysis, so theories and data are typically used much more flexibly than they are with quantitative methods. The limitation is that, since the theory is developed in part directly from the data in hand, data can't be used to test the credibility of the theory – since the data led to the theory, the data must match the theory. Again, we emphasize that science is a social process, so in the case of inductive work the confirmation of the theories that result comes from replication by other researchers or by the same researcher in a new study.

Identifying a research topic and research questions

Research questions are the core of all research designs. Ideas about what to study often come from our personal experiences and curiosities. The challenge is to take those ideas and identify a specific topic of inquiry and then ask 'good' questions. An initial step in formulating a qualitative project is to select a topic that interests us. The topic is the starting point, which we then need to refine into a question or problem. Unlike quantitative research, in qualitative the research question is *defined and redefined continually* while the data are being collected and analysed. This does not mean a qualitative researcher begins collecting data with no research questions. The researcher usually begins with a general or broad question. Initial qualitative questions are just not framed too precisely or narrowly because the goal is for the researcher to keep an open mind and to let insights emerge from the data that help reshape the research questions.

If we want to learn about patients with dementia, our research topic could be the everyday challenges facing patients with dementia, experiences of family members of dementia patients, or cultural variations in the significance of dementia. Designing questions with a qualitative lens is very flexible, and again, to reiterate, the research question typically begins broad and is redefined several times as data are collected and analysed. A qualitative researcher will usually start by identifying a general question around the topic, with the goal tending to be to *explore*, *describe*, or *explain* something. Consider the topic of cultural variations in dementia. Our initial research question is: 'How do different cultures treat older people who have dementia?' Researchers have found that in some cultures the concept of dementia does not exist; declining memory and cognitive abilities that accompany the ageing process are viewed as natural changes rather than as disease states. With this information, our research question may be redefined to ask: 'How do different cultures view older adults and their cognitive changes, and in what cultural circumstances are patients identified as having dementia?' This question in turn may be refocused or refined as we establish our sampling frame and begin to collect data.

There are also practical issues to consider when designing research questions; the questions should be able to be answered by the type of study the researcher can do. We can all think of questions that interest us, but is it possible for us to study these things? Realistically, we cannot study every culture in the world to identify how they view ageing and cognitive decline. Therefore, our question would be specified to reflect the cultures we can actually investigate.

Researchers sometimes unintentionally impose a framework on their project that does not fit what they are studying or leads strongly in a particular direction when the researcher is trying to follow an exploratory, inductive approach. For instance, for our question about gender differences in mathematics and science skills, we may pose this question: 'How does teaching style lead to different levels of mathematics and science skills for male and female students?' This question assumes that teaching style is the cause of the gender differences, which may lead us to focus exclusively on observations of teaching style and overlook other (perhaps more salient) factors, such as how students interact with and react to each other. A better question to begin this study would be: 'What factors in the classroom may impact male and female students' mathematics and science skills?'

Strauss and Corbin (1990) summarize *four types of questions* that qualitative researchers use when carrying out their research. First, they ask **theoretical questions**, which help identify relationships and patterns in the data and understand whether and why differences between cases are found (e.g. what is the relationship between X and Y?). Returning to our example of classroom observations to explore gender differences in mathematics and science skills, a theoretical question we may ask is, 'How do our observations of teaching styles, student behaviours and test performance match theories of gender role socialization?' These theoretical questions link data and theory together. Researchers also ask **sensitizing questions**, which help the researcher determine what the data are indicating. Sensitizing questions focus on things like, 'What is the meaning of something to individuals?' and 'What does that behaviour signify?' We could ask, 'How do boys and girls react to in-class comments by peers who are good in mathematics and science and do these reactions differ by gender?' Third are **guiding questions**, which direct the course of data collection and analysis and are likely to change over time as theory and empirical data evolve. For instance, if a particular theme begins to emerge in interviews with respondents, the researcher may add a series of questions to further understand that theme among the remaining set of respondents. If we noticed differences in how often girls and boys volunteer to answer questions in their mathematics and science lessons, we may direct our attention to the students' behaviours during the lessons to identify any non-verbal cues students may be giving that would help us better understand the origins or reasons for the difference. Finally there are **practical questions**, which is a broad category encompassing questions about the particularities of the research design. How will selecting a particular data collection technique over another affect the type of data to be collected? What should the sampling frame be? Is my theory logical? Continuing with our classroom observation example, we may have contemplated conducting interviews with students and teachers about the gender differences but decided that it is not likely that students, for instance, would be very cognizant that they may be acting in specific gender-socialized ways. Such a thought would lead us to give greater consideration to an observational study instead (or in addition to interviews).

Grounded theory

In 1967 Glaser and Strauss developed rigorous techniques for generating theoretical ideas from empirical data, which they termed grounded theory.

Grounded theory is thus an inductive approach, and the term reflects the fact that the theory is rooted in or 'grounded' in the data. Grounded theory was developed at a time when, unfortunately, researchers following primarily qualitative or quantitative lines heavily critiqued each other's work and approaches to understanding the world. Grounded theory offered researchers investigating qualitative questions a concrete method for carrying out a study. While some interpretive scholars have critiqued grounded theory for unnecessarily trying to resemble quantitative methods by establishing a detailed approach for conducting research, grounded theory remains popular today. This brief introduction to grounded theory aims to give you a better sense of this popular qualitative approach to studying the social world.

Grounded theory is an iterative process and involves simultaneous data collection and analysis. A project begins with a general guiding research question. As data are initially gathered, the researcher identifies core themes and concepts from the data. Data collection may shift to focus on learning more about these themes. At the same time, the researcher remains open to identifying other important issues. The early stages of the research tend to be very open as far as what information is collected since there are usually no theoretical restrictions on what is considered relevant. Data collection consequently can take a long period of time. Later phases are spent verifying data and putting data into meaningful categories.

Coding of data, making comparisons, and theoretical sampling are central to grounded theory. We introduced theoretical sampling in Chapter 2 and discuss coding and other strategies for analysing and summarizing data later in this chapter, so we will only briefly describe them here. With ongoing analysis of data, researchers can monitor their data collection, selecting additional study participants based on insights gained from earlier participant data and stopping data collection once new information is no longer generated from additional cases. We may, for instance, while examining how divorced parents and their children interact, identify three general types of familial interactions: parents who have considerable direct contact with each other, parents who largely interact through their children only and a lack of familial participation among the non-custodial parent. Having identified these three groups during early data collection, we might then be sure to sample a reasonable number of families from each group to have enough data to compare how their interaction patterns impact the children.

Grounded theory methodology places special emphasis on a process of finding similarities and differences in the data. A pattern of similarity in data is given a unique **theme**, which is a term for a name or label that reflects the substantive concept. These themes are redefined and delineated from one another as additional empirical information becomes available for analysis. When doing grounded theory, we look not only for data that are similar but also for data that do not fit with a pattern or concept that is identified. By looking at divergent data – the outliers – we can better understand what distinguishes one concept from other concepts.

Drawing on the example of divorced families, we may label one pattern of child-parent interactions in the data 'emotional manipulation' (i.e. the theme). This term describes a child's use of a parent's guilt about breaking up the marriage to acquire something the child wishes. We arrived at this theme by identifying examples of emotional manipulation in our interviews with or observations of divorced families. By recognizing the commonalities between examples (e.g. playing on a parent's guilt in various ways to obtain something desirable to the child), we are able to recognize a pattern, which we then label 'emotional manipulation'. This interaction pattern would be distinguished from other types of behaviour that do not employ guilt as a tactic such as a child asking the second parent for something they want after the first parent says no.

In the grounded theory approach, theories are formed by identifying relationships between concepts (i.e. themes). In other words, existing concepts are not imposed on the data when applying grounded theory principles, but rather concepts that emerge from the data are used. While grounded theory has become synonymous with induction, Strauss (1987) points out that grounded theory also involves some deductive techniques since continuous theoretical analysis of the data suggests avenues of research that seem fruitful for further development as the study progresses.

The qualitative and quantitative divide

Qualitative research has been a formal methodological approach since the beginning of the twentieth century, with roots in anthropology.[4] Today qualitative methods are used across the social sciences. While we view qualitative and quantitative methods as complementary approaches to studying the world and this position is increasingly common among the social science community, not everyone agrees. Until recently, most researchers were trained in either qualitative or quantitative approaches. This led to a strong division between qualitative and quantitative researchers, who denied the value of the other approach. Some have characterized qualitative research as 'soft' science or 'merely' journalism because of the frequent use of quotes and detailed descriptions. A more serious concern with qualitative research has been the inability to verify the data.

---

[4]   See Denzin and Lincoln (2000) for a concise history of qualitative research and the challenges the field has faced since its origins.

When researchers engage in participant observation in a particular community, for instance, we must rely on the truthfulness of the researcher to accurately report her observations and trust that the researcher made rigorous observations and analyses. Criticisms have also been made about quantitative research. Some have argued that quantitative methods pay so much attention to identifying patterns of relationships and understanding variation that they miss the 'outliers' and what some feel is the core issue in the social sciences: what individuals themselves think, feel and do and how they interpret the world. To study this adequately, researchers advocating a qualitative approach argue that more than numbers are needed; perspectives from individuals themselves and in-depth examinations of subject matter are warranted. What we need to remember when evaluating either approach is that their goals, orientations and methods differ, so it's unfair to evaluate one by the other's approach.

Throughout this book, we advocate the importance of using multiple methods whenever doing social science research. We have already introduced the concept of triangulation, which recognizes the value of using multiple theories, data collection strategies, data analytic techniques, and both qualitative and quantitative methods to obtain a more complete understanding of the social world. Laurel Richardson (1994), a qualitative researcher, deconstructs the metaphor of triangulation, advocating a shift toward **crystallization**. She argues that the crystal is a more appropriate metaphor for describing the research process because triangulation implies there are only three sides or vantage points from which social phenomena can be approached. The shape of a crystal suggests the use of multiple angles and dimensions to address research questions. Regardless of whether you prefer the concept of triangulation or crystallization, the important point is that there are numerous ways to look at the social world.

Procedures of qualitative research: Moving from data to theory

Most commonly, observational methods and in-depth interviews are used to explore qualitative-based research questions. In some cases, as we will discuss in Chapter 5, comparative techniques and analysis of media images and other forms of communication are also used to study qualitative topics. The resulting data for qualitative research are not numbers but rather text – in the form of interview transcripts, a researcher's observational notes, and archival documents – and in some instances images. Researchers are then faced with organizing and interpreting a large amount of text. Let's say 20 one-hour interviews were conducted. It would not be uncommon for each interview transcript to be 40 pages. In just this small example, the researchers would have to synthesize 800 pages of text. While quantitative data are analysed using a well-defined set of statistical tools, analysis of qualitative data is a much less rigid process because it involves synthesis of text. This is not to say that qualitative data analysis is not rigorous, but it applies a more flexible set of procedures compared to quantitative studies.

Analysis and interpretation are conceptually separate processes, although they are done simultaneously in qualitative research. The main goal of qualitative analysis is to organize data (text) into a meaningful format. Then the data can be reduced into a meaningful set of patterns, categories, and/or themes. Words, phrases, tone, non-verbal communications and the context of comments, among other aspects of text, are analysed. **Interpretation** is the process by which meaning and significance is attached to the analysis. Interpretation leads to explanations for descriptive patterns, identification of relationships between categories, and theoretical developments.

Box 4.1: 'Qualitative' versus 'quantitative' data analysis

Qualitative researchers distinguish the type of in-depth interview data they code and analyse from the coding that is done with open-ended survey questions that are analysed quantitatively. In Chapter 5, we describe in-depth (qualitative) interviews, which are aimed at obtaining as much information from individuals as possible in their own words. Surveys and interviews are also used in quantitative studies. While quantitative survey instruments most often have closed-ended questions with discrete response options, they also sometimes include **open-ended questions** that allow respondents to answer freely without a set of predesignated responses. Quantitative researchers usually develop a series of codes from open-ended responses that can be analysed with statistics, like responses to closed-ended questions. Consider these two open-ended questions: 'What health problems have you had in the past year (e.g. heart disease, arthritis)?' and 'What was your most enjoyable experience this past year?' A quantitative researcher would create a list of health problems and give each respondent a 'yes' or 'no' code for each condition (e.g. for diabetes, respondent #1 would be given a code of 'yes' if he mentioned having diabetes; otherwise he would be given a 'no' code). Each health problem becomes a variable with dichotomous (two) answers that can be analysed with statistical tools. Answers to the second question, most enjoyable experience, are more likely to vary than are health conditions. However, they too can be coded into a set of variables for statistical analyses. We could create variables for spouse/significant other experiences (yes/no), family-oriented events (yes/no), vacations (yes/no), work-related events (yes/no), and so forth. The

cont.

Box 4.1: 'Qualitative' versus 'quantitative' data analysis cont.

researcher may find that most responses fall into significant other or family-related events, in which case the codes may be refined to reflect more specific experiences (e.g. distinguishing significant events in a family like a birth or anniversary, reconnection with family member).

Some scholars have referred to this transformation of open-ended questions into quantitative variables as qualitative research. But most qualitative-oriented researchers reject this classification. They argue that their research and analytic techniques differ significantly from the ones just described. While qualitative researchers also code their data into meaningful themes and categories, their data are much more in depth and the intention of the coding is vastly different as discussed in this chapter. Colloquially, the coding of open-ended data for quantitative research is known as 'qualitative research with a lower case "q"' and coding for the purposes of qualitative research is 'Qualitative research with a capital "Q"'.

Unlike quantitative research, analysis of qualitative data begins early in the research process, essentially as the data are being collected. As the researcher begins observational work, interviewing individuals or collecting archival documents or text for content analysis, she begins to identify themes or ideas that are common to individuals, the setting or the documents. This helps shape the direction of the remaining data collection. Unlike quantitative data collection, qualitative data collection is a very flexible and continually changing process as the researcher explores one avenue and then refocuses in another direction and so forth. If an interviewer detects certain issues are common to many respondents, for instance, she may specifically ask other respondents about them. If an observer witnesses something that may be meaningful to group members (e.g. a ritual, pattern of interactions), she may hone her observations to better understand it. If analysing media images, the researcher may identify an item in the communication form that is interesting or potentially meaningful and look for more evidence of it in the remaining text. And finally, with historical documents, if the researcher uncovers an event or piece of evidence in one document, she may then search for more evidence to support or counter it.

While qualitative data analysis varies by topic, method of data collection and researchers' preferences, coding and diagramming are the common approaches qualitative researchers use when analysing their data. These will be briefly summarized.

Coding

Coding is the process of organizing and interpreting data. Specifically, coding is mapping the data into a set of categories that a researcher develops to summarize the text and make theoretical statements. A code can represent a very specific topic or can be a broader theme, depending on the aims of the study. It is common to begin the coding process by reading through the interview transcripts or field notes multiple times to obtain an overall sense of the data and identify key themes. Since data analysis is initiated shortly after data collection commences, the researcher often develops ideas about themes early in the process. In addition, scientists tend to enter into a research setting or interview process with some preconceived ideas. Typically however a researcher's ideas become modified, expanded and refined once data collection begins.

Identifying some initial themes or patterns is the first step to organizing the data. These patterns, ideas, and themes are each labelled with a name, which is often called a **code**. All the text pertaining to one particular code is given a similar marking or combined into a common computer file or simply a pile if hard copies are used. The researcher sometimes makes comments throughout the copies of notes, transcripts or documents or transfers key phrases, ideas, or quotes to index cards or a computer file to organize information by themes. The coding of text can be done line-by-line, paragraph-by-paragraph or by larger sections of text. When the goal is to do a detailed analysis of conversational patterns, for instance, line-by-line analysis is preferred (even pauses in speech are examined in conversational analysis!). In other cases, the researcher's goal is to analyse broader patterns or themes so larger 'chunks' of text are examined. Whenever coding, it is important to step back from the details or one can become too immersed in the data and miss the larger picture.

Once text begins to be coded, the researcher should keep a running log of his thoughts about how the code was used. This is not only important for working through the meaning of the codes but also later on to help the researcher remember coding decisions. When two parts of the data, for example comments by two different respondents, are given the same code, the researcher then examines the data together to look for similarities and differences. The properties and dimensions of the categories/codes can then be refined. Once a number of codes are developed, the researcher examines the commonalities and distinguishing characteristics of the codes. This helps identify whether new categories or subcategories should be created or whether codes should be combined. After this iterative coding process of comparing and refining categories is done several times, the researcher tries to see if any codes can be linked to reflect a broader overarching theme.

A special type of research note is called a **memo**. In a memo, the researcher writes out his thoughts and ideas throughout the research process; this is typically done while codes, themes and theoretical concepts are being developed. Often memos start very broad and tend to be reviewed and re-focused during the research process as key concepts and themes are identified and reworked. Sometimes memoing is thought of as extensive marginal notes.

The best way to understand how coding is done is with an example. In Box 4.2, we present an example of a qualitative study of patients with early stage dementia. Each participant completed a face-to-face in-depth interview concerning how the diagnosis of dementia and the disease impacted their lives, how others have responded to the disease and personal fears about the disease. When reading through interview transcripts, the researchers recognized that the respondents commonly discussed issues of driving and helping others. Excerpts from transcripts are presented in Box 4.2 that illustrate the context in which respondents discussed these issues. Once the researchers recognized that helping others and driving were mentioned in multiple interviews, they looked for whether or not related comments were made in all the interviews. In examining the contexts in which driving and helping others were mentioned, the researchers realized these were important ways for the dementia patients to maintain the activities and sense of independence and altruism they felt before being diagnosed with dementia. Therefore, the overarching theme from these two codes was the importance of continuity of activities and sense of worth. As is often the case, the researcher first coded very specific issues respondents discussed and then recognized that both categories reflect continuity of pre-diagnosis lifestyle.

Box 4.2: Example of coding

Menne and colleagues (2002) conducted in-depth interviews with six individuals who had early stage dementia. Study participants were recruited from an early stage memory loss support group. After transcribing the interviews, the researchers read through the transcripts to identify common themes respondents mentioned. They found that it was very important to the individuals to continue to live their lives as they had before they had dementia. Two themes used as examples of maintaining continuity with pre-dementia lifestyle are driving and helping others.

Code #1: driving
Respondent #1: 'Not because anybody is trying to hurt anybody, but because we have the laws which say we don't want people to drive, and the fact is that there is a lot of people who can still drive, but they haven't hurt anybody, but on that same score it's almost going like this.'

cont.

Box 4.2: Example of coding cont.

Respondent #2: No I don't know ... sometimes I may ask him [the doctor], I may ask him again, I said, ' I feel fine. And my car has all the modern things and it's easy to drive yeah it is. You just get in there and turn a few switches and you go.' He said, 'No, no driving.' So you know for a while you sort of give in to the powers that be.'

Code #2: helping others/contributing to the world
Respondent #1: A teacher said, 'I certainly would like to help people who can be helped and that's why I did most of my time as a teacher ... and I've been working on that "what can I do" "What can I be of value?"' This respondent also thought he was helping by participating in research.

Respondent #2: 'Well, I guess I'd like to be able to ... do more things but I just know I can't ... I mean I'd like to go and, at one time before I was going to see if I could go and help somebody but then realized that I couldn't ...'

Respondent #3: 'I make everybody laugh ... well, that's the only thing left for us.'

If you look at the comment from the third respondent under helping others, you may not immediately think that having a sense of humour represents 'helping others'. This respondent though stated that humor was one way he could still make a positive contribution to others' lives. It is often necessary to step back from the actual words being said to attempt to understand the significance and meaning in the words (or observations). The researcher may not have initially coded humour as helping others but upon recognizing that others were concerned about still being able to help others looked to see if this respondent also stated anything related to that issue.

When analysing interview data, it is beneficial for at least two people to code the same text so comparisons can be made between the coders. This increases the reliability of the data by confirming that repeated analysis of the same data produce the same findings (codes). Two (or more) people independently review the data and code the text using the codebook that has been designed. After coding is completed, the researchers compare their analyses and try to reconcile any differences that they find in their coding. It is desirable to have at least 90 percent agreement between coders, which is known as **inter-coder reliability**. If the coders have many differences in their work, the codebook should be reworked. In many instances, multiple codes may potentially overlap or be too vague; narrower and clearer definitions can enhance the likelihood that multiple coders will have similar sets of codes. It is common to have multiple coders review a small percent (e.g. ten percent) of the data and code them, which helps identify the areas of the codebook that are problematic. Adjustments are then made and the process is repeated until there is high rater agreement. The first iteration of the codebook is usually not the final one. Once the inter-rater reliability has been established, the set of codes is applied to the entire set of data.

Software programmes have been designed to help qualitative researchers code their interview data. These programmes can be used to identify words (e.g. driving) and related words (e.g. car) to help a research locate text that may be related, assuming the text is in a digital format. One of the drawbacks though is that a programme does not understand nuances and the underlying meaning of what was said. Rather, it is an automated process. In the humour example in Box 4.2, a computer programme would not have detected that statement as reflecting helping others. However, qualitative software is typically multilayered; a user can attach a note at a particular place and click on it later to review. While many researchers use software to help with their organization of data and coding, there is no substitute though for an individual's insights and interpretive abilities.

Diagramming

Diagrams are a useful way for qualitative researchers to show their data. Diagrams are visual displays that organize and systematically present data (see Miles and Huberman (1994) for many examples of diagrams that qualitative researchers use). A table is one way of charting and classifying information using columns and rows. A complex table with several columns and rows is referred to as a matrix. Tables and matrices are well suited for depicting a variety of information, including a typology. We could develop a typology of household division of labour with different categories. Table 4.1 presents five types of division of labour for households with two adults. In the first column, 'traditional division,' we see that the male is primarily responsible for working, while the female is primarily responsible for childcare and household duties. In the second column, 'equitable work-female home', both the male and female work and the female also assumes primary responsibility for the household and childcare. This table provides a reader with a quick overview. We could add to this table or have a separate table to depict the patterns we found in the data that distinguish the households by individuals' characteristics such as age or education. There may be age differences, with older couples having a more traditional division of labour, or education levels of women may impact the division with more highly educated women tending to have reverse traditional or equitable divisions of labour.

Concept charts and flow charts can also help researchers organize their data and categories. These charts are often not presented in the final reports for the study but are used throughout the data analysis process. The set of codes that are developed may be laid out on a piece of paper or the computer screen. This visual presentation can often help the researcher see what codes can be combined or what may be related to each other. When a person is studying a sequence of events and instances that have a time or causal ordering, flow charts or timelines can be used to succinctly present the data. **Social network analysis** often uses diagrams to map out how people are connected to each other. Decision trees can also be used to show how people make decisions, and diagrams of 'mental models' show how people are conceptualizing the topic being studied.

Table 4.1: Table depicting household division of labour typology

	Traditional division	Equitable work – female home	Equitable division	Equitable work – male home	Reverse traditional
Work responsibilities	Male primarily	Male and female	Male and female	Male and female	Female primarily
Household responsibilities	Female primarily	Female primarily	Male and female	Male primarily	Male primarily
Childcare responsibilities	Female primarily	Female primarily	Male and female	Male primarily	Male primarily

Reporting qualitative findings

Qualitative and quantitative research reports are presented in rather distinct ways. Quantitative articles usually have a similar structure. They tend to be divided into four sections: 1) introduction outlining the theory and prior research related to the topic; 2) research design section that describes the sample and data collection strategies; 3) summary of statistical results; and 4) discussion of findings and conclusions. While qualitative-based research articles also include theory, descriptions of sampling and data collection techniques, summary of results and conclusions, their format varies considerably across studies and there are a variety of ways of summarizing results.

Qualitative reports are full of direct quotes from individuals and rich descriptions. Qualitative researchers are particularly likely to use quotes from individuals that include specialized vocabulary (i.e. words or phrases that are specific to a particular group or region). Findings are usually presented in the words of the study participants and the researcher herself (in the first person, 'I found ...'), rather than in the third person ('the research found ...'). These strategies allow the reader to not only have a greater understanding of the person or event being described, but also to gain an insider's view on the topic. The reader is thus more likely to feel as though she is at the scene or listening to the person firsthand.

Researchers frequently use more than just quotes to describe their conclusions. They use detailed narratives from an individual's perspective to illustrate points. Let's return to the household division of labour typology we (hypothetically) designed in Table 4.1. We could draw on our interview data with the couples who we would classify as having an 'equitable division of labour'. We could select one representative couple and use their experiences and decision-making processes, as well as their own words, to describe to the reader how couples with equitable division of labour establish this division and how they manage their roles. Alternatively, we could create a fictional narrative of a couple with equitable division of labour that combines elements common to multiple couples we interviewed. This narrative technique is usually very effective and is more engaging to the reader than a traditional summary of findings (e.g. 'An equitable division of labour involves the following characteristics ...').

Qualitative researchers have used other very creative techniques to portray their findings. Bluebond-Langner (1978), for example, conducted a qualitative study of families with children who had a terminal illness. She wrote a play based on her field notes to describe the everyday experiences of terminally ill children, beginning with diagnosis through to death. Richardson (1992) wrote a poem to summarize the thoughts and feelings of a woman she interviewed as part of a project to explore the perspectives of unmarried women. The poem was written in the woman's words only and conveyed her diction, tone and thoughts.

When reporting qualitative research, the researcher must carefully decide how much description to include. Detailed descriptions and direct quotes are the heart of qualitative work and should be used to provide readers a sense of the setting and insights into people's perspectives and thinking. What is included by way of description will depend on what questions the researcher is attempting to answer. Often an entire event will be reported in detail because it represents a typical experience. Too much detail, though, can become too tedious. The most appealing accounts give sufficient detail and interpretation of the information. Qualitative studies, particularly field research, are often turned into books, which provide sufficient space for elaboration. Standard scientific journal articles are between fifteen and forty double-spaced manuscript pages and thus for many studies are too short to adequately describe the setting and the researcher's experiences in the field. Qualitative books can be very interesting and even catch the attention of readers outside university walls!

Applications

1   Time use among adolescents

In Chapter 3 you designed a quantitative study focused on how adolescents spend their time. Now design a qualitative study on this same theme. You can either modify your original topic or design a completely new question related to adolescents' time use. What makes this a qualitative rather than a quantitative study? In what ways can the research question benefit from a qualitative orientation?

2   The experiences of older adults with dementia

In the last chapter, we considered caregiver stress. Since you are really interested in how adult children may be affected by their parents living with dementia, you decide to do more research. You come upon an article by Hodgson and Cutler (1997), in which they propose a concept called anticipatory dementia. According to this concept, individuals may have a fear that normal, age-related memory changes are actually signs of dementia. Anticipatory dementia may be more commonly experienced among adult children of dementia patients than among adults who do not have a loved one who has had dementia.

Would qualitative methods be appropriate for studying the topic of anticipatory dementia? Or would you propose to study it using quantitative methods? Why do you say this?

3   The death penalty as a deterrent to crime

We can use a qualitative research design to better understand whether the death penalty is a deterrent to crime. A researcher may conduct a series of in-depth interviews with convicted murderers from their jail cells to explore their motivations for committing the crimes and whether or not they considered the possible consequences before they acted.

a)   What makes this a qualitative study?

b)   The researcher reports taking an inductive approach to studying this topic. What does she mean?

c)   If the researcher used grounded theory to investigate murderers' motivations for their crimes, what did she do?

4 Ecological modernization theory

In this chapter, we discussed how some qualitative studies build off existing theories or quantitative research. Consider ecological modernization theory and give an example of how a qualitative design could be used to better understand an aspect of this theory.

5 Gender differences in mathematics, science and language skills

This has already been covered in this chapter, so there will be no additional exercises.

6 Work and family balance issues/opportunity costs theory

a) How could qualitative methods help us better understand women's decisions regarding family and pursuing a career and how they balance their roles? In other words, what would be the advantages of studying this topic from a qualitative perspective?

b) We have explored a variety of issues related to family and career decisions and balancing these roles in this book. Let's return to our study where we conduct in-depth interviews with couples to better understand how they make family and work decisions and divide the family, household and work responsibilities between themselves. Outline a basic strategy we could use to analyze the data we collect.

c) Qualitative researchers are often creative in how they present their findings. Give an example, using this research topic, of a 'creative' way to summarize the data (do not use an example already given in the text).

7 Sexual and contraceptive behaviour and the threat of HIV/AIDS

Design a qualitative research project using the broad topic of contraceptive behaviour and the threat of HIV/AIDS. What makes this a qualitative rather than a quantitative design? How is investigating this research question from a qualitative orientation beneficial?

5   Collecting the data

- Introduction
- Content analysis
- Historical-comparative
- Field research/naturalistic observation
- Surveys, interviews and focus groups
- Experiments and quasi-experiments
- Triangulation, mixed methods and emergent methods
- Case study
- Internet research
- Applications

Introduction

In this chapter we introduce you to different strategies social scientists use to collect their data. The data collection techniques vary almost as much as do the topics social scientists investigate. When deciding what method to use, there is no right or wrong answer, but some methods will be better choices than others for particular research topics. Several factors determine the 'best' data collection strategy for a topic. Some methods, like surveys and experiments, are more suitable for collecting quantitative data, while others, such as in-depth interviewing and participant observation, lend themselves to gathering qualitative data. Certain techniques are more appropriate for collecting data for research questions about individuals, while others are better for addressing questions about institutions, cultures and nation-states. Sampling issues are a consideration as well, and they have an impact on which methods of data collection can be used. If it is important to obtain a probability sample of citizens in a given region in order to make statements about the whole population, the researcher will not be able to conduct the research with a web survey since computer knowledge and Internet access isn't universal. And of course personal preferences, background and talents also play a role in a researcher's choice of methods. Some of us really enjoy conducting surveys; others find experimental research appealing; and others prefer to get a first-hand look at a social problem by integrating themselves into a group or setting. In addition to conceptual, theoretical, sampling and personal factors, practical issues must be considered. Some methods take a considerable amount of time to carry out, and some are more expensive to undertake than others. For example, in large surveys meant to collect data on a representative national sample, it's very expensive to conduct face-to-face interviews compared to phone, mail or internet based data collection, so only a handful of national surveys use face-to-face interviews. This chapter provides an overview of common methods of data collection, including the advantages and disadvantages of each and the types of topics for which they are most appropriate (see Table 5.1 for a comparison of the six most common techniques).

Table 5.1 Comparison of types of data, observation and sampling for six data collection strategies

	Content Analysis	Archival Research	Historical–Comparative	Field Research	Surveys and Interviews	Experiments
Primary and Secondary	Secondary	Secondary	Secondary	Primary	Primary	Primary
Longitudinal and Cross sectional	Longitudinal and Cross sectional	Longitudinal and Cross sectional	Longitudinal	Longitudinal and Cross sectional	Longitudinal and Cross sectional	Cross sectional
Macro and Micro	Macro and Micro	Macro and Micro	Macro	Micro and Micro	Micro	Micro
Quantitative and Qualitative	Quantitative and Qualitative	Quantitative and Qualitative	Quantitative and Qualitative	Qualitative	Quantitative and Qualitative	Quantitative
Unobtrusive and obtrusive	Unobtrusive	Unobtrusive	Unobtrusive	Unobtrusive	Obtrusive	Obtrusive
Sample	Probability and Non-probability	Probability and Non-probability	Probability and Non-probability	Non-probability	Probability and Non-probability	Non-probability

Content analysis

One way to learn about a particular culture is to examine the language and symbols by which people communicate. Visual art, songs, books, photos and other forms of communication (called **texts**) can provide a wealth of information about a society, subgroups within it, and specific historical time periods. Content analysis is a technique used to analyse texts, whether written, spoken or visual, and the analysis can be either quantitative or qualitative. The main goal of content analysis is to systematically classify words, phrases, sentences and other units of text into a series of meaningful categories. Content analysis has been used to study a wide range of topics including song lyrics, gender stereotypes in children's books and media depictions of old age. Types of communication or texts that have been analysed include magazines, videos, personal diaries, advertisements, poetry, government documents, recorded conversations and speeches. Analysis of recorded forms of communication allows us to not only understand a culture or phenomena in the present or in the past but also trends over time and across societies.

Let's return to our research topic of HIV/AIDS education. The prevalence of AIDS varies by country. We could hypothesize that one reason for differential prevalence rates is AIDS education. In countries where citizens have little knowledge about the route of disease transmission, they may be more likely to engage in risky behaviours, which in turn lead to higher incidence of HIV/AIDS. The HIV/AIDS information presented in the mass media of a society can provide one indication of how much AIDS is discussed and what types of information about transmission are addressed. We will use India as our example. An estimated five million Indian adults and children have HIV/AIDS (UNAIDS/WHO, 2004). A recent report (UNAIDS/WHO, 2004) suggested many young Indian adults do not have accurate information about AIDS transmission. Only one in five adults aged 15–24 correctly identified two ways to prevent the sexual transmission of HIV and correctly identified three HIV transmission misconceptions. Additionally, only about half of those aged 15–24 reported using a condom when having sex with a non-regular partner. Clearly there is a knowledge gap among a group who are at risk. We could use content analysis to examine the type and extent of AIDS information young people are exposed to in the various media to see what kind of information is being conveyed to them.

When conducting a content analysis, the sampling unit and unit of analysis must be clearly defined. Television programmes, newspapers, and magazines could all be used as our sources of text. To simplify, we may decide to analyse the three magazines most widely read by adolescent girls and boys, and look at all issues from the past five years. The magazine issues are the sampling unit. The sample should be carefully selected for content analysis, or the resulting findings can be biased. For instance, the results of analysing a magazine aimed at a population of older adults might yield very different results than would be obtained from those targeting youth.

Having identified the sampling unit – magazines with top circulation among youth, we need to decide exactly what to analyse. What in the magazines will help answer our research question? We can consider how many articles over the five years dealt with AIDS and what about AIDS was discussed – route of transmission, prevalence, effects of the disease on patients, etc.; how much space was devoted to AIDS in each magazine per year (e.g. number of pages). Such analysis of the visible aspects of text, without considering the connotation of the text, is called **manifest coding**. Manifest coding can include counts of whether something occurs or not and how often, usually a quantitative strategy.

Latent coding, on the other hand, is the analysis of the more implicit meaning of text, a qualitative strategy. What does the text mean? If the data are images, such as magazine covers, what do the images signify? If the data are personal diary entries, what was the person trying to convey? What ideas – themes – are common across people's diary entries at a particular time in history? The direction (e.g. positive or negative statements about something or optimistic or pessimistic) and strength of messages (e.g. highly pessimistic, somewhat pessimistic, relatively neutral, somewhat optimistic, highly optimistic) are also forms of latent coding. One tricky issue in latent coding comes from differences in interpretation between the researchers and the target audience of the media being analysed. In our example, we would not want to assume that researchers from the US would see the same messages in the magazine texts as do Indian adolescents. In doing such a study we would want to supplement our reading of the texts with interviews or focus groups with some members of the target audience to make sure our readings were well calibrated to what they are seeing.

Carrying out a content analysis requires a **coding scheme**, which is a well-defined set of rules on how to systematically analyse and characterize the text. In the AIDS example, what messages regarding route of transmission are we interested in? How much of an article has to address AIDS to be counted as an AIDS focused article (e.g. what if AIDS is just mentioned among a list of several diseases)? Rules and coding categories are typically developed using an iterative process. Modifications to the coding scheme are made as analysis begins because researchers identify additional themes or categories and redefine and clarify coding rules as new or unusual instances arise. A 'good' – reliable – coding scheme is one that many researchers could use with the same data and produce coding that would be similar (e.g. multiple researchers identify the same number of articles as mentioning AIDS or as focused on AIDS). When the coding between multiple researchers is very similar, we call this high **inter-coder reliability**, a topic we discussed in Chapter 4. Such reliability increases our confidence that our findings are meaningful. It is more difficult to develop reliable rules for latent coding than it is for manifest coding because latent coding requires more subjective judgments than manifest coding.

The research question drives the type of data that are collected and analysed. Data such as counts of articles dealing with AIDS can be analysed with quantitative statistical techniques, just as survey data are. We could test whether the number of times each route of transmission of the AIDS virus in the magazines is mentioned relates to changes in the Indian public's knowledge about those routes of transmission over time. Other data like themes and implicit meaning of themes could be analysed with qualitative techniques such as thematic analysis, whereby coders read line-by-line and continually ask themselves what the content means. Therefore, content analysis can be used with both qualitative and quantitative research approaches.

One of the reasons content analysis is advantageous is because the data are already available, and the researcher's role in data collection is unobtrusive. By **unobtrusive**, we mean the researcher does not have an impact on the data that are collected; for some of the strategies we'll discuss in this chapter the research process and researcher's presence can impact the social processes being studied and the data collected. We can use content analysis when other forms of data collection are impossible – for example, much of our knowledge of the past is based on content analysis. A limitation of content analysis is that the results of a content analysis are purely a description of the text; we cannot determine why the text is how it is, how people reacted to it, or the social significance of the text from content analysis alone. But mixing content analysis with other forms of research can strengthen each. For example, we might interview authors, editors and graphic designers for the teen magazines to see what meaning they intended to convey in various articles and illustrations. And as noted above we could examine the reaction of the target audience to the teen magazines.

Secondary data

Many of the data collection techniques in this chapter involve primary data. (We discussed the difference between primary and secondary data in Chapter 2.) By collecting our own data, we have a great deal of control over the kind of information that is gathered. But we are limited in where we can collect the data and how much data we can collect. We might be able to conduct in-depth interviews or surveys in our local community but we might not be able to use these methods with a national sample. And with few exceptions we can't collect primary data about the past.[1] As a result many researchers use secondary data (data that have been collected previously by others). Today an incredible amount of data and statistics are routinely collected by governments, public and private organizations, and universities. For example, most countries gather demographic, economic, crime and consumer data at regular time intervals (see Box 5.1 for an example). At universities, research groups and individual scientists also routinely collect data on a variety of social science topics, as do polling firms and research companies. In Chapter 1, we used secondary data from Uniform Crime Reports, a crime reporting programme of the US Federal Bureau of Investigation, to begin to test the deterrence theory. Much of this secondary data, whether written documents, official statistics collected by government or the results of the thousands of surveys conducted every year are archived to make the data readily accessible to researchers and to insure that the data are preserved in well documented forms. Much of the most important secondary data are now available on the web, a point we will return to below.

Box 5.1: Examples of secondary data
National statistics
Governments often collect data regularly on their citizens, institutions, and activities. The *Statistical Abstract of the United States* is an annual compre-hensive summary of political, economic, and social statistics in the US that is published by the US Census Bureau (http://www.census.gov/compendia/statab/). It has been compiled since 1878. A wide range of national data and some state-level data are available, such as statistics on educational attainment, children currently in school, health care utilization (e.g. hospital use rates, prescription drug use), motor vehicle accidents and fatalities, demographic characteristics, participation in and expenditures on recreational and tourism activities, labour force status of citizens, federal budget expenditures and oil and gas extraction and production. When examining statistics on a topic over multiple time points or for multiple nations, even if the data were collected by the same organization like the US Census Bureau, it is necessary to consider how the statistics were compiled

cont.

---

[1]   Archaeology is an exception in that an archaeological dig collects what might be thought of as primary data about life in the past by careful examination of the physical traces left by past lives. But for the most part, social science research on the past relies on secondary data.

Box 5.1: Examples of secondary data cont.
each year to identify any changes or differences in measurement. For example if you are interested in the types of occupations Americans had throughout the twentieth century, you would find that service and computer-related jobs came about in the later part of the twentieth century and were not even occupational categories earlier in century. The World Bank and the United Nations compile extensive data on the economic, social, health and environmental conditions in many nations that are very useful for research comparing countries.

Cross-cultural data
The *International Social Survey Program* (ISSP) was initiated in 1984 to collect data from residents of different countries to be able to make comparisons across countries. A wealth of data is available from the ISSP on a variety of social topics (http://www.issp.org/). Each year, a topic (such as social inequality, family and gender roles, the environment, or religion) is identified, and a series of common questions is created and translated into each country's primary language(s). Each participating country conducts and pays for its own surveys. The data that are collected are then combined together into one data set. Today, 43 nations participate in the ISSP survey, including Germany, the United States, Great Britain, Australia, Poland, Sweden, Mexico, Brazil, South Africa, South Korea, and Taiwan.

Archived data sets
Many large, expensive to collect, high quality data sets are available from data archives. If you wanted to find empirical data for our research topic on adolescent time use, you could turn to existing data sets. A longitudinal study, entitled *The Michigan Study of Adolescent and Adult Life Transitions* (MSALT), was initiated in 1984 with thousands of sixth graders in schools in Southeastern Michigan. The students were followed through high school and then periodically re-interviewed as they transitioned to adulthood to track their educational and work pathways. The goal of the study was to examine how changes in families and classrooms impact adolescents' achievement related attitudes and behaviours, such as occupational and educational planning. In addition to interviews with students, data were also collected from student academic records and interviews with parents and teachers (http://www.rcgd.isr.umich.edu/msalt/home.htm). This is just one example of a data set that is available for use by the research community. Such data

cont.

> **Box 5.1: Examples of secondary data cont.**
> sets can be found by a simple Internet search or searching archival databases (e.g. the Inter-university Consortium on Political and Social Research (http://www.icpsr.umich.edu/). Data can also be found by perusing articles and books related to the topic of interest to see what data sets were used. There is a strong norm in the social sciences that data sets should be available for re-analysis, and most important data sets are available in archives.

What are the advantages of secondary data? Collecting primary data can be very time-consuming and expensive. It is typically much cheaper to use existing data. In many cases, data have already been collected on a topic of interest and can often allow students and researchers to expand the scope of their projects beyond what they could accomplish with primary data.

For example, it is often not feasible for students or researchers to collect data themselves from residents in several countries or from a large sample. Secondary data can often be useful in such cases. Box 5.1 gives an example of a collection of cross-cultural social science data. If we want to test the ecological modernization theory we have been discussing, we could search to see if any data exists on countries' carbon dioxide emissions and national economic indicators. In our search, we would find that the Statistics Division of the United Nations has these data available for many countries at multiple time points (http://unstats.un.org/unsd/default.htm).[2] As noted, archival data are also useful for exploring historical topics. When studying something from the past, researchers do not have the option to interview people who experienced a particular event or time period, and the historical event may have occurred so long ago that accurate recollection would be difficult.

The Internet and growth of digital media have simplified the process of identifying and accessing secondary data. Data collected in the latter part of the twentieth century typically have been stored electronically and are therefore more readily accessible compared to information collected prior to the electronic age. In some instances, data are easily accessible online from organization and government websites, such as the data needed to test ecological modernization theory that we described above. Existing data are often available free of charge, although some organizations charge a fee to access their databases. Many offer subscriptions to institutions like universities, so that access is free for students and faculty. It's also possible to

---

[2]   If you did a generic Internet search for these data, you would find several websites with data (or information about how to access these data) on countries' carbon dioxide emissions and economic indicators. The website for the World Resources Institute, an environmental think tank in the US, is one example (www.wri.org/).

contact other researchers directly to see if they have data that can be shared. Central storage of social science data has also become increasingly common in recent years. For example, the Inter-university Consortium for Political and Social Research (ICPSR) at The University of Michigan is a large repository for social science data. The data from many large scale research projects and the data collected by many individual researchers are stored at the ICPSR. Individuals can conduct searches of data sets or by topics to see what data are available for use; much of the consortium's archives are now online. The Council of European Social Science Data Archives (http://www.nsd.uib.no/cessda/home.html) plays a similar role for European data. In the case of historical and rare documents, it has been necessary to visit libraries or museums for data access but increasingly these materials too are available on the web.

While we have mentioned data available through public archives, **private documents** can also be valuable for social research. Personal diaries and letters are two important types of documents useful in social science research. They can provide valuable insights into how people were feeling and what they were doing at a particular time period in a particular society. Of course, letters and diaries do not necessarily reflect objective reality since they are based on personal interpretations of events.

Secondary data have some disadvantages. When we use already existing data, we do not have control over how the data were collected, what data were collected and what problems may have occurred during the collection. We can only use what is there, which may not be exactly what we are looking for. We cannot go back and ask people about the circumstances or the meaning of their responses; we have to make interpretations based solely on what is available. Careful documentation of how the sample and data collection were done (called **meta-data**) is sometimes not available or not thorough enough. Most professional societies, government agencies funding research and data archives are working to improve the quality of such meta-data, but little can be done to improve limited documentation on previous studies. And perhaps most important, collection of primary data is often interesting and even fun. Observing behaviours, asking people questions, or conducting experiments with individuals gives a sense of accomplishment and makes it easier to be sure you have the data you wanted.

Historical-comparative

Many techniques described in this chapter help us study micro (individual) level social issues. Social scientists are also interested in understanding larger-scale, macro-level phenomena. How did a major societal change

occur, like a political upheaval, a revolution, or women's increased participation in government? What are the commonalities among governments
that have remained in power for a large number of years? How have social
institutions such as a criminal justice system changed over time in a
country and what lead to and resulted from the changes? Historical-
comparative research is a method for studying such questions. These
methods have a long history in the social sciences. Karl Marx (1867/1999),
for instance, used historical-comparative methods in the mid-nineteenth
century to investigate how economic systems changed from slave based to
feudal to capitalist systems and to describe the nature of capitalism.

Historical-comparative research typically involves the analysis of
multiple nations, of a particular period of time in-depth, and/or societal
changes in one or a few places over a number of years. Historical-
comparative methods can be used to address either qualitative or quantitative research questions. Studies looking at societal and institutional
changes over time or comparisons across different nations are particularly
challenging, and therefore specific strategies have been developed for
addresing such issues. Several issues distinguish historical-comparative
studies from other social science research: the complexities arising from
studying large social systems or institutions, the incomplete nature of
archival data, and the required synthesis and interpretation of vast
amounts of very diverse data.

Researchers rely on secondary data for their research into the past and
across nations. To reconstruct a past event or time period, they may turn to
official government documents and items kept in museums, libraries or
individuals' private archives. In some cases, works of journalists, historians
and other writers (e.g. biographers) can be useful in identifying details of
the past and people's lives. Finally, personal recollections in the form of
diaries and autobiographies can also be used as data. Working with
historical data, as previously mentioned, is a challenge. Personal accounts
and works of historians and writers are biased since the writers' perspectives
influence their accounts. On the other hand, diaries and other personal
documents from a particular historical period give a sense of how people
thought and lived in that period. In addition to biases reflecting the
perspective of the writer, historical data are typically incomplete. Paper and
artworks are vulnerable and over time can fade or be ruined. Some
documents have been destroyed because of wars, natural disasters, or
individuals who did not want others to have certain information (e.g.
politically corrupt leaders). Some records are simply misplaced and some
are thrown out because they are not seen as important. The biases and
incompleteness of historical data can lead to many barriers in doing the
research. It can be very time-consuming to try to locate 'missing'
information and even then the researcher may not find anything. Another

challenge is that if the research indicates that X happened before Y but another source reports Y happened before X, there is no way to know for sure which account is true. This example points to the importance of using multiple sources when possible to piece together past events and circumstances. When studying multiple countries, information is not always available in our primary language, so it may be necessary to find a translator or to learn the language or else the information available will be quite limited.

Historical-comparative research typically involves examination of a considerable volume of documents, statistics and other data, which must be organized into a meaningful framework for analysis. Data collection and theory building are often done simultaneously. Let's say we want to identify factors that lead Eastern European countries to come under communist rule after World War II. We may have some initial ideas about what factors from the war contributed to certain countries becoming communist, including seriously weakened economies and widespread death and famine. As we begin researching the World War II and post-war periods, our data may identify other factors as well, such as the strength of the Communist led anti-Nazi resistance movements during World War II. Our theory would then be adjusted based on the evidence and data collection and analysis would resume.

As you can imagine a vast amount of information is available on this topic. In accumulating potential sources of information, we would take notes and would then try to organize the details into a meaningful timeline, set of categories (factors contributing to the rise of Communist rule, in this example) or themes. The ultimate goal is to organize all the information into an explanatory model. We would decide early on in the research process whether to focus on one country for our study or to draw comparisons across countries that became communist. Alternatively, we could compare countries that became communist to other countries that did not become communist.

Comparative research can be incredibly labour intensive. In some cases, it is necessary to travel to different countries, museums or historical sites to gather information, which is time-consuming and expensive. Findings from historical-comparative studies cannot typically be applied to our understanding of other countries or time periods since usually only a few countries are compared. Nonetheless, this is a very important approach to research in the social sciences and the only approach that allows us to look at large scale social change over long time periods.

Field research/naturalistic observation

As social scientists, we are interested in human behaviour. We try to understand how people act, the motivations for and influences on behaviours and the nature of social interactions. One way to study these topics is to observe people directly as they carry out their daily lives. This technique for collecting data is called **naturalistic observation** and is also known as **field research** or **ethnography**. 'Naturalistic' refers to observations made in the subject's natural settings (e.g. homes, places of employment, public places, the rainforest), as opposed to a research laboratory or other controlled setting. A researcher goes to a location to collect data, which is called going into the 'field'.

The idea of field research often brings to mind studies done by anthropologists on 'exotic' cultures or by sociologists on deviant groups. Some field research matches this image. The anthropologist, Colin Turnbull, for instance, spent a few years in the late 1960s studying a small Ugandan group called the Ik. His research, reported in the book *The Mountain People* (1972), described how this hunting and gathering society survived through droughts and near starvation and how they even turned on their family members to survive the extremely harsh conditions.[3] Laud Humphreys (1975) conducted a famous sociological study of male homosexual encounters in public restrooms, known as the *Tearoom Trade*, using participation observation. Acting as a lookout in public bathrooms, Humphreys observed men engaging in sexual acts and then tracked the men's identifications using license plates to describe the men and their behaviours.[4] But observational research is also used to study more 'usual' settings and groups, such as restaurants (Fine, 1996), fishing communities (Ellis, 1986) and a retirement community (Jacobs, 1974), as well as mundane activities such as waiting room experiences (Lofland, 1972) and children's baseball teams (Fine, 1987).

Observation is a useful method for collecting data because people are often unaware of many of their behaviours, so independent observation may be the only way to link what people say to what they do.[5] As

---

[3] Turnbull's work has been the subject of some criticism. See for example Heine (1985).

[4] Humphreys' study is often remembered for its serious ethical problems, including deception on the researcher's part and lack of consent by the men. In addition, tracking the actual identities of these men, many of whom were married, could have caused serious personal problems for them.

[5] One of us (Dietz) did a study of household energy use. One of the interview questions was 'During a typical day during the summer, about how many hours does your air conditioner run?' One person being interviewed in their living room said: 'I never use the air conditioner' even while the air conditioner was running full blast during the interview. A very large literature examines the best ways to ask questions in surveys and interviews to get accurate information about things that may be hard to recall or embarrassing to report and about how much error we will find in reports on such things.

mentioned, it is also valuable for studying groups that would otherwise be difficult to access, such as sex workers. In **fieldwork**, the researcher is far more directly involved in the social world being studied than he is when using other data collection techniques. Behaviour is observed in natural settings, and most researchers have found that after they have been in the setting for a while, the people being studied tend to 'let down their guard' and show typical behaviours and discuss issues honestly. Thus fieldwork can usually avoid concerns with **artificial responses** that can occur when people are studied in a research laboratory or respond to questionnaires because the researcher becomes a routine part of the local social scene. However, fieldwork, like all methods, also has its limitations. Fieldwork takes longer than most other types of data collection, with observational periods typically ranging from several weeks to several years. It is very sensitive to an observer's accounts and interpretations so there is always a concern that a different researcher might have seen different things. And field research makes the researcher a participant to some degree in the activities being studied, and that can lead to ethical concerns that must be addressed, as well as a need to be sensitive to how the process of doing the research may have influenced what was being studied.

There are basically two forms of observational research: participant and direct. With **participant observation**, the researchers immerse themselves in the research site, become acquainted with the people they are observing, and are active members (or participants) in the setting. In **direct observation**, the researchers watch people but do not become participants in the setting. A direct observer tries to disrupt a field site as little as possible to minimize the impact of their presence on those being observed. Researchers may videotape a setting or make observations from behind a one-way mirror. The use of visual and audio devices can have an impact on how people behave, so they should only be used when unobtrusive. And of course ethical rules for conducting research generally preclude recording people without their consent. In some cases, it is necessary for the researcher to do participant rather than direct observation to gain access to a group or setting. While there is little question today that Humphrey's study of sex acts in men's bathrooms is ethically questionable, it is very unlikely that the men would have behaved normally if Humphreys just sat in the restroom taking notes. Acting as a lookout allowed Humphreys to make observations in a way that was not threatening to the men.

Returning to our question about gender differences in mathematics and science skills, we could observe interactions among children and between children and teachers in classrooms. We could get permission to videotape each classroom for a number of days or perhaps sit in the back of the classroom to observe daily behaviours. Both are forms of direct observation. In contrast, participant observation in such a situation would involve becoming a student or a teacher in the classroom and learning from the statements and actions of other students and/or teachers.

As we noted in Chapter 4, qualitative researchers often seek to understand individuals' lives from the individuals' own perspectives. Fieldwork is particularly suited for this form of inquiry. Through observation a researcher can understand how people create and define their social world by interacting with others and how they develop shared meanings using language and other symbols. By spending lengthy periods of time watching how a group interacts, the researcher can gain an **insider** or **emic perspective** into people's lives. Anthropologists regularly immerse themselves into different cultures and subgroups to uncover patterns of behaviours, interactions, thoughts and rituals.

Participant observation begins with a broad idea about a particular group, culture or setting. The researcher then identifies a site for observation. Selecting and gaining access to field sites is a critical step. A site that will provide a range of interactions and experiences of the group of interest is desirable. If we are carrying out a study with dementia patients, we could do observations in their homes or at their physician appointments. If we limited observations to physician appointments, we would have a very narrow perspective on the patients. Making observations in the homes of individual patients is not very feasible since the researcher's presence would likely be disruptive and the time needed for data collection would be quite extensive since only one patient would be observed at a time. We could find a centre where dementia patients go during the day when their loved ones are working or need a break or a facility where dementia patients live. Both sites would allow us to watch several patients at one time. It is always important to weigh the benefits and disadvantages of possible sites in terms of what can be observed, how intrusive the observation will be and how difficult it will be to obtain data.

Another consideration for site selection is that some locations can be difficult to access, especially when we wish to study deviant and vulnerable groups (Laud Humphrey's research on sex in public bathrooms is a good example of this limitation in access). Unless a public setting, like a shopping centre, is used, it usually is necessary to negotiate with a person, referred to as a '**gatekeeper**', to gain access to the site. How a researcher is presented to group members and by whom can have a strong effect on how open individuals will be with the researcher and the type of access the researcher will have to the location. A researcher must decide how involved to become in a group or setting and should take on a role that does not compromise a group's functioning. One can become a complete, active participant in the field, called 'going **native**'. For example, one might study a social movement in which one is an active participant. The researcher can also take on a slightly more detached role, where she is not active in all aspects of the group and maintains some distance from members. Some researchers studying social movements have helped out in movement activities but not become full members. The type of role assumed is not solely up to the researcher though; the gatekeeper largely influences this decision. If we decide to conduct our study of Alzheimer's patients in a full-time care facility, we would have to gain access to the facility from the owner or manager of the facility. While an introduction by a member of the group is the best way to gain entry, we may not want the administration to formally present us to the patients and family members. Patients may be more likely to be open and comfortable if we take on the role of a worker, such as a nursing assistant or a volunteer. Even though ethical consider-ations would usually require that patients and families be informed about the study, participating in a typical role in the setting provides an effective way to become unobtrusive. We then would be able to watch patients doing their day-to-day activities and at the same time would be providing assistance to the patients, making our presence as researchers in the situation more normal than would be the case if we were only observers.

Once access is granted, the researcher adapts a role within the setting and begins observations. Typically a researcher begins by becoming acclimated to the setting and becoming comfortable with group members rather than worrying too much about collecting data in the first days in the setting. Much of this time is often spent developing contacts with 'insiders'. Insiders provide a wide range of information to the researcher, and are usually found as the researcher builds rapport and trust with group members. Often one or a few people become especially helpful to the researcher, and are referred to as '**key informants**'. These people are not always representative of the group because they may be leaders or they may be people who link the group to other parts of the social world. So while the information they provide is invaluable, researchers must also keep in mind that their perspectives may differ from those of other group members.

A researcher's notes about the setting and individuals' behaviours and interactions are the core data of fieldwork. While video and audio recorders can be helpful, they can be very intrusive when used to record routine activities. (However, audio recorders are nearly always used to capture interviews so that the exact words spoken as well as pauses and intonations are available as data.) Therefore, observational methods largely rely on a researcher's notes and the transcripts of interviews. **Notetaking** should be done systematically and should be as detailed as possible. The goal of notetaking is to provide a rich and accurate description of all observations to enable maximum recall later. Rather than writing something vague like 'The patients had a group meal at noon', the researcher would describe the meal in great detail ('At noon, all the residents but Joe were seated in the dining hall. Sue sat next to Bob at table 1 ... '.). Detailed notetaking is a very time consuming activity, and participant observers often report spending as much or more time writing notes as they do observing.

In a natural setting, we must take notes in an unobtrusive manner to disturb the setting as little as possible. It would be distracting to group members if we were constantly frantically writing notes on paper; we would also miss things when doing so. Field researchers give accounts of going to bathrooms, their cars and other places of privacy to jot down notes discreetly during the day. As soon as it is possible though, we should report everything that we witnessed. We should also record our own feelings and impressions in our notes because it is important to distinguish between what is witnessed and how one feels or reacts to something. After leaving the field locale, we review and prepare written summaries of the observations. Field researchers sometimes also use visual aids, such as maps of the field site or diagrams outlining how people are interconnected in social networks (see Box 5.5, page 140) or to chart a group's schedule. Observers also may conduct in-depth interviews with select group members, which often occur in the form of conversations rather than formal interviews.

Overt observation, when the researcher reveals her identity to the observed group, is generally preferable to **covert observation** due to ethical problems with deception (as discussed in Chapter 2). With covert observation, the researcher's presence is unknown to the subjects. However, there are circumstances where covert observation is ethical. Sometimes we do observational studies in public settings, such as parks and restaurants, and it is impractical to inform all people in these settings that research is being conducted. In most situations though, the researcher should reveal her identity to the group under observation. Usually after a period of adjustment, group members become used to the researcher's presence and as a result that presence has minimal impact on their behaviour.

Surveys, interviews and focus groups

You have probably been interviewed or have been given a survey before, perhaps in a class, while shopping or over the phone. It is also likely that you frequently hear, read and see survey results in the media: who are people voting for in the next election? How happy are citizens with current national economic conditions? Surveys are the most popular form of data collection in the social sciences. A survey consists of a series of questions that individuals answer. Surveys can be used to study a variety of topics, including attitudes, beliefs, characteristics, traits, knowledge, behaviours, and anything else that can be reported by respondents. They can be used to provide data for quantitative and qualitative research and can be administered in various ways – by mail, on the phone, in person and over the Internet. Surveys are beneficial because information can be gathered from a large number of people in a relatively short period of time.

Surveys are used by researchers in many disciplines, including sociology, psychology, criminology, demography, epidemiology, medicine, political science, education, and economics. Governments also conduct surveys regularly to track the size and characteristics of their population, to monitor economic activities and to assess public health trends. Opinion polling agencies, non-profit research organizations and marketing firms also routinely carry out surveys, as do news-paper, television and other media outlets. As we will discuss shortly, questionnaires and interviews are two forms of surveys. A **questionnaire** consists of a series of questions that respondents read themselves and answer. In an **interview** a person (the interviewer) reads the set of questions from an interview guide to a respondent and records the responses. The questionnaire and interview guide are similar but the questionnaire has to be designed so as to insure that the respondent can accurately complete the survey without assistance, while the interview guide has to direct the interviewer through the process of asking questions of the respondent.

Quantitative researchers frequently use data from surveys. The aim of a quantitative-oriented survey is to measure variables so hypotheses can be tested, although sometimes surveys are used just to describe the population. Surveys are useful for estimating the prevalence of attitudes and behaviours in a population, examining relationships among variables and determining causal links between variables. Theory-driven quantitative surveys usually follow a deductive approach. As described in Chapter 3, a researcher takes conceptual ideas derived from one or more theories and creates a series of hypotheses. Hypotheses describe variables, each of which are measured with one or more survey question. For our hypothesis that gender differences exist in children's science and mathematics skills, the variables are gender, science knowledge and mathematics knowledge. These three variables can be measured in a survey. We can ask respondents their gender and give them questions that test their science and mathematics knowledge. We might also ask questions about gender roles or about how the respondents perceive boys who are good at mathematics and science and how they perceive girls who are good at these subjects. Because the goal of this kind of research is to make comparisons between respondents based on the characteristics we measure in the survey, everyone in the sample should be given an identical survey, with the same questions, response options and question ordering. We want differences across responses to be the result of things we measure, not a result of having asked different questions of different people.

Surveys can have two types of questions: closed-ended or open-ended.

Closed-ended questions ask respondents to select a response(s) from a series of pre-designated choices and as a result are easy to quantify. For example, we might ask: 'How religious are you?' (1) not at all religious, (2) a little religious, (3) somewhat religious, and (4) very religious. **Open-ended questions** ask respondents to provide their own answer, such as 'Please describe how religious you are.' The respondent then would decide how to answer this question. The open-ended questions allow for responses that the researcher did not anticipate and allow respondents to answer in their own words. However, it can make it very difficult to compare responses across respondents and difficult to find ways to quantify the responses. A survey with a quantitative orientation tends to have mostly closed-ended questions so that direct comparisons can be made between respondents' answers. Open-ended questions are also sometimes used but require a great deal of work to analyse compared to closed-ended questions. Surveys designed for qualitative purposes primarily rely on open-ended questions. Surveys used to develop data from quantitative research have sample sizes ranging from a few dozen to several thousand, and in some cases more than a hundred thousand responses. Surveys used to develop data for qualitative research usually have sample sizes of less than a hundred and often only a few dozen respondents because the data from each respondent takes much more time to analyse. Again, the lines between qualitative and quantitative approaches are not rigid. Sometimes we include an open-ended question in a survey with mostly closed-ended questions to get a sense of the ways people answer. Then an exploratory or inductive analysis of that question can be used to develop a closed-ended item for later questions. We often use **focus groups** (to be discussed below) to get qualitative data on what people are thinking about when they answer closed-ended questions to make sure the questions are getting at what we intend.

Qualitative researchers often use observational methods, archival data and content analysis. They also use survey methods, in particular in-depth interviews. An **in-depth interview** is a series of mostly open-ended questions that is used to obtain detailed or descriptive information from individuals about a research topic. The intention of these surveys is not to test relationships between variables or quantify behaviours or attitudes. Rather, the goal is to learn about a research topic from an individual's own perspective, in her own words, and in detail. The gender-mathematics/science skills topic can also be studied with a qualitative approach. We could conduct in-depth interviews with a sample of teachers to understand their thinking about the academic strengths and weaknesses of girls and boys. We could also inform the teachers that there is some empirical evidence that gender differences exist in boys' and girls' mathematics and science skills and ask their thoughts about why this might be. As you can see from this brief example, surveys can be used for either qualitative or quantitative oriented research and thus provide a very flexible way to look at a topic.

You may think that surveys are an easy way to collect data. A person can write a number of questions and mail them to people, call people and ask them the questions, or post the questions on a website. While it's true that a survey can be done quickly, designing a good survey is truly a craft, and it takes work to avoid the 'garbage in, garbage out' problem. If questions are poorly written, the information we receive back will be meaningless. For decades researchers have given considerable attention to improving the design and implementation of surveys. Box 5.2 provides an overview of how to write survey questions based on this body of research. Before administering a survey to a sample, it is a good idea to give the survey to at least a small group of people to make sure the questions are clear and that there are no other problems with survey. This is called **pilot testing** or **pre-testing**.

Box 5.2: Constructing a survey instrument

It is important to carefully design a survey so as to enhance the quality of the data. Questions that are confusing, misleading or just poorly constructed will yield useless information. Here we give a brief introduction to some of the 'dos' and 'don'ts' of crafting survey questions, including examples of problematic questions. Question writing is challenging because our goal is for each question to have the same meaning to all people (a lofty goal indeed). When doing research, it is best to begin by searching for previous surveys that may have measured the variables of interest. In many cases, researchers have already done work to validate that their questions accurately reflect the concept they are trying to measure. This can greatly simplify the task of writing questions and if we use exactly the same question then comparisons can be made across surveys. Measuring variables like gender in a survey is reasonably straightforward. If we are interested in studying psychological well-being or aggressiveness, however, writing questions that accurately measure the concepts we are studying is more difficult. For new questions, it is very important to test them with at least a small group of people before doing the full survey to make sure the questions make sense to those you will be sampling. Even the most seasoned survey researcher finds that what is clear to them is not necessarily clear to others!

- A survey should have a brief introduction to the purpose of the survey including a statement about the right of the respondent not to participate and how the data will be kept confidential. The initial questions should

cont.

Box 5.2: Constructing a survey instrument cont.

be of a non-sensitive nature and on topics that respondents may find interesting (making them more likely to complete the survey). Typically, demographic questions such as race and age, and sensitive questions like income, are asked at the end of a survey. When sampling the general population, a good rule of thumb is that survey questions should be able to be understood by individuals with only a sixth grade level of education; complex phrasings and high-level vocabulary should be avoided.

- Question wording should be neutral and should not suggest how a person should respond or what is socially desirable.
  Poorly worded: Protecting the environment is important, especially for future generations. How concerned are you about the environment?
  Better choice: How concerned are you about the environment?
- Do not ask multiple questions within one question. This is called a double-barrelled question.
  Poorly worded: How often do you eat vegetables and fruits?
  Better choice: How often do you eat vegetables? How often do you eat fruit?
- Do not use abbreviations or jargon in questions.
  Poorly worded: To what extent do you think NAFTA has affected Mexico's economy since its initiation?
  Better choice: The North American Free Trade Agreement (NAFTA) was initiated in 1994 between Canada, the United States and Mexico. The agreement eliminates most tariffs on products traded between the countries in an effort to encourage trade and stimulate their economies. Since its adoption, how much do you think NAFTA has affected the economic circumstances in Mexico?
- Do not ask respondents to answer a question on something they do not know much about or the answers will not be meaningful. The previous question about NAFTA is an example of this – many people in the general population won't have given NAFTA much thought.
- Ask clear and concrete questions; don't be vague or ambiguous. Always give a specific time frame or quantity if applicable.
  Poor choice: How often do you eat?
  Better choice: On an average day this past year, how many meals did you eat (this does not include small snacks)?
- Questions should be asked to maximize recall, especially if it is a question about the distant past or over a period of time. The following question uses an unrealistic time period for people to give accurate information. The revised question uses a smaller time frame, which is likely to result in more accurate estimates.

cont.

Box 5.2: Constructing a survey instrument cont.

Poor choice: How many nappies did your child use in the past year?

Better choice: On an average day this past year, how many nappies did your child use?

- Ask mutually exclusive questions in which the response choices do no overlap. With the initial question, one person with an income of $50,000 may select category b, while another could select category c.

Overlapping response options: What is your current annual household income?

a) Under $25,000   b) $25,000–$50,000   c) $50,000–$75,000
d) $75,000 and over

Mutually exclusive response options: What is your current annual household income?

a) Under $25,000   b) $25,000–$49,999   c) $50,000–$74,999
d) $75,000 and over

- Ask mutually exhaustive questions in which all respondents can select at least one option.

Poor choice: What is your race?   ____ White ____ Black
Better choice: What is your race?   ____ White ____ Black
                                          ____ Asian ____ American Indian
                                          ____ Other race; please specify:

- If asking the same questions across cultures, we need to be sure the questions have the same meaning across cultures. For instance, the Center for Epidemiologic Studies Depression (CES-D) Scale (Radloff, 1977) is a commonly-used 20-item scale that assesses depressive symptoms. Each question asks how often a person feels a particular way in the past week. One question is: 'I felt I could not shake off the blues even with help from my family and friends'. When this question was asked with samples outside the US, some respondents did not understand what 'feeling blue' meant.

- When asking questions about sensitive topics, such as a person's sexual behaviours or history of abuse, question wording is critical. Many respondents will decide not to answer sensitive questions or will not be truthful in the answers they do give. If an interviewer is administering a survey about sensitive issues, it is important for the interviewer to sound neutral and non-judgmental to increase a person's comfort level. For example, survey researchers know that people don't like to report their income. Research has shown that people are more likely to indicate their income when they are given categories to choose from rather than being asked directly, 'What is your annual household income?' Additionally, the

cont.

Box 5.2: Constructing a survey instrument cont.

larger the income categories, the more likely respondents are to answer (a question with categories such as under $25,000, $25,000–$50,000, etc. is more likely to be answered than a question with more detailed categories such as $0–$4,999; $5,000–$10,000, etc.). Of course with smaller income ranges, we know one's income more precisely than with larger income ranges.

Survey collection techniques

Surveys are administered by mail, over the telephone, in person and on the Internet. Financial costs, time allocated for data collection, sampling frame, the kind of survey questions and researchers' preferences all influence the mode by which surveys are conducted. Here we briefly describe the advantages and disadvantages of each technique.

Mail. Mail surveys are well suited for a relatively short questionnaire (usually less than 10 pages). With mail surveys, we can obtain information from a large sample quickly and relatively inexpensively. This survey modality is very popular because it can be used to study a wide variety of topics. Another advantage of mail surveys is that they can be filled out at participants' convenience, unlike telephone interviews, which often lose respondents since calls may come at an inconvenient time. Since mail surveys do not involve direct contact with any researchers, respondents may be more inclined to answer questions on sensitive topics honestly than if the questions were asked by an interviewer. However lengthy surveys should not be administered by mail because many people will likely opt not to return the survey or will return it incomplete. Surveys with mostly close-ended questions work best; people do not tend to write lengthy answers to open-ended questions with mail surveys. Another major disadvantage of mail surveys is that there is no opportunity for quality control over the data; you cannot influence how many questions each respondent will complete, cannot ensure they understand the questions, cannot clarify answers given, and cannot ensure surveys are returned at all.

Don Dillman (1978, 2000) has developed and tested techniques to maximize participation in a mail survey, which are now widely utilized. Dillman's methodology involves sending a packet to each potential participant containing the survey instrument, an invitation to participate, a stamped return envelope and a small token of appreciation for partici-pation. Three follow-up letters and postcards are sent to non-responders every two weeks, with the second follow-up once again including a copy of the survey and return envelope. An alternative to this approach is to send a letter to the sample inviting their participation before sending the first survey packet as a 'heads-up' notice. These strategies have been found to achieve a 50 percent response rate in many studies, which means that at least half of the sample completes the survey. Methods to improve response rates using mail surveys have been widely studied, and issues like questionnaire length, personalization of mailings and even types of stamps used on the envelopes have been found to affect response rate.[6]

Telephone. Telephone interviews are a popular data collection technique because they allow information to be gathered quickly. An interviewer calls a person, usually at home, asks a series of questions and records the answers. Polling organizations and media in particular rely on phone interviews because they can call a sample of households about a topic and have feedback from many respondents within a few hours. Phone interviews are advantageous when a research question seeks to collect data using a probability sample of a population since telephone access is now almost universal in many parts of the world. Since answers are recorded as the interview is being administered, it's best to use closed-ended or short-answer questions, rather than seeking in-depth information. And since most telephone interviews have the interview guide built into Computer Assisted Telephone Interviewing software, the data are entered into the computer even as the interview is being conducted, so data analysis can begin immediately.

A telephone interview should be short to avoid respondent fatigue. Since telephone surveys are typically conducted in people's homes, it's easy for people to be distracted if the survey is long and as a result they may feel imposed upon. Survey questions should have as few response choices as possible, since it is difficult for respondents to remember many choices when read to them over the phone. Unlike mail and web surveys, the interviewer is able to clarify responses, ask follow-up questions if needed, and can answer questions participants may have. This enhances the quality of the data obtained and can also reduce the number of questions that respondents do not answer or leave incomplete. Another advantage of telephone interviews is that since there is no face-to-face contact between the **interviewee** and interviewer, a person may feel more comfortable answering some questions than if the interview were in-person. However, unlike web and mail surveys, phone surveys cannot use maps or other graphics as part of questions.

Telephone surveys are often used because a random sample of a population can be generated from a process called random digit dialling at

---

[6]   See Mangione, 1995, 1998; Dillman, 2000; Dillman *et al.*, 1974 for detailed information on ways to improve mail survey response rates.

less cost than a random sample can be developed for mail, Internet or face-to-face interviews. The exact procedures for random digit dialing reflect substantial research on how to obtain a **representative sample** of the population via the phone system but the basic idea is simple. All potential working telephone numbers in a designated area are identified. Then numbers are selected at random. Because there are unlisted phones and new numbers that might not be in the listing, a random number is added to each real phone number to generate a list of numbers that can include new and unlisted numbers.[7]

One of the challenges of conducting surveys over the telephone is that it is often difficult to reach certain segments of the population, especially those working full time, while it is easier to reach others. Problems unique to telephone interviewing include exclusion of households that do not have phones, biases in terms of who is likely to be home at certain times of day, and increased frequency of phone call screening, cell phones and multiple phone lines in many households. Finding ways to work around these problems to obtain a representative sample remains an active area of research. Protocols for maximizing telephone survey participation require several call backs to each household, which can be time-consuming.

In-person. Some interviews are conducted face-to-face, with the interviewer and interviewee meeting at an agreed upon location (often the interviewee's home) where the interview occurs. While in-person interviews usually include closed-ended questions, compared to other survey modalities they are better suited for in-depth, open-ended questions. They permit longer questionnaire length than the other survey modalities. Unlike mail and web surveys, a face-to-face interview allows the interviewer to probe, clarify, and ask follow-up questions. The main disadvantage is that in-person interviews can be very time-consuming and expensive. Interview appointments have to be scheduled and if the sample is geographically dispersed, travel expenses can become large or interviewers at multiple sites must be employed. For very large surveys based on national populations, in-person interviews may require a team of many dozen interviewers, all of whom have to be trained and supervised. However, with some segments of the population it is easier to conduct in-person interviews than to use mail, web or telephone surveys. When surveying a sample of older adults, many of whom may have visual or hearing problems and in some cases short-term memory problems, in-person interviews are far more effective than other modalities. An interviewer can show the

---

[7]   We could simply dial random numbers. But research has shown that the process of adding a random digit to an existing number is more likely to turn up valid phone numbers (old and new listed numbers and unlisted numbers) than using purely random phone numbers. This saves time in the survey process as there are fewer calls to non-working numbers.

interviewee cards with response choices or the actual questions to help respondents with memory and hearing problems. This improves the interview experience for the respondent and interviewer.

In-person interviews are usually recorded, especially those consisting mostly of open-ended questions. This allows the interviewer to focus on what the interviewee is saying. The interviewer typically just jots down key points that the respondent makes. While audio recorders can seem imposing, most respondents do not mind them after being assured no one but the researchers will be able to access the recording and that no identifying information will be linked to the recording.

With face-to-face interviews, the interviewer's role is critical to having a successful interview. The interviewer must build rapport and connect with respondents so they will feel comfortable. At the same time though, the interviewer needs to stay neutral. The interviewer's role is to determine the topic, pacing and relevance of what is discussed, while the interviewee's role is to provide coherent and truthful responses. The interviewer needs to keep the respondent on track to maintain a reasonable interview length, which is not always easy to do.

Box 5.3: Intervewing techniques

- Be familiar with the interview instrument so you can pay attention to what the interviewee is saying.
- Always dress professionally but in a way that makes the interviewee feel comfortable.
- Always carry identification (i.e. your university or professional affiliation) to the interview.
- The beginning of an interview is important for setting a positive tone and for making the participant feel comfortable. If a respondent is not comfortable, they are unlikely to talk openly and honestly.
- Provide a general description of the purpose of the interview. You don't want to give away too much information lest it impact how the participant responds to questions.
- Begin with questions that will catch a person's attention and establish their interest.
- For a structured interview, each interview must be conducted in the same manner; the interviewer should ask the same questions in the same order and use the same wording.
- An interviewer should always look and sound interested in what the interviewee is saying. If it is an unstructured or in-depth interview, the interviewer should consider tape recording the interview to avoid constant notetaking during the interview, which can be very distracting.

cont.

Box 5.3: Intervewing techniques cont.

- Be sure to ask follow up questions to clarify any confusing or contra-dictory statements that respondents make.
- With unstructured interviews, interviewers need a strategy to encourage respondents to talk. An interviewer can sometimes remain silent and wait for a response, can repeat the question in a different way, and have a series of follow up questions, called probes, to keep the interview going.
- Conclude each interview by asking the interviewee if they have any remaining comments, questions or concerns.

Web surveys. Increasingly researchers are using the Internet to carry out their surveys. The popularity of online surveys has extended beyond academic research to marketing companies, businesses, news services and pollsters. Early Internet surveys tended to consist of a series of questions that would be sent and returned within email messages. Today, many surveys are designed on websites where respondents can view and respond to the questions. Several companies and software programmes have even been created specifically for web survey design and implementation. The appeal of web surveys is the ability to obtain data from many individuals – even globally – rapidly and with lower costs compared to mail, telephone, and in-person interviews. The data collection period tends to be much shorter than other survey modalities. For instance, if email addresses are used to recruit respondents, reminder emails are typically sent to non-responders every few days rather than every two weeks as would be the case with mail surveys. When respondents complete the surveys, the researcher can instantaneously receive their data. Web surveys can also be structured to minimize the amount of incomplete data in each person's survey; respondents may not be able to proceed through the survey until they have answered particular questions. Web surveys are well suited to incorporate audio, visual and interactive components into the survey instrument (e.g. showing respondents a map on an area or two images to evaluate).

The greatest disadvantage of web surveys, however, is that not everybody has Internet access or computer skills, which limits who can participate. The number of people with computers and Internet access and knowledge grows rapidly each year. While access has grown, Internet users tend to be higher educated and wealthier than non-users (Newburger, 2001; Day *et al.*, 2005). Convenience samples are typically used when conducting web surveys. It is common to sample a group of people who have email access (and therefore have knowledge of the Internet), such as college students, university professors,and subscribers to listserves. Some private organizations have created panels of Internet users who have agreed to participate occasionally in surveys; for a fee a sample of their panels can be used for a web survey. Most of these panels seem to be convenience samples and thus it is not clear how results can be generalized to a larger population. A particularly innovative organization, Knowledge Networks, recruited a randomly selected sample of US households for participation in an Internet panel (www.knowledgenetworks.com). Computer and Internet training was provided to sample members, and web televisions were given to households that did not have computer access. As members of this panel, individuals are asked to participate every so often in various surveys. Fees for using this sample are substantial though. Given the many benefits of web surveys, it is likely that innovative sampling techniques, such as those used by Knowledge Networks, will emerge.

Survey structure

Surveys range from being completely structured to unstructured. A **structured survey** has a predetermined set of questions that are administered in a designated order. While the questions can be closed-ended or open-ended, the purpose of a structured interview is standardization. If we vary the questions asked across respondents, or we ask questions in different orders, then when we make comparisons across respondents we can't know if the differences we see are due to characteristics of the respondents or to differences in question wording and ordering. By asking each respondent the same questions in the same order direct comparisons can reveal how the characteristics of the respondent are linked to her answers to the questions. Structured surveys are most commonly used in quantitative research, when the goal is to understand patterns of variation and examine relationships between variables. If structured surveys are conducted by interviewers, the interviewer asks each question the same way, using the same response options and follow-up questions (if applicable) and in the same manner (e.g. tone of voice). The interviewer also records the information verbatim without interpreting what the interviewee says or guiding their responses.

Unstructured interviews lend themselves more to qualitative research. While a researcher usually has some initial questions to ask respondents as well as a mental list of topics to pursue, there is no formal survey instrument. Rather, the **interview guide** begins with introductory questions and includes an outline of key topics that should be covered in the interview to prompt the interviewee's memory. This lack of structure allows for a topic to be explored broadly and to follow whatever direction the respondent and interviewer take. An unstructured interview is particularly well suited for giving individuals the opportunity to express themselves in their own words. Interviewers conducting these surveys typically use respondents' comments to guide the flow of the interview and determine what follow-up questions are asked. Consequently, while the general topic and perhaps certain aspects of the topic of interest are predetermined, the specific questions and question wording vary by respondent. When we are interested in learning about something about which little is known or we are seeking an in-depth understanding of a phenomenon, broad and flexible questions are more appropriate for obtaining information than a series of very specific (and thus potentially limiting) questions. Conducting unstructured interviews is challenging because the interviewer must listen carefully and determine when to pursue a new topic that arises in the interview, when to change directions, and when to ask follow-up questions. Unstructured interview data, however, are more difficult to analyse and synthesize since there are no standardized set of questions. Respondents aren't asked the same questions, and completion of some interviews may lead to new questions and topics to be covered in future interviews. Data from unstructured interviews then should not be used to make direct comparisons between cases since not all respondents are asked the same questions.

Group surveys

Some research topics can benefit from obtaining data from a group of people responding together rather than from single individuals. These groups are commonly referred to as focus groups. Small group processes have been used for years by market researchers to assess an audience's reaction to a television show, a commercial, a slogan, a new product and so forth. Social scientists use focus groups too. A reason focus groups are popular is that you can receive instantaneous feedback about something – you get a lot of data very quickly.

A focus group is a group interview designed to explore what a specific group of people think about a topic (Krueger, 1988; Morgan, 1997). A trained moderator asks questions and facilitates the group's discussion, while a second person may observe the meeting and take notes. The notetaker typically documents not only the content of the discussion but any significant nonverbal cues given by group members and overall impressions of the session. Similar to interviews, focus groups can have a very structured format or can be quite flexible depending on the research goals. It is much easier to use an unstructured format if a topic is well known to participants. If participants know little about a topic, a structured session is more likely to yield information; participants may go off topic if they know little about an issue and are asked to discuss it or there could be long periods of silence during the group meeting.

Whether structured or unstructured, focus group research uses an interview guide, which contains a series of questions or topics that direct group conversations. The questions are typically broad and general to encourage group discussion. A series of yes-no or agree-disagree questions will not likely yield information exchange between group members. Sessions typically last no more than one or two hours. The moderator's role is critical in **small group research** because group dynamics need to be carefully managed. It is common for groups to have members with radical opinions or dominating personalities, but it is important for everyone to participate and to feel comfortable sharing their opinions, even if dissenting. The moderator also needs to know when to probe for more information from the group, when to move the discussion along, and when to step in to limit silence.

Focus groups are beneficial when we are interested in people sharing their opinions with each other. Researchers commonly use data from small groups to help develop their survey instruments, especially if the topic has not been previously studied. If we are interested in understanding how adolescents in four countries – let's say Germany, Turkey, Japan and Sri Lanka – spend their time on a weekly basis, it is likely that adolescents in these countries allocate time differently, and youth in some countries may commonly engage in activities rare or unknown in other countries. If we made a list of questions about time allocation using our best logic about the topic, we may miss some important questions that would capture cultural differences. We could ask a group of adolescents in each country to identify as many activities they can think of that others their age participate in. The advantage of the small group research strategy in this context is that we may learn more from the groups about adolescents' time use than from individual interviews – ideas shared by group members may spark other ideas that individuals would not have thought of on their own.

Focus groups should be considered whenever researchers are interested in how people make decisions, how they interact with each other and if they are interested in broadening people's perspectives and generating new ideas among members. Focus groups can also be to study how discussion with others can change people's viewpoints about a topic. It is important to note though that the data resulting from small groups are not equivalent to individual level data received using surveys. We can only make conclusions about the small groups, not the individuals in the groups. In the group setting, people may think of things they wouldn't have otherwise, and the dynamics of each group can influence individuals' responses at the time of the meeting. Focus group information is not generalizable to the population since they are typically conducted with a small number of individuals who are not representative of the larger population.

Usually more than one focus group should be conducted to study a topic because any one group may have participants who have particular characteristics or ideas or the dynamics of the group may bias the data. With multiple groups we can identify not only a greater diversity of ideas but those ideas that are consistent across groups. While the number of groups that should be carried out varies by research question, a rule of thumb is to stop conducting focus groups once theoretical saturation is reached (i.e. when no new data are found). Selecting participants for focus groups can be challenging because a group that is too homogeneous will likely result in a very limited discussion. A very heterogeneous group (e.g. some who are professionals about the topic and others who are 'lay' persons) also has its disadvantages because the differences between individuals may be too great to have a productive meeting. There is some evidence that mixed gender groups can be troublesome; some women may be reluctant to talk in groups dominated by men. Sampling for focus groups varies, but often convenience samples are used. Recommended group size is between six to twelve people. This size group is small enough so all group members have the opportunity to participate and large enough so that one person will not dominate the discussion. This size also increases the likelihood that there will be diverse viewpoints and a lively discussion.

Alternatives to focus groups have been developed, including the Nominal Group Technique and Delphi Survey Technique. A goal of these approaches is to carefully structure the process of group interaction so that the desirable features of that interaction are enhanced (e.g. creativity, diversity of views) while the less desirable features are minimized (e.g. dominance by one or a few members, 'group think'). The **Nominal Group Technique** also engages small groups in discussions about a topic but is structured to maximize every member's participation and minimize conflict and the dominance of any group member (Delbecq *et al.*, 1975). A well-defined topic or question is initially presented to each small group, and members are asked to silently write down their responses to the question. The moderator then goes around to every participant asking each to share an idea. This listing process is repeated several times until all ideas are shared. After the moderator records everything said, each idea is discussed and clarified by the group as needed. Finally, participants can be asked to rank order their preferences; the votes are then tallied and results are discussed. By the conclusion of each session, ideas receiving the greatest and least support are identified. This technique is commonly employed to foster citizen participation in public policy decision-making scenarios.

The **Delphi Survey Technique** combines questionnaires and group discussions (Linstone and Turoff, 1975). Typically a questionnaire is first administered to a group of respondents. The results of the first survey are then synthesized and given back to the participants. The participants then complete another questionnaire and are then given a summary of those results. Several rounds of opinion collection and feedback take place. This procedure is used to encourage the exchange of ideas between individuals and in some cases to establish consensus about an issue among participants. The logic of this approach is that individuals will reevaluate viewpoints after exposure to others' views (or to test if opinions indeed do change).

Experiments and quasi-experiments

An experiment is a research design in which the researcher divides the objects to be studied (called 'subjects') into at least two groups (called 'treatment' or 'experimental' and 'control' groups). The experimenter structures the situation so that the experimental and control groups are 'exposed' to different levels of the independent variable that is the focus of the research and then observes the effect of the manipulation (i.e. different levels of exposure) on a dependent variable. The researcher ensures that both groups have exactly the same experiences except for the one thing being studied – the independent variable. In most experimental studies, you can think of the independent variable as something (such as a stimulus) that is given to the **treatment group** but withheld from the control group. For example, one of us (Kalof, 1999) conducted an experiment on the effect of gender stereotyped video content on viewers' gender attitudes. She randomly assigned a group of subjects into one of two subgroups, an experimental or treatment group that watched a gender stereotyped video clip and a control group that watched a video clip with no gender stereotyped content. By comparing the two groups afterwards, she could see what effect the one thing that was different (the manipulated independent variable – the content of the video) had on individual attitudes.

The best way to design a simple experiment is to divide subjects into groups using a random process, such as a flip of a coin, a toss of dice or a random number table (found in the appendix of most statistics books and on the Internet). Random assignment is the essential element in a 'true' experiment because it ensures that each subject has an equal chance of ending up in either group. This maximizes the chance that the groups are 'equivalent,' (in other words, each group will have the same number of pre-existing differences). In the video experiment, that means both experimental and control groups had an equivalent number of subjects with prior exposure to stereotyped videos, prior experience with coercion and even prior experience with psychology experiments. This is accomplished by the randomization process. The random assignment ensures the two groups will differ only by chance and statistical procedures allow us to take account of those chance differences. After watching the video, all subjects were given a survey questionnaire that measured gender attitudes. The researcher found that there were differences between the two groups in gender attitudes. There are two reasonable explanations for the differences. First, it may be that at the start, the two groups differed in their attitudes. Or it may be that the video had an effect. We can calculate how large the difference in attitudes between the two groups is likely due to chance (the luck of a coin toss). This calculation tells us that if the difference between the two groups is substantially larger than the result of a coin toss, we can conclude that the differences were not just luck, but rather the video had an impact on gender attitudes.

If we assign subjects to treatment or control groups by some other method that is not random – by gender, by age, by time of day the students are free to watch the video (which may be related to their major and what classes they are taking) – then it is impossible to separate the effect of the video from these other subject characteristics. But the coin flip (a random selection process) is powerful because it should make the groups roughly the same in all characteristics. The value of the experiment with random assignment to treatment and control groups is that we can establish that the experimental treatment caused the change in the subjects. It does this because the coin flip provides a basis of comparison between what we see and what would happen by chance. Because we formed the groups by chance, all differences between the groups must be the result of either chance or the experimental treatment of the two groups.

While the ability to get very strong evidence about causal effects makes experiments appealing, they have their limitations too. First, randomized experiments usually take place in laboratory (artificial) settings, rather than in natural settings, so there is always a chance people will behave differently in an artificial setting than they would in their normal environments. Second, many experiments are based on samples of convenience, often college students, so the ability to generalize to the larger population is compromised. Both of these are considered 'threats to external validity,' that is, threats to our ability to generalize outside of the exact context of the experiment. Third, there are many important topics for which it is either unethical or impractical to conduct an experiment with randomization. For example, we neither could nor should randomly assign states to either have or not have a death penalty.

Experiments conducted without random assignment are called quasi-experiments. **Quasi-experiments** are 'experimental' in that an independent variable is manipulated, but the experimental and control groups are not equivalent. Most public policies can be thought of as quasi-experiments (Campbell, 1969). Quasi-experiments are appealing because the intentional change in the world allows us to examine what happens and what doesn't happen as a result. Thus, the analysis of quasi-experiments has become a major area for methodological research (Cook and Campbell, 1979; Cook *et al.*, 2002). However, because there is no random assignment to treatment and control groups, analysis of quasi-experiments must take into consideration things other than the intentional change that might have produced the results. A great deal has been written about the logic of quasi-experiments and sometimes rather advanced statistical methods are deployed to do the best job possible of separating the effects of the manipulation from everything else.

Our death penalty analysis in Chapter 3 is a simple example of how we try to do this kind of analysis. We can treat the adoption of a death penalty as a quasi-experiment. We then try to make comparisons across states and take account of other factors that might drive the homicide rate to get a sound assessment of the effects, if any, of the death penalty. In an actual research project we would do much more extensive analysis than we presented in Chapter 3. But a quasi-experiment will always be subject to criticisms that it hasn't captured the true causal effects of the manipulated variable. However, sometimes, with careful design and analysis, we can be reasonably certain that we've estimated what actually happened.

Triangulation, mixed methods and emergent methods

When we have a specific research topic and are trying to decide how to collect our data, we are likely to be able to quickly eliminate as unsuitable or impractical for that project several data collection strategies discussed in this chapter. But usually more than one technique can provide data needed to address our research question. Decisions about which data collection method to use are based on several theoretical, conceptual, personal and practical factors. The choice is easier for some research questions than for others. If we are interested in studying what people know about AIDS, then official statistics are not going to be of much help, but primary or secondary data from surveys might be useful, and in-depth interviews or content analysis of popular media would be as well. If we want to understand consumption that has an impact on the environment, official statistics could be very useful but so would surveys, participant observation or content analysis, depending on how we wanted to approach the issue.

As we have highlighted in this chapter, each method has its advantages and disadvantages. Every data collection technique can provide important insights into a research question but offers a limited vantage point. If observational methods are used, data are based on a researcher's interpretation of events and situations. If survey methods are used, data are based solely on what individuals say; it is always possible that a respondent's recollection is poor, that they inaccurately report information, that they misunderstand a question, or that a question was poorly worded. If content analysis is used, the intention of text is usually unknown as is how people who were the target audience for the text interpreted and responded to the text.

Triangulation, which we introduced in the first chapter, points to the value of utilizing multiple data collection techniques, such as a combination of interviews, government data, and observation to explore a research question. Each additional method that is used to address a particular research question provides another way of looking at a problem and can help offset the limitations of any one approach. A multi-faceted perspective contributes to a richer, more complete understanding of the social world. The concept of mixing methods is often credited to the work of Campbell and Fiske when they used multiple methods to study psychological traits (Campbell and Fiske, 1959). It has only been since the late 1990s, however, that serious attention has been given to **mixed methods**, as entire books have begun emerging on mixed method strategies (e.g. Tashakkori and Teddlie, 2003).

Mixed methods can be used to enhance our understanding of a topic typically studied from just a qualitative or quantitative perspective. Alongside social scientists' increasing shift toward thinking that qualitative and quantitative orientations are complementary rather than competing perspectives, there has been interest in developing strategies to combine qualitative and quantitative data collection and analytical approaches. Researchers can consider *both* causal (quantitative) and interpretive (qualitative) questions when designing their research projects. We can use our example of how families balance the demands of work and family to highlight the benefits of mixed methods. Let's restrict our thinking to two-parent families to simplify the example. We may want to know if there are gender differences in how time is divided between family, home and childcare responsibilities. This is a question we can test with quantitative methods: does gender influence household division of labour? We would conduct a survey to get data on this topic. We may also want to know how couples interpret their division of labour and/or whether or not they are happy with the division. Or we might take the outliers in the quantitative analysis – those with highly egalitarian or highly non-egalitarian divisions of labour, and conduct in-depth interviews to learn more about their family life. This approach allows us to understand how variables are related and then answer why they may be related. Mixed methods studies can be conducted sequentially, as in this example, where one method is used first and provides a base for a second method of inquiry. Mixed methodologies can also be conducted where data collection using different techniques is done simultaneously.

Therefore, triangulation of methods helps us combine qualitative and quantitative approaches to a research topic, provides a richer understanding of an issue and helps overcome the limitations of any one data collection strategy. Mixed methods can also give us greater confidence in our findings (it increases the validity of the results, a topic we will discuss in the next chapter). If we use multiple methods and they reveal similar information, we can be more confident in our conclusions. And if we find different results across methods we can learn a great deal from considering why the results differ. Despite all these advantages, triangulation of methods can be expensive and time-consuming, which is why they are not more frequently used.

Sometimes a single approach is seen as combining aspects of qualitative and quantitative approaches. For example, **Q methodology** is a mixed method with the potential for developing a deeper understanding of social attitudes, values and beliefs (see Box 5.4 for more details). Q methodology was introduced in the 1930s by William Stephenson (a physicist, psychologist and protégé of Charles Spearman) and revitalized by Steven Brown, who reports that the method has become particularly popular among the younger generation of academicians.[8] The popularity of Q reflects a much needed multi-method approach to social science research that focuses on uncovering how people structure discourses. Many streams of social science now embrace the concept of discourses (made ever more popular by renowned scholars such as Haraway, Habermas and Derrida) providing fertile ground for an explosion of interest in Q methodology. Q explores social discourses by combining the openness of qualitative methods with the statistical rigour of quantitative analysis (Addams, 2000). It uncovers the way statements or images are patterned into coherent collections by people and which people endorse or reject these patterns. In that sense it combines inductive and deductive strategies in the study of the subjective world of respondents. The list of topical areas that have been fruitfully examined with Q methodology is long and diverse. Among other things Q has been used to study national identity in Europe (Robyn, 2000), democratic deliberation in Australian politics (Dryzek and Braithwaite, 2000), strategic planning in hospitals (Popovich and Popovich, 2000), feminist methodology (Gallivan, 1994 and Kitzinger, 1986), jealousy (Stenner and Rogers, 1998), US television's portrayal of a fictionalized racial incident (Carlson and Trichtinger, 2001), and numerous environmental issues such as global climate change (Dayton, 2000) and public participation in watershed management (Webler and Tuler, 2001).

---

[8]   See Brown, Steven R. The History and Principles of Q Methodology in Psychology and the Social Sciences. http://facstaff.uww.edu/cottlec/QArchive/Bps.htm

Finally, emergent methods are state of the art research designs that cross disciplines and address the gap between methods and theory.[9] One of the most useful emergent methods in quantitative research, applicable to a wide range of social issues, is social network analysis (see Box 5.5). **Social network analysis** explores the structure of group relationships to discover informal connections between people – in the business world, for example, these links drive how work gets done and how decisions are made.[10] Social network analysts have studied a wide variety of topics, such as social interaction in classrooms in Spain (Martínez *et al.*, 2003), HIV transmission (Rothenberg *et al.*, 1998), elite social circles (Alba and Moore, 1983), urban black communities (Oliver, 1988), and recruitment into cults and sects (Stark and Bainbridge, 1980).

Box 5.4: Q methodology: A mixed method

Q method is a technique for investigating individuals' subjective attitudes and beliefs on an issue or topic for the purpose of identifying differing social perspectives or, in the language of Q, social discourses. Discourses are the ways in which individuals structure their thinking and discussion about the topics under study. The Q method can be used to identify both what discourses exist within a community and who subscribes to or rejects which discourses.

In a Q study researchers first try to identify all the statements that are part of the discussion the topic being studied. This full listing is referred to as a 'concourse'. The concourse can be assembled from existing text (e.g. newspapers, websites, public records) or it can be created via interviews. Typically, 20–60 statements are selected to make up the Q sample of statements from the concourse. Ideally, Q statements are short, easy to understand 'stand-alone' sentences. Unlike survey questions, which should have singular meaning, Q statements can have 'excess meaning'. In other words, they can be interpreted in different ways by different people.

Researchers then ask individuals to rank order a group of statements that represent the diversity of the concourse in terms of whether they agree or disagree with the items. This is known as a 'Q sort'. The statistical analysis of the resulting data indicates which statements 'hang together' as a discourse thus indicating how many discourses are present in the population from

cont.

---

9   For an excellent overview of emergent methods for qualitative research, see Hesse-Biber and Leavy, 2006.

10 Kate Ehrlich and Inga Carboni, Inside Social Network Analysis (http://domino.watson. ibm.com/cambridge/research.nsf/c9ef590d6d00291a85257141004a5c19/3f23b2d424be0da 6852570a500709975/$FILE/TR_2005-10.pdf)

Box 5.4: Q methodology: A mixed method cont.

which respondents were drawn and the content of each. The analysis also indicates which respondents endorse which discourses, and thus can help understand patterns of support and opposition within the group being studied.

A recent study to reveal social perspectives in environmental decision-making processes included (among a longer list of statements) the following Q items about how to enhance public participation:

- Hold meetings at different times and places so no one is excluded from participating.
- Participants should attend meetings regularly and see tasks through to completion.
- Discuss the values underlying people's opinions about the issues.
- All important stakeholders are taking part in the process.
- The process taps the knowledge and experiences of local people.

The Q participants are a small number of people with different, but well-formed opinions. Q participants are not selected to be a sample of a population, but are exemplary cases selected to represent the breadth of opinions present in a concourse. Typically, one or two dozen people are ideal for a Q study. If we were using Q to study people's preferences for a public involvement process the statistical analysis might reveal one idealized narrative that emphasizes producing clear progress on the problem through a science-led process. A second may express little care for actual progress on the problem, but instead focus on improving trust, social capital, and power relations by guaranteeing participants access to information and meaningful control over the agenda and the process. A third might start from a belief that agencies possess legitimacy and need to consult or cooperate with stakeholders in a limited and controlled fashion. Such a result would indicate that there are three discourses about the appropriate role for public engagement in environmental policy. Any individual's Q sort might correlate highly with one or the other of these perspectives; it might correlate moderately with two perspectives or it might not correlate with any (suggesting the person has a totally different point of view). This is because the factors are understood to represent idealized conceptual schema, which means that an individual may legitimately hold aspects of multiple perspectives.

There are several aspects of Q that can make it an appealing choice of method for investigating subjective attitudes and beliefs on an issue or topic.

cont.

Box 5.4: Q methodology: A mixed method cont.

First, it allows participants to define their own viewpoints. Second, it is a technique that forces people to prioritize their preferences, in a way that is challenging to accomplish with interviews or focus groups. Third, Q method can clarify areas of agreement and disagreement by putting people's specific views in the larger context of their overall viewpoint. Fourth, it summarizes the many viewpoints held by individuals into a few shared perspectives. Like all methods, Q also has some weaknesses. First, it is not designed to measure frequencies in a population, the way a well-designed survey can. Second, important social perspectives may be missed if the people participating do not fully represent the breadth of views held in the population of interest. Third, Q studies cannot prove that the revealed perspectives are the only perspectives that exist within the population. A larger Q study may reveal more perspectives and more detail because additional people with these different views are included.

Seth Tuler and Thomas Webler

Box 5.5: Social network analysis: An emergent method

A common theme in the social sciences is that behaviour is dependent both on attributes of the individual and on surrounding social influences. These surrounding influences are often quantified using the concept of social networks. Networks are simply maps of social interactions consisting of nodes (or 'vertices') connected by links (or 'edges'). Nodes represent individual agents (either people or more aggregate groups, such as nation-states), while links represent any type of social relationship between agents, such as social support, information sharing, trust or friendship.

While the concept of networks has permeated many social science disciplines for several years, their rigorous mathematical treatment is a more recent development. 'Social network analysis' refers to the set of quantitative methods used to describe networks and to make predictions regarding the commingling influences between individual and collective behaviours. As a descriptive tool, social network analysis helps us to understand three broad characteristics of networks: structure, process and function.

Network structure refers to the patterns of interrelationships amongst a set of nodes. While many scholars have used the term 'network' to describe a particular organizational form (as opposed to, for example, hierarchies or markets), a social network perspective emphasizes that networks *reflect* forms of organization and are not, in of themselves, organizational forms. Thus, hierarchies and markets can be identified as networks of a certain type

cont.

Box 5.5: Social network analysis: An emergent method cont.

– we can then look to certain properties of the network to tell us more about the type of organization that is reflected in the network. Common measures of structure at the network level reflect the aggregate number of interactions (density), the frequency with which interactions are reciprocated (reciprocity), and the largest separation between any two nodes in the network (diameter). The network analyst may also shift to a smaller scale of analysis using a clique or cluster analysis, revealing the ways in which networks are made up of a collection of cohesive subgroups. Yet another set of network measures seeks to describe the positions of individual nodes with networks. These node-level measures often focus on the 'centrality' of network actors, or how closely actors are positioned to the center of a network structure. Examples of commonly-employed centrality measures include degree centrality (total number of relationships), eigenvector centrality (the extent to which a node's relationships also have a large number of relationships, and so on), and closeness centrality (the extent to which a node is positioned close to many other nodes in the network).

Network process refers to the ways in which adjacent nodes interact and influence one another. Within a friendship network, for example, we may be interested in the spread of values or behavioural norms. If I have many friends who do not eat meat, then I may also stop eating meat. Network structure places constraints on these processes; insofar as norms spread on friendship networks through a process of social influence, we may expect to find very different types of shared norms evolve where networks are clustered into relatively isolated units. On the other hand, processes that occur in a network can also influence structure. Within *elastic* social networks, agents have many opportunities to reposition themselves, cut some links and form others. Thus, friendship networks tend to be highly elastic while kinship networks are highly inelastic (hence the saying, 'you can choose your friends but not your family'). In elastic networks, processes that occur along network links can cause changes in actor traits, which in turn cause actors to seek new network positions. This co-evolution of network structure and individual attributes is an important area of research on social networks, but requires longitudinal data to tease apart these causal relationships.

Network function refers to the system-level performance of the network. Sometimes networks are fabricated to achieve a specific purpose, such as the production of new knowledge (as was the case in the selection of young minds to participate in the Manhattan Project). But more often, the analyst is interested in applying a specific performance criterion to an arbitrary social network structure. Some prominent examples come from the epidemiology

cont.

Box 5.5: Social network analysis: An emergent method cont.

literature, where scholars are interested in knowing how quickly infections can spread through a population. While certain types of network structures facilitate the rapid infection of an entire population, other types of networks attenuate this system-level process. This lends practical insight into how interventions may be used to change system performance. If we know the structure of a social network, and we know how disease spreads on the network, then we can efficiently target agents to vaccinate or quarantine such that we maximize system-level resistance to infection. Similarly, a network perspective can reveal the most important linkages to form within a network if the function we are concerned with is not the spread of disease, for example, but the efficient transmission of information.

As a predictive tool, social network analysis has benefited from recent advances in the statistical modeling of network structure. One problem the network analyst faces in trying to explain observed patterns of interaction is that network linkages are quite interdependent. Thus, methods that assume independence of observations (the statistical tools that are most commonly used in the social sciences) are inappropriate for network data. An example of such dependencies is the common phenomenon of clustering, or transitivity: the friends of my friends are often my friends. Another example is reciprocity: I love my baby, so my baby most likely loves me. A new class of statistical models, known alternatively as *p** or *exponential random graph models*, is a powerful tool for explaining observed network structures while preserving the inherent interdependencies of network data. This class of models allows the analyst to estimate the strength of a particular attribute – such as shared ethnicity or cultural norms – in driving network structures conditional on other effects that drive the cohesion of networks, such as clustering and reciprocity.

Adam Douglas Henry

Triangulation of data sources

Just as it is valuable to use multiple methods, it is also valuable to combine multiple sources of data. To study children's behaviours, we could interview children's parents or teachers. (Interviewing young children themselves is ethically challenging given their age and in any event the accuracy of children's descriptions of their own behaviour and that of other children would be limited.) Since parents and teachers have different roles and interact with children in two different environments, interviewing both would provide a more complete picture about each child's activities and behaviours. We could also use records from the school to find information about a child, including report cards, teacher's notes and disciplinary reports. Returning to our example of Alzheimer's patients, it is difficult to obtain information from Alzheimer's patients themselves, especially if they are in later stages of the disease. It is common to interview the spouse or main caregiver of the patient. We may also consider collecting data from other loved ones and perhaps the patients' primary physician or a paid helper (i.e. formal caregiver). In addition to providing a wider range of information about the patient, relying on multiple sources for the same information can increase the accuracy of the data. When we collect data from individuals, it is always possible that their perspectives are biased, their recollection is poor and so on. If we collect data from more than one source, we can compare how closely the sources align in their assessments. If multiple sources report similar information, we can be more confident about the findings. Of course, we must always be cognizant of the characteristics and relationships of the sources. We couldn't expect information about daily life challenges from Alzheimer's patient's physicians to be as complete as would be the information from the person living with the patient. But the primary caregiver and physician would both provide data on a patient's physical and cognitive health status, the progression of the illness and so forth. Therefore, multiple sources can be invaluable in the right circumstances. While we have used the example of different sources in interview based research, researchers conducting historical-comparative research nearly always use multiple sources when they are available. Observational research can also benefit from seeking information from multiple sources (e.g. not just relying on one or two informants or observing only a few members of a group).

Case study

Many of the data collection techniques we've discussed help us identify general patterns and trends in the social world. But sometimes we are interested in studying a single instance, such as a natural disaster, unusual illness symptoms, an extraordinary person or a historical event. An in-depth study of a single person, event, community or group is called a **case study**. Case studies have a long history in the social sciences as well as in other fields. Case studies have also been the subject of recent methodological research (Ragin and Becker, 1992; Brady and Collier, 2004; George and Bennett, 2004). Medical journals frequently publish reports of patients who have unusual symptoms, disease circumstances or recovery trajectories. Some of the earliest and most famous psychologists did case studies. Many of Sigmund Freud's insights that lead to his psychosexual theory of development came from case studies of his clients. Jean Piaget, who is known for his work in cognitive development, drew on observations made of his own children to advance his theories. Case studies can be useful when we want to examine how a particular programme or intervention will unfold in use; the intervention can be introduced in one setting before applying it broadly.

Not all case studies are done with single cases; sometimes comparisons are made between multiple cases to draw insights. For instance, a criminologist interested in understanding the thoughts and behaviours of serial killers may do an in-depth analysis of three or four serial killers to try to establish some commonalities. Often multiple data collection techniques are used to collect information about a case, including observation, interviews and archival data. The greatest limitation of case study research is the lack of generalizability. **Generalizability** is the ability to draw conclusions about a population based on data from a sample. Findings based on one case cannot be used to make larger statements about the population. We may have new understandings of the minds of three serial killers but we don't know how those results generalize to other serial killers.

Internet research

The growth of the Internet in the past few decades has had a large impact on how social scientists do research. Some of these changes have already been mentioned in this chapter. Web surveys are increasingly used to collect data. A simple search on the Internet can result in locating a considerable amount of social science data and statistics. Data are available that have been collected by scientists, private and public organizations, polling and marketing agencies and individuals. Journal articles, conference presentations and even books are available online to help us with our research. The Internet has undoubtedly made it easier for social scientists to access information for their research. A common mistake, however, especially among beginning students, is relying too heavily on the Internet when doing research. Many books, journal issues, data sets and statistics are not available online. It is still necessary to go to the library and to request information from other universities, organizations, libraries or researchers. Just because information is not readily available on the Internet does not mean it does not exist. And one must be cautious about information found on the Internet. While many high quality data sources and publications are available online, so are data sets of dubious quality and publications that don't meet the standards of social science research.

Social scientists have also begun to utilize the Internet as a direct *source of data*. Chat rooms and other Internet sites where people interact with each other about a particular topic can be used as data. We could, for instance, consider using postings from patients in chat rooms to better understand how a particular disease impacts individuals' lives and identify the salient illness issues by seeing what they discuss with other patients. A recent study (Marcum, 2007) used chat room transcripts to identify tactics child predators use online to manipulate children. It is difficult to find other ways to collect data about child predators. Experimental research is sometimes now conducted on the Internet. Does establishing support groups online help people stop smoking or help them remain on a weight-loss diet? When given the opportunity to obtain information online about a survey topic individuals agreed to participate in, do they seek further information? Some researchers are also exploring the possibility of using online virtual worlds and online multi-player games both as sites of observation and places to conduct experiments (Bainbridge, 2007). The use of the Internet as a source of data raises several new ethical issues. First, while individuals are posting their information on websites that are available for public viewing, individuals do not know their information is being used for research purposes. Second, if utilizing data from chat rooms, when researchers log into a room, should they tell members that they are a researcher interested in using their data or should they take on a more covert role in the chat room?

Applications

1 Time use among adolescents

a) In Chapter 3, you designed a quantitative study pertaining to time use among adolescents. Identify two additional ways you could collect data to test your hypothesis. What are the advantages and disadvantages of these two techniques?
b) Now return to the qualitative study you designed in Chapter 4. Identify two ways you could collect data for this study and state the benefits and drawbacks of these data collection strategies.
c) If you are asked to triangulate data sources for either your qualitative or quantitative study, how would you proceed?

2 The experiences of older adults with dementia

a) In Chapter 4, you were introduced to the concept of anticipatory dementia. Do you think observational methods would be useful for collecting data about this topic? Why or why not?
b) What data collection strategy would you recommend using to collect data for the qualitative study you proposed in the last chapter?

c) If you wanted to examine whether or not exposure to information about symptoms of dementia makes people more likely to experience anticipatory dementia, what type of data collection strategy would you use?

3 The death penalty as a deterrent to crime

Explain how a mixed method approach to collecting data related to deterrence theory could be valuable.

4 Ecological modernization theory

In this chapter, we mentioned that data have been collected by countries on their carbon dioxide emissions and a variety of national economic indicators. What are some of the advantages and challenges involved in working with this type of secondary data?

5 Gender differences in mathematics, science and language skills

Design a study in which content analysis would be the most appropriate method of collecting data.

6 Work and family balance issues/opportunity costs theory

We have discussed opportunity costs theory throughout this book. Identify a hypothesis or circumstance related to this theory that would benefit from the use of the following data collection techniques. In other words, how could these strategies be used to collect data on this topic?
a) Group surveys
b) Field research
c) Historical-comparative

7 Sexual and contraceptive behaviour and the threat of HIV/AIDS

Return to the two research projects you designed in Chapters 3 and 4 to better understand individuals' sexual and contraceptive behaviours and the threat of HIV/AIDS. In your opinion, for both research questions what would be the 'best' method of collecting relevant data? Why did you select these approaches?

6   Assessing the findings

- Introduction
- Critical thinking concepts and tools
- Problems with subjects
- Problems with design
- Some assessments specific for quantitative findings
- Some assessments specific for qualitative findings
- Applications

Introduction

In previous chapters we have examined the two most common approaches to social science research – quantitative and qualitative analysis – and have introduced you to the many methods researchers deploy to gather data. In this chapter we will inventory the problems that can lead to inaccurate conclusions from research. When we began this book, we proposed that social science should really be thought of as a 'hard' science because of the many challenges involved in trying to understand and explain human behaviours, thoughts and interactions. You have no doubt seen this first hand with the examples and exercises we have used throughout this book. We may think, for instance, that gender differences in children's mathematics and science performance are due in part to children being socialized into gender stereotyped roles. But testing that hypothesis is not easy, and the way we construct our research study has everything to do with what types of conclusions we can make. As we will see, many problems with research design can occur whether we use qualitative or quantitative approaches and can plague many different types of data collection strategies even though different approaches to research sometimes use different language to deal with similar problems. In diagnosing potential sources of problems, we can often design studies to limit the harm these problems do to our ability to draw solid conclusions. And as always, triangulation allows us to complement studies with one set of potential flaws with studies that don't have those particular flaws, leading to greater overall confidence in what we have learned across methods.

One way to think about these problems is to consider what one can conclude from a study. As a starting point, we can think about a study that interviews family caregivers of Alzheimer's patients. One form of reporting such a study is simply to say that 'I spoke to a dozen caregivers and this is what they said'. No claim is made that what is reported is true for anyone except those to whom one spoke – the results are not claimed to apply to (in other words, be generalizable to) a larger population. Further, no claim is made about the accuracy of what was said – the report is simply stating what the caregivers said. No link to theory is made either by arguing that there are theories consistent with what you found or by arguing that there are patterns in the data that can be abstracted into theory – the study is neither inductive nor deductive. If the goals of a study are restricted in these ways, most of the methodological problems we will discuss in this chapter don't apply. Many fine studies do remain this restrictive, including Dornenburg and Page's (1998, 2003) fascinating books on chefs, food critics and restaurants and Barbara Ehrenreich's examinations of working life in the US (Ehrenreich, 2005; Ehrenreich *et al.*, 2002). The value of this descriptive work is indisputable, as Bruno Latour reminds us, 'for every hundred books of commentaries, arguments, glosses, there is only one of description'.[1]

However, most social science research is intended to expand beyond simple reports of what one saw or heard in at least two related ways. First, we often want to make statements about a larger group than those from whom we collected data. One would like to feel that the interviews with the dozen caregivers provide some insight into the situation of more than just those dozen people. This is the reason we use probability sampling methods – we often cannot interview an entire population about whom we are interested but we want the people we do interview to be representative of a larger population. Second, we usually would like to test existing theory or develop new theory based on the evidence gathered. The theoretical use of the data is not just to make generalizations beyond the sample. Theories describe the conditions under which social processes unfold and link pieces of evidence together to create a greater understanding of the issue at hand. Often several studies have to be conducted about a topic using different methods of inquiry and data collection strategies to gain an accurate understanding of the problem. If these are all standalone studies that aren't linked together in any way, all we have are a series of individual studies.

---

[1]   See Bruno Latour's A Prologue in the form of a dialogue between a student and his (somewhat) Socratic professor (http://www.ensmp.fr/~latour/articles/article/090.html).

When we create new theories or link data to existing theories, thus to other pieces of empirical evidence (i.e. data), we contribute to the larger body of scientific knowledge.

What might lead us astray in either generalizing to a larger group or testing or developing theory from the accounts of our dozen caregivers? In this chapter we discuss some key issues in the assessment of research findings. We will learn that all studies are flawed, but that different approaches to collecting and analysing data are differentially vulnerable to each flaw, and that special care in how we design research can minimize some of the problems that might occur.

As we have noted, the qualitative and quantitative traditions have developed somewhat independently, and there have been tensions between the two approaches. Much of this tension centers on methodological critiques of quantitative and qualitative work by those who are sceptical of one approach or the other. These tensions are easing as multiple methods and triangulation are applied by more and more researchers who are interested in common social phenomena. Consequently, we believe that the criteria for assessing research quality and for honing research design will become common across both qualitative and quantitative approaches. For example, some influential methodologists have argued that a number of criteria developed for quantitative research could be fruitfully applied to qualitative studies, especially case study methods (King *et al.*, 1994; but also see Brady and Collier, 2004). Of course there has been debate about some of the specific proposals. But despite some progress in the development of the social sciences we have to acknowledge that the tensions continue to exist.

Therefore, we present our discussion of assessing findings in three sections. The first is a brief discussion of **critical thinking**, the art of evaluating and analysing the claims of others. This discussion applies to quantitative and qualitative methods and in fact to all arguments about the state of the world. We then discuss the most commonly used criteria that researchers in the quantitative traditions use for assessing research, followed by a discussion of criteria that are used in the qualitative traditions. In each case we offer examples that illustrate the ways in which the criteria can be used to hone a design and also to understand its limits. In doing so, we let each tradition have its own 'voice' rather than applying an overarching set of criteria to both approaches. We have some sense of regret in this structure. If we are all engaged in a common enterprise of understanding the social world, then we should, as a community of researchers, have a common set of criteria for what constitutes strong evidence and the limits of that evidence. But in writing this text, we also have to be honest with our readers and admit that such a common vision does not reflect the current state of methodological discourse. In part this is because quantitative and qualitative research traditions typically are asking rather different questions about the social world and thus must deploy different approaches and be attentive to different problems to answer those questions well. But in part the current situation represents a rather fractured (and all too often fractious) discourse that has not yet reached consensus on how to assess studies. We hope that subsequent editions of this text might be able to reflect such a consensus and discuss more universal criteria.

Critical thinking concepts and tools[2]

Critical thinking is an intellectual tool that helps evaluate an argument and helps check the quality of reasoning about a problem, issue or situation. Richard Paul and Linda Elder of the Foundation for Critical Thinking have developed a guide to critical thinking that is useful in every domain of learning, particularly those focused on evaluation and assessment. Critical thinkers question information, conclusions and points of view and always strive to be clear, accurate, precise and relevant. Paul and Elder's Universal Intellectual Standards provide a way to check the quality of reasoning, and the most significant of those standards and the questions associated with each are given in Box 6.1.

Box 6.1: Critical thinking standards

Clarity
- Could you elaborate further?
- Could you give me an example?
- Could you illustrate what you mean?

Accuracy
- How can we check on that?
- How can we find out if that is true?
- How can we verify or test that?

cont.

---

[2] The text in this section is adapted from Richard Paul and Linda Elder's Critical thinking: Concepts and tools. The Foundation for Critical Thinking (http://www.critical thinking.org/articles/universal-intellectual-standards.cfm)

Box 6.1: Critical thinking standards cont.

Precision
- Could you be more specific?
- Could you give me more details?
- Could you be more exact?

Relevance
- How does that relate to the problem?
- How does that bear on the question?
- How does that help us with the issue?

Depth
- What factors make this a difficult problem?
- What are some of the complexities of this question?
- What are some of the difficulties we need to deal with?

Breadth
- Do we need to look at this from another perspective?
- Do we need to consider another point of view?
- Do we need to look at this in other ways?

Logic
- Does all this make sense together?
- Does your first paragraph fit in with your last?
- Does what you say follow from the evidence?

Significance
- Is this the most important problem to consider?
- Is this the central idea to focus on?
- Which of these facts are most important?

Fairness
- Do I have any vested interest in this issue?
- Am I sympathetically representing the viewpoints of others?

Source: Richard Paul and Linda Elder, *The Miniature Guide to Critical Thinking Concepts and Tools* (http://www.criticalthinking.org/files/Concepts_Tools.pdf)

We provide a brief explication of some of these standards below (quoted from Paul & Elder, http://www.criticalthinking.org/articles/universal-intellectual-standards.cfm):

1 Clarity: Could you elaborate further on that point? Could you express that point in another way? Could you give me an illustration? Could you give me an example?

Clarity is the gateway standard. If a statement is unclear, we cannot determine whether it is accurate or relevant. In fact, we cannot tell anything about it because we don't yet know what it is saying. For example, the question, 'What can be done about the education system in America?' is unclear. In order to address the question adequately, we would need to have clearer understanding of what the person asking the question is considering the 'problem' to be. A clearer question might be, 'What can educators do to ensure that students learn the skills and abilities which help them function successfully on the job and in their daily decision-making?'

2 Accuracy: Is that really true? How could we check that? How could we find out if that is true?

A statement can be clear but not accurate, as in 'Most dogs are over 300 pounds in weight'.

3 Precision: Could you give more details? Could you be more specific?

A statement can be both clear and accurate, but not precise, as in 'Jack is overweight'. (We don't know how overweight Jack is, one pound or 500 pounds.)

4 Relevance: How is that connected to the question? How does that bear on the issue?

A statement can be clear, accurate, and precise, but not relevant to the question at issue. For example, students often think that the amount of effort they put into a course should be taken into account in their course grades. Often, however, the 'effort' does not measure the quality of student learning; and when this is so, effort is irrelevant to their appropriate grade.

5 Depth: How does your answer address the complexities in the question? How are you taking into account the problems in the question? Is that dealing with the most significant factors?

A statement can be clear, accurate, precise, and relevant, but superficial (that is, lack depth). For example, the statement, 'Just say No!' which is often used to discourage children and teens from using drugs, is clear, accurate, precise, and relevant. Nevertheless, it lacks depth because it treats an extremely complex issue, the pervasive problem of drug use among young people, superficially. It fails to deal with the complexities of the issue.

6 Breadth: Do we need to consider another point of view? Is there another way to look at this question? What would this look like from a conservative standpoint? What would this look like from the point of view of ...?

A line of reasoning may be clear accurate, precise, relevant, and deep, but lack breadth (as in an argument from either the conservative or liberal standpoint which gets deeply into an issue, but only recognizes the insights of one side of the question).

7 **Logic**: Does this really make sense? Does that follow from what you said? How does that follow? But before you implied this, and now you are saying that; how can both be true?

When we think, we bring a variety of thoughts together into some order. When the combination of thoughts are mutually supporting and make sense in combination, the thinking is 'logical'. When the combination is not mutually supporting, is contradictory in some sense or does not 'make sense', the combination is not logical.

The critical thinking standards in Box 6.1 will be useful in the following discussion of the major categories of limitations of both quantitative and qualitative research.

Problems with subjects

Problems with subjects take several forms. They all lead to the same ultimate problem – we have to be cautious in assuming that what we have observed with our respondents can be generalized to a larger population. It is easiest to think of these problems of taking two forms. One is getting the 'wrong' subjects. The other is respondents giving us the 'wrong' information.

The 'wrong' subjects

If we care about generalizing to a larger population, we want to choose subjects who are typical of that larger population. In statistics, we can define in a formal, mathematical sense what we mean by typical. But a commonsense understanding will suffice for our discussion. In selecting caregivers to interview, we would want them to be like other caregivers in all the ways that matter for the purposes of understanding the activities, frustrations and satisfactions of providing care to family members with Alzheimer's. We wouldn't want mostly people who feel they are doing a great job, or mostly people who are deeply frustrated and angry, nor mostly people who have a lot of time or money to support their caregiving. We want people who are more or less like most people giving care. Or put differently, we want the range of confidence, frustration, anger, time and money in our subjects to look like the range in the overall population of caregivers.

One of the main reasons we often use probability samples is to be sure we are getting samples that are representative in just this way. A probability sample matches the characteristics of the population from which it is drawn except for 'luck of the draw' and since statisticians understand the 'luck of the draw' very well, we can use statistical procedures to ensure that we have a representative sample.

However, sometimes we can't draw a probability sample, either because there is no feasible way of doing so or because the costs and complexities of such a sample are beyond the means of our research budget. In the case of the hypothetical caregiver study, it might be possible to develop a random sample of caregivers in a particular country or in a particular community by tracking down individuals diagnosed with Alzheimer's and finding family caregivers. But this would be an expensive and complex operation. Let's assume that in our hypothetical study we used a convenience sample. We used support groups, health care centres and other means to find family caregivers. We then ask them if they would be willing to be interviewed. We would probably find that most will say 'yes' but some will say 'no'.

This suggests we will have to be careful in generalizing from our sample to the population of all caregivers in the community. First, the method we used to find respondents, while entirely reasonable, does not ensure that we have a group representative of the larger population of family caregivers. It may be that those who are most happy with their role, or those that are least happy, are less likely to be in touch with support groups or health care centres or other caregivers. So the process of selecting the sample may have introduced some discrepancies between the sample and the population we want to be able to speak about.

Second, not all those we contact will agree to an interview. People who volunteer for studies are by definition somewhat different from those who don't. So we always have to worry about whether or not the differences between those who volunteered and those who didn't may make it impossible to generalize from the volunteers to everyone else. It is useful to think of the problems introduced by the subject as belonging primarily to what we could call the 'baggage' of individuals – *subject/respondent charac-teristics or attributes* that they bring with them into the research project (such as propensity for volunteering, gender, age, prior experiences, religion). In our example, it may be those with the best or with the worst experiences, and probably those with the most time available are most likely to agree to participate. This again will make our sample deviate in some ways from the overall population of caregivers. So in such a study we would have to pay special attention to who we recruit and also be properly cautious in interpreting our findings.

The 'wrong' information

Third, some interviewees may decide not to answer some of the questions they are asked. Instead of getting the information we need, we get what researchers call a 'non-response'. Most people are reluctant to discuss financial matters. Family conflicts may also be a taboo subject for many, and so too might be the behaviours of the loved one that are most frustrating to the caregiver. And, fourth, even when a question is answered, the respondent may feel that she or he is 'on stage' and should give a 'performance' that reflects well on them and on the loved one being cared for. It may be difficult for a caregiver to admit to feeling overwhelming frustration or resentment with the dementia patient. Sometimes these inaccuracies will be intentional; often they will simply be the reality as constructed in the interview. Here again, special care and caution are required.

These four problems – discrepancies between the sample and the population, differences between those who participate and those who don't, missing data from questions not answered and inaccurate answers – are problematic in the context of in-depth interviews with a small convenience sample, but they apply to all forms of data collection. In Chapter 5 we discussed some of these issues in the context of survey research. In national surveys, we may wish to have a representative sample of the adult population of a country. But in practice, all our methods of drawing a sample will miss some parts of the population. Many people drawn in the sample will refuse to participate in the survey. Many people who agree to be interviewed refuse to answer some questions. And the answers to some questions may be inaccurate through either intent or error on the part of the respondent.

We can see the same problems with the small analysis of opportunity costs and fertility in Chapter 3. In most cross-national studies, researchers use all countries for which data are available. But as we saw when we had to remove Iraq and Bahrain from some analyses, some countries are 'non-respondents' in the sense that we can't include them in the analysis because the data for them are not available. For cross-national research, this is a mix of problems one, two and three. And those using archived statistical data from many nations are well aware that some national statistics are not very accurate, often because of limited abilities of some countries to measure these things, sometimes because there is intentional misreporting. So problem four – inaccurate data – is of concern too. International agencies spend considerable effort on developing comparable and accurate ways of measuring key variables to minimize this problem, but it still exists, just as it does in in-depth interviewing or in survey research.

Problems with design

Design problems include a variety of issues that can threaten the confidence we have in the findings because we have measured or observed the wrong things, or have not measured or observed things very accurately. Key among these problems are invalid operational definitions (to be defined shortly), poor measurement and designs that don't allow accurate conclusions, including researcher bias. Here we describe these most common design issues.

Reliability and validity

The assessment of research findings is in large part centred around the issues of validity and reliability. **Reliability** is concerned with *consistency*. Research findings are considered reliable if similar findings are revealed time after time in repeated applications of the research. At least since Galileo scientists have worked hard to develop reliable measures. Galileo noticed that when he observed the stars and other celestial objects, his measurements would vary slightly each time he made them. The assumption was that there was a true value of what was being measured but that each measurement was influenced by some error. A reliable measure is one that keeps the error small. The development of reliable measures in social research is a major field in social statistics. Often we try to ensure reliability by asking multiple questions on the same subject, as is done in most standardized tests. These multiple observations can be combined into an overall measure that is more reliable than any single question would be by itself. If we want to assess pain experiences among a patient group, for instance, we may ask two questions that measure pain at different points in a survey instrument, which would be a more reliable measure of pain than just one question. As we saw in Chapter 5 and will discuss later in this chapter, qualitative researchers have developed careful protocols to ensure the reliability of field observations and in-depth interviews.

Validity is concerned with *congruence*, or a 'goodness of fit' between the details of the research, the evidence, and the conclusions drawn by the researchers. We usually consider two aspects of validity – internal validity and external validity. **Internal validity** means that the study is drawing appropriate conclusions from the data at hand. For example, if the variables in a study do not measure what they were intended to measure, there are problems with *invalid operational definitions*. When we have the wrong operational definitions, we don't have internal validity. Obviously we would not use a bathroom scale to measure an individual's IQ – that would be an extreme example of an invalid operational definition. But often problems with the relationship between the theoretical concept being discussed and the thing that has been measured can be subtle. For example, in designing a test of aptitude in mathematics or science, we would have to be careful not to build questions that tap more into experiences common among young men than among young women. If we were not sufficiently careful, we might think we were measuring aptitude when in fact we were measuring experience. A great deal of debate in the research literature centres on this kind of problem – does the study really measure what the theory describes? This problem can occur both when theory is used to form hypotheses in a deductive approach or when theory is developed from observation in an inductive approach. Another threat to internal validity comes from drawing causal inferences incorrectly. We have discussed this problem in the previous chapter when we examined the merits of experiments and quasi-experiments. In the absence of a true experiment with randomization, it can be hard to determine the effects of an independent variable. A researcher may claim that her analysis shows that opportunity costs lead to lower fertility, or that the death penalty reduces homicide. But without randomization, other creative researchers can usually make arguments as to why any particular study has missed an alternative explanation for what was found. This is why our understanding advances by the accumulation of studies rather than from any single study – in the absence of randomization we must always have some concern with alternative explanations of what was observed as a threat to the internal validity of our conclusions in a particular study.

However, as we also noted in Chapter 5, experiments also have their own limits, primarily as the result of threats to external validity. **External validity** is the ability to generalize from a study to a larger population. While experiments can achieve a high degree of internal validity with respect to determining what is causing what, they usually require somewhat artificial circumstances that may produce atypical behaviour of the subjects and often have to draw on non-representative samples. Thus the ability to generalize from experiments to the rest of the world is often problematic and as a result, experiments may have limited external validity.[3]

It is important to remember that we can sometimes measure things with great reliability but the measures actually have little validity (such as the bathroom scale as a measure of IQ). An example of this is the controversy over large gender and race gaps in college placement tests. We know that these tests are very reliable in the sense that if we gave the same test (or different versions of the same test) to the same people several times,

---

[3] Another type of validity refers to the reproducibility of situations, or how well an experimental (or interview) situation corresponds to real-world referents; people may behave differently in experiments or interviews than in corresponding settings where performance evaluation is reduced (see Druckman, 2005, 69, for further discussion).

the scores of individuals would not change much.[4] The debate about them centres on validity. In the US men have consistently been scoring higher than women on the SAT exam's verbal and mathematics sections for almost four decades; in 2004 the College Board reported an average score of 1049 for males and 1005 for females nationwide. The race gap in scores on the Graduate Record Examination (GRE) is even more severe. In 1996, whites scored 236 points higher than blacks in the combined GRE exam, and 10 years later the gap had increased by another 5 points.[5] But while these measurements are reliable, it is not clear how well the tests actually tap what they are intended to tap – the ability to succeed in college or in graduate school. Or to put it differently, it seems that the tests are accurate in that they predict with reasonable accuracy the success of white males but are less successful at predicting the success of women and minorities. So their validity when applied to the larger and more diverse population is considerably less than when applied only to white men.

Sampling bias

The link between respondent problems and design problems can be understood by thinking about sampling bias. **Sampling bias** is the difference between what we observe in our sample and what we would have observed if we collected data for the entire population. Without a random, representative sample, research findings cannot be generalized beyond the sample in the study. As we have seen, there are many sources of sampling bias. One of the most obvious is the use of volunteers in research (one of the most popular sampling strategies in psychological studies). This introduces a *self-selection* sampling problem that reduces the external validity of the study. One reason social science research is often based on probability samples is that such samples allow us to generalize to the population because, at least ideally, we are choosing who is in the data set and thus eliminating 'volunteer' effects. But as we have seen, in a survey we still have to persuade people to participate. So in any survey a great deal of effort is spent on trying to get everyone drawn into the probability sample to complete the survey. Indeed, factors that influence participation in

---

4 One thing these tests certainly measure is the ability to take standardized tests. So taking the same kind of test over and over is likely to improve your skills at test taking and thus yield somewhat higher scores with practice. This is the basis of many commercial programmes intended to help students improve their scores. But if you take a test only a couple of times without practice in between, for most people the score won't change much.

5 Gender gap data are from www.womensenews.org/article.cfm/dyn/aid/2220; racial gap data are from the Journal of Blacks in Higher Education, www.jbhe.com/news_views/51_graduate_admissions_test.htm, accessed December 30, 2007.

surveys and the effects of **non-response** on survey results is a major topic of methodological research.

The problem of bias based on self-selection can also be thought about in the context of experiments. If we randomly assign people to the experimental and control group we know the two groups differ only by chance, and we can use statistics to calculate how big those differences are. This gives us a high degree of internal validity. If we let people pick their group, we don't know what influenced those choices and how the groups differ as a result and we may not have much internal validity. This is a special case of the more general problem of comparing those who agreed to participate at all with those who didn't.

Subjects who know that they are being studied could 'act' for the researcher as if performing on a stage, thus introducing bias into the study called **on-stage effects**. This can sometimes manifest itself as a **social desirability** effect; study participants may want to please the researcher by acting in ways they think the researcher wants them to or answering questions in line with the researcher's expectations. Study participants may also try to portray a positive image of themselves to the researcher. One way to minimize on-stage effects is to give respondents only a general sense of what the goal of the research project is, rather than telling them the specific issues the researcher is investigating. If doing survey research, as discussed briefly in the last chapter, questions should be designed in a neutral manner so respondents are more likely to answer them honestly rather than as they think they should. Another problematic subject problem is **selective** or **distorted memory**, which might occur when researchers ask subjects to recall events that happened long ago or events that are painful to remember (such as sexual abuse).

Researcher bias

From time to time researchers have been documented to have either intentionally or unintentionally designed research that is biased towards upholding a particular theory or hypothesis about the relationship between variables. We have mentioned Stephen Jay Gould's *The Mismeasure of Man* (1981/1996) which provides an excellent exposé of the early research on intelligence in which he chronicled researcher bias in the design of studies and in the presentation of research results. In evaluation and intervention research, those conducting the research may have a vested interest in seeing the policy or programme of interest succeed, and that may have an impact on how they evaluate the programme. Research bias can also occur more subtly. A researcher may be so convinced that a hypothesis is true that they unintentionally slant their observations to find evidence supporting the hypothesis and ignore or discount negative evidence as outliers.

We can never make these effects disappear. But we work very hard to minimize them as best as we can. Again, no study is perfect, but by thinking carefully about possible sources of error and bias in each study, we can develop a robust understanding of the world by looking across studies.

Some assessments specific for quantitative findings

With survey research, the researcher must try to think of potential alternative explanations to the theory being tested and then measure those factors in the survey. Surveys tend to be expensive and time-consuming, and we work hard to think through all the issues before we start to collect data. Statistical techniques can then be used to examine the effects of the variables that represent alternative explanations and potentially rule them out as reasons for the relationships we observe. In the case of gender-mathematics/science skills, it may not be that males and females are born with different aptitudes for mathematics and science. Rather it may be that parents and teachers encourage young men and women to excel in different subjects in school. So we would include in our survey measures of how much parents and teachers encouraged a person to study science and to study mathematics, for instance, as a measure of these variables. If we found a relationship between gender and mathematics/science skills but did not include parent and teacher influences (assuming they are a factor), our findings about gender would be overly simplistic. But if we found that the relationship between gender and mathematics and science skills persisted after we took account of the level of parental and teacher encouragement, we have more confidence in the assertion that there is a real gender difference. Alternatively, if controlling for level of encouragement makes the relationship between gender and mathematics/science skills disappear, then the theory is discredited by the data.

An important issue with most quantitative studies is the interpretation of the procedures we use to assess the effects of random processes. There are two very common ways that random effects occur in quantitative research. One is the effects of random assignment to experimental and control groups in experiments. The other is the random selection of respondents in a survey. In the case of experiments, a statistical analysis will tell us how likely it is that the differences we see between the experimental and control groups are the result of random assignment of subjects to one of the two groups. If the chances are very small, then we assume that the experimental treatment has had an effect. If the chances are reasonably high that the differences could have been generated by the flip of a coin or other random assignment making the groups somewhat different, then it is hard to argue the experimental treatment has had any effect. In the case of the survey, we observe various patterns in the sample. The statistical analysis tells us how likely it is that the results are just a chance effect of drawing a sample and not something we should expect to see if we had data on the whole population. For example if we observe a gender difference in the attitudes towards mathematics in a sample and statistical analysis says the difference 'has a p value less than 0.05', we know that there is less than one chance in 20 that there is no gender difference in the population.

Quantitative studies make extensive use of p (probability) values. By convention, we call a p value less than 0.05 'statistically significant'.[6] It is important to be clear about what that means. In an experiment, it means that there is less than 1 chance in 20 (5 percent or 0.05) that the differences between the groups were due to the random assignment. Therefore the difference is reasonably believed to be a result of the treatment. In the case of a survey, it means that there is less than 1 chance in 20 that the result is an artifact of the particular sample we have drawn and would not be seen if we had data on the whole population. Technically, the p value for survey results is the probability that the sample came from a population in which the effect we see in the sample does not exist.

If we don't find statistically significant effects, it's hard to argue that much of anything is going on. Of course, in deductive research if a theory says an effect should be there, and we find no evidence that it is, that can be an important result. On the other hand, if we find a statistically significant effect, we have established, with reasonable certainty, that something is going on. But the quantitative researcher must then move back to considerations of theory to interpret what is going on. Statistical significance (and the lack of statistical significance) is an important tool but it is important precisely because it guides our discussion of what we have found, not because it substitutes for that discussion.

Some assessments specific for qualitative findings

Judging the value of qualitative research is just as important as evaluating the quality of quantitative research. Many of the criteria we described above regarding subject and design problems do not easily apply to qualitative research. Probability samples, for example, are not typically used with qualitative research because the goal of much qualitative research is not to make statements about the larger population but to understand things

---

6   Sometimes we use small p values, such as 0.01 when we want to be really certain that the effect we have found is 'real'. But the more cautious we are, the more often we'll miss findings because they aren't sufficiently different from random effects. So if we view the analysis as rather exploratory, we may use a p value of 0.1.

in-depth and directly from the perspectives of those being studied. Thus, subject limitations and external validity, according to the criteria outlined above, are typically a 'problem' with qualitative research. Lincoln and Guba (1985) and Guba and Lincoln (1989) propose four criteria for judging qualitative research that better reflect the issues confronting this orientation: credibility, transferability, dependability and confirmability. These build on the general concepts of reliability and validity, as we described earlier, but develop them in the context of qualitative research.

Credibility is how accurately the data reflect reality. When collecting data, triangulation of methods and data sources can create a more complete understanding of the group or setting of interest. If conducting an observational study, for instance, the researcher may also informally conduct interviews with group members to gain additional insights. Combining both a researcher's observations and information obtained directly from individuals can improve the credibility of findings. Since accurately representing the perspectives of individuals is key to qualitative research, member checking is an important strategy to ensure credibility. In **member checking**, a researcher can ask study participants to review the researcher's notes, interview transcripts or even preliminary analyses and summaries of findings to see if they agree with the data and if they have anything else to add. **Peer debriefing** is also used to increase credibility. The researcher can discuss various stages of the research process with an uninvolved person (typically a colleague). This peer can give the researcher another perspective on the project and can help make clarifications and help identify what the researcher may have overlooked. Qualitative researchers also engage in **negative case analysis** to improve credibility. This means searching for cases or instances that are exceptions or run counter to the research findings. If studying household division of labour, identifying a subsample of households where the male does primary caregiving for children and the home (**unusual cases**) can help us better understand the more common circumstances in which there is an equal division of household labour and traditional division of labour (male is primary breadwinner and female is primary caretaker of children and home).

Generalizability, which is the extent claims can be made from the findings to a population, is a component for a strong research design. With quantitative studies, sampling is used to be able to generalize findings. Typically, qualitative studies use non-probability samples and small sample sizes, both of which limit the ability to generalize. Findings from field research do not tend to be generalizable because only one site or one group is studied. Making observations in more than one setting can increase the ability to generalize findings but this is often not practical. Guba and Lincoln called the extent that results can be applied to other settings or situations transferability. Qualitative researchers should provide rich ('thick') descriptions of the research site and characteristics of the sample to help others understand the sample and setting.

Dependability is most similar to the quantitative emphasis on reliability or how accurate the data are. Quantitative researchers focus on whether results can be replicated. With an observational study this would mean that if a second researcher would witness the same events, both sets of observations would match. Multiple observers can increase reliability, although it is not practical to have two observers in a setting. It is also unlikely that two researchers' observations would match perfectly because each researcher has a unique perspective and is likely to focus on some things more than others. In addition, many observational studies take months or years to conduct, making replication unrealistic. Since reliability (as quantitative researchers apply it) is not a fair way to judge qualitative studies, Guba and Lincoln proposed dependability. Dependability reflects how truthful the researcher is and how truthful the research is. It is the researcher's responsibility to accurately present the data, to be honest in the collection and presentation of data, and to be thorough in how they conduct their research. This includes describing the changes that inevitably occur in a setting and how changes impacted the research. The researcher should ensure the amount of data collected is adequate; did the researcher reach theoretical saturation?

Interviewer-interviewee dynamics can also influence research results. First, there is always concern about attachments the researcher forms with their subjects. Such attachments are natural since the researcher will become well acquainted with group members through daily interactions, especially when the observational period lasts several months or years. However, attachment can influence the researcher's views of the group members and setting, rendering the observations biased. One way to help ensure that our observations remain as unbiased as possible is for us to engage in theoretical and data triangulation. We should test one source of information against others to see if they match; this can help confirm information or identify alternative information. We should try to change perspectives frequently and look at both the details of a group and setting, as well as the larger picture. We should constantly strive to be aware of what we are witnessing objectively and what we are interpreting. Objective and subjective experiences should be kept distinct as much as possible. Another challenge with face-to-face interviews is interviewer bias. How we ask a question, such as our tone and wording choices, can impact how a person responds to a question. Consider this question: 'How many glasses of alcohol do you consume on an average day?' If we ask this in a judgmental tone, a person who drinks heavily may be hesitant to admit her behaviour. Or, in an effort to seem friendly and causal, we may decide to introduce the question with, 'I am sure this does not really apply to you, but … .' One way to minimize the influence of the interviewer is to be sure all interviewers are well trained and that all interviewers carry out every interview in an identical manner. This is particularly important if the interviews are going to be directly compared.

Other dynamics between the interviewer and interviewee can influence responses, including the social characteristics of the interviewer. If we want to interview a White American about stereotypes of African–Americans, and the interviewer is African–American, the interviewee may be hesitant to say anything that could be potentially offensive to the interviewer rather than just being truthful. The setting of the interview can also affect the results. If the interview takes place in a public location, such as a library, or if other people are present during the interview (e.g. spouse), the respondent may not be as forthcoming with information as if the interview were conducted in a more private setting.

Confirmability is the degree to which others can confirm the results. Observational methods, in particular, have an element of subjectivity since they rely largely on researchers' accounts, notes, and interpretations. The researcher needs to have a carefully documented trail of the data (e.g. sources, detailed notes, transcripts, tapes, dates on everything), which is called an **audit trail**. Documentation can be very time-consuming but is very important. Triangulation of data can also increase confirmability; checking with other sources of data can provide additional support for the observations.

Applications

1   Time use among adolescents

Select either the qualitative or quantitative research question you designed in the previous chapters. Drawing on the information presented in this chapter, identify several strategies you would use to improve the quality of your research (e.g. minimize design limitations, improve validity).

2   The experiences of older adults with dementia

a)   We have considered various issues related to dementia throughout this book. Let's think about the daily challenges dementia patients may face (e.g. confusion, inability to complete simple tasks, short-term memory problems like forgetting the oven is on). We construct a questionnaire to assess the types of challenges dementia patients experience daily and the extent these challenges are problematic. Our sample consists of patients in the early stages of dementia. We triangulate our data by also interviewing each patient's primary caregiver (or if the patient does not yet need a caregiver, we will define this person as the individual who spends the most time with the patient). Identify any design or respondent problems we may face with this study. Is there anything we can do to overcome these limitations?

b) How could we enhance the reliability and validity of this study?

3 The death penalty as a deterrent to crime

In Chapter 1, using scatterplots and descriptive data, we found that, in contrast to deterrence theory, death penalty states had higher rates of homicide than did states without the death penalty. Using information presented throughout the book (not just this chapter), what steps would you take to better understand this unexpected finding? In other words, is there enough evidence here that would convince us that deterrence theory is invalid?

4 Ecological modernization theory

We have discussed the availability of secondary data to test the premise of ecological modernization theory. Are there any design problems you can think of with these data?

5 Gender differences in mathematics, science and language skills

Throughout the book, we have proposed a study where a researcher goes into classrooms and makes observations of teachers and children to better understand gender differences in mathematics, science and language performance. If you are the researcher carrying out this study, what would you do to convince other scientists that you did valid and reliable research?

6 Work and family balance issues/opportunity costs theory

We have discussed opportunity costs theory throughout this book. In Chapter 3, we provided some quantitative data to test this theory preliminarily. Identify any potential study or design limitations with that project.

7 Sexual and contraceptive behaviour and the threat of HIV/AIDS

You were asked for the first research topic to consider either the qualitative or quantitative research question you created. For this exercise, select the research question you designed in previous chapters reflecting the orientation you did not select for the first question (e.g. if you selected qualitative for application #1, now select your quantitative question).

Drawing on the information presented in this chapter, identify several strategies you would use to improve the quality of your research (e.g. minimize design limitations, improve validity).

7 Exercises using research from the published literature

In this chapter we present abbreviated research scenarios from the literature that students can use to exercise their skills in applying the concepts discussed in the book. Each study is outlined as a problem and includes basic information from the published article. It is our intention to have students work these problems with just the information provided here (in most cases, the abstract and details from the method sections of each article). The problems differ not only in the depth of information provided, but also in the structure of the presentation, reflecting the diversity of formats used in the literature for reporting empirical research. For a more comprehensive assessment of each article, students may access the full text by locating the article in their library or on the Internet.

Problem 1

Kulik (2007) compared perceptions of gender-based equality in the division of household labour among Jewish women ($n = 60$) and Arab Muslim women ($n = 62$) from dual-earner families in Israel. Guided by theories regarding the division of household labour, the author also explored the impact of three sets of variables – resources (e.g. education), gender-role attitudes, and job flexibility (flextime) – on perceived equality in the division of household labour. The results are based on a comprehensive survey of Jewish and Arab Muslim families in Israel, in which the author examined various aspects of family and work life. Data were collected from October 2000 to April 2001. Participants were married mothers who work outside the home. The Arab Muslim participants were Hebrew-speaking residents of five villages in the central and northern regions of Israel. The initial sample consisted of 79 Jewish women and 87 Arab Muslim women. The women in both groups held senior administrative positions in the education system or the municipality. The findings revealed that the Jewish women tended to perceive the division of household labour as more egalitarian than did their Arab Muslim counterparts. Furthermore, the Jewish women had more egalitarian gender-role attitudes and more job flexibility than did the Arab Muslim women. However, all three sets of variables predicted perceived equality in the division of household labour to the same extent for both groups of women. Moreover, for both groups, education level correlated with attitudes toward household labour and with extent of job flexibility. Overall, the findings suggest that education may contribute to improving women's quality of life in both traditional and modern sociocultural contexts.

(From: Kulik, L. (2007). Equality in the division of household labour: a comparative study of Jewish women and Arab Muslim women in Israel, *The Journal of Social Psychology* 147(4): 423–40.)

Exercise for Chapter 1

Is this a deductive or inductive research design? Explain your answer.

Exercises for Chapter 2

What is the unit of analysis (who or what was observed)?
Describe the sample (include as much information as you can from the above scenario).
Do you know how the sample was selected and whether it is a probability sample? What is the population?
What type of data did the author collect (Primary or secondary? Cross-sectional or longitudinal?)
State the hypothesis in words.
Restate the hypothesis as a mathematical formula.

Exercises for Chapter 3

Explain how the hypothesis is causal.
Name the dependent variable(s).
    Any operationalization (definition) available?
Explanatory variable(s):
    Name the independent variable(s) in the scenario.
        Any operationalization (definition) available?
Extraneous variables:
    Name any controlled variables.
    Name at least 4 uncontrolled variables (what could influence the
        dependent variables other than the independent variable and the
        controlled variables?)

Draw a diagram of the hypothesis using the boxes in Figure 7.1.

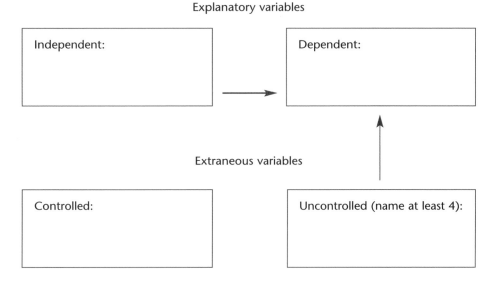

Figure 7.1 Hypothesis framework

Exercise for Chapter 4

Briefly rewrite the method of the study to adhere to an inductive qualitative design.

Exercise for Chapter 5

This research used a survey design. Rewrite the study as one of the other deductive data collection strategies described in Chapter 5. What are the advantages and disadvantages of using this strategy over the current survey design?

Exercise for Chapter 6

Identify any limitations of the research because of
    a)   subject/respondent problems.
    b)   design problems.

Problem 2

The fishing industry in the US and most industrialized nations is composed almost exclusively of men. Yodanis (2000) examined how the process of gender construction keeps women from being fishers. The researcher lived and worked in a fishing town in an eastern coastal region in the US for two summers and one autumn season. This allowed the researcher to informally meet and get to know fishermen and their spouses and children. This work was supplemented with in-depth interviews with 54 men and women in fishing families who were selected due to particular characteristics they had that were of interest (e.g. work reputation). The article discusses common explanations for occupational sex segregation to explain why women do not fish, including biology, gender role socialization, cultural traditions and discrimination. However, an alternative explanation is proposed based on the data – the social construction of gender. In fishing communities, the researcher proposes, gender is defined in relation to fishing. Women are 'women' because they do not fish; they define their role as 'not fishing'. 'Man', on the other hand, is defined as a person who fishes. These differential gender role definitions help women keep the boundaries between themselves and fishing as they construct gender. The social construction of gender helps explain why women do not strive to succeed in the most lucrative industry in rural coastal communities.

(From: Yodanis, C.L. (2000). Constructing gender and occupational segregation: a study of women and work in fishing communities, *Qualitative Sociology* 23(3): 267–90.)

Exercise for Chapter 1

Is this a deductive or inductive research design? Explain your answer.

Exercises for Chapter 2

What is the unit of analysis (who or what was observed)?
Describe the sample (include as much information as you can from the above scenario).
Do you know how the sample was selected and whether it is a probability sample? What sampling strategy was used? What is the population?
What type of data did the author collect (Primary or secondary? Cross-sectional or longitudinal?)

Exercise for Chapter 3

Briefly rewrite the study as a quantitative design.

Exercises for Chapter 4

Describe how this study uses an inductive approach.
What are the advantages of using a qualitative approach to studying this topic?
Does it seem that the researcher was able to obtain an emic perspective into the topic? What does this mean?

Exercises for Chapter 5

What technique(s) was used to collect the data in this study?
Was the data collection process obtrusive or unobtrusive?
Was the observation direct or participant?

Exercise for Chapter 6

Identify possible limitations of this study. What could the researcher do to minimize these limitations?

Problem 3

An experimental design was used by McGarva *et al.* (2006) to examine the effect of driver cell-phone use on roadway aggression. Subjects were 135 drivers traveling in a small city in North Dakota. The authors videotaped the subjects while a confederate driver in a low-status vehicle (a sun-faded 1970 hatchback) frustrated them by remaining motionless at a stoplight that had turned green. When the confederate visibly talked on a hand-held cell-phone ($n = 67$, the experimental condition was determined by a coin toss) male subjects who were held up behind the confederate's motionless car exhibited their frustration by honking their horns more quickly and frequently than did drivers in no-cell-phone trials, and female subjects who were held up behind the confederate were more angry according to blind judgments of videotaped facial expressions (1 = no reaction to 7 = very angry) when compared with those of drivers in no-cell-phone trials ($n = 68$) The results suggest that driver cell-phone use contributes to the growing crisis of roadway aggression.

(From: McGarva, A.R., Ramsey, M. and Shear, S.A. (2006) Effects of driver cell-phone use on driver aggression, *The Journal of Social Psychology* 146(2): 133–46.)

Exercise for Chapter 1

Is this a deductive or inductive research design? Explain your answer.

Exercises for Chapter 2

What is the unit of analysis (who or what was observed)?
Describe the sample (include as much information as you can from the above scenario).
Do you know how the sample was selected and whether it is a probability sample? What is the population?
What type of data did the authors collect (Primary or secondary? Cross-sectional or longitudinal?)
State the hypothesis in words.
Restate the hypothesis as a mathematical formula, $y = f(x)$.

Exercises for Chapter 3

Explain how the hypothesis is causal.
Name the dependent variable(s).
    Any operationalization (definition) available?
Explanatory variable(s):
    Name the independent variable(s) in the scenario.
        Any operationalization (definition) available?
Extraneous variables:
    Name any controlled variables.
    Name at least 4 uncontrolled variables (what could influence the
        dependent variables other than the independent variable and the
        controlled variables?)
Draw a diagram of the hypothesis using the boxes in Figure 7.1.

Exercise for Chapter 4

Briefly rewrite the method of the study to adhere to an inductive qualitative design.

Exercises for Chapter 5

This is an experiment. Did the researchers use random assignment?
What are the manipulated conditions of the independent variable?
Was the data collection process obtrusive or unobtrusive?

Exercise for Chapter 6

Identify any limitations of the research because of
   a)   subject/respondent problems.
   b)   design problems.

Problem 4

Walker (1996) explored how partners in close relationships 'do gender' (i.e. define and construct gender roles) and exercise power even in their ordinary everyday behaviour, such as in their selection of television programming via a remote control device.

Participants

The sample for this study consisted of 36 American couples recruited primarily by students enrolled in an upper-division undergraduate course on gender and family relationships. In recruiting respondent pairs, students worked in groups of four to maximize diversity. Couples were chosen so that each group of four students would select a diverse set of pairs. All respondents were in a romantic (i.e. heterosexual married, heterosexual cohabiting or cohabiting gay or lesbian) relationship in which both individuals were at least 18 years old. All couples had been living together for at least one year and had a television set with a remote control device. Within each group, however, participants included (a) couples varying in relationship length, from shorter (1 year) to longer (15 years or more); (b) a lesbian or gay couple; (c) at least one married couple; (d) at least one heterosexual, cohabiting, or unmarried couple; (e) couples with and without children; (f) at least one couple in which at least one partner was Asian American, African American, Latino, or of mixed race; and (g) couples in which both partners were employed and couples in which only one partner was employed. Fourteen percent (n = 5 pairs) of the 36 couples (72 individuals) were gay or lesbian. This report focuses on the 31 heterosexual pairs. Women and men in these heterosexual couples did not differ significantly on sociodemographic characteristics. The typical respondent was 34 years old (standard deviation = 12.69). Most (77%) were White, although nearly one quarter were either African American, Hispanic, or of mixed race. Nearly three quarters (74%) were married; one quarter was cohabiting. On average, their relationships had been in existence for 10 years. Most (77%) respondents were employed, and just over 30% were students; only 16% of the sample, however, were nonemployed, nonretired students. Heterosexual respondents represented three income groups. Just over one third earned less than $20,000 annually, one third reported an annual household income between $20,000 and $39,999, and just under one third earned $40,000 or more. One third had children living at home.

Measures

A semi-structured interview was administered to each member of the couple. In addition to sociodemographic questions, respondents were asked about the number and location of television sets and videocassette recorders in the home, the frequency with which they and their partners watched television, and other activities they engage in while watching television. They were asked about use of the television remote control, in general, while watching with their partner and during the programme most recently watched with the partner. They were also asked if their most recent experience was typical of their joint television watching. These questions were quantitative in nature, and included questions about relationship happiness, happiness with the way things are regarding watching television with the partner, and how much partners enjoy the time they spend together. Other questions focused on issues of power. These questions were open-ended and concerned changed expectations about watching television with the partner over the history of the relationship, how the couple decides on a programme to watch together, how partners get each other to watch programmes that they want to watch, and their frustrations with watching television with their partner. Respondents were asked if they would like to change anything about the way they watch television together, if they thought they would be successful at making these changes, whether it would be worth it for them to make the changes, and how their partner would react to the changes. In addition, any changes they had already made in their joint television watching behaviour were described.

Procedures

A coin toss was used to determine which partner to interview first. Partners were interviewed separately, usually in their own homes, by trained student interviewers. Interviews were audio-taped and transcribed. A statistical software programme was used to analyse the quantitative data, and transcriptions were read and reread for analysis of the open-ended data.

Results

Men in heterosexual couples use and control the remote control device more than women, and their partners find remote control use more frustrating than they do. Heterosexual women also are less able than men to get their partners to watch a desired show. The results confirm that couples create and strengthen stereotypical notions of gender through the exercise of power even in the leisure activity of watching television.

   (From: Walker, A.J. (1996) Couples watching television: gender, power, and the remote control, *Journal of Marriage and the Family* 58(4): 813–23).

Exercise for Chapter 1

Is this a deductive or inductive research design? Explain your answer.

Exercises for Chapter 2

What is the unit of analysis (who or what was observed)?
Describe the sample (include as much information as you can from the above scenario).
Do you know how the sample was selected and whether it is a probability sample? What is the population?
What type of data was collected (Primary or secondary? Cross-sectional or longitudinal?)

Exercises for Chapter 3

Name any controlled variables.
Name at least 4 uncontrolled variables.

Exercises for Chapter 4

Did this study use a qualitative orientation? If yes, how? If no, how would a qualitative approach contribute to a greater understanding of this topic? How did the researcher gain an insider's perspective?

Exercises for Chapter 5

This research used a multi-method design. Based on the data collection strategies discussed in Chapter 5, can you identify which methods were used? What are the advantages of a multi-method design?
What technique(s) was used to collect the data in this study?
Was the data collection process obtrusive or unobtrusive?
Was the observation direct or participant?

Exercise for Chapter 6

Identify any limitations of the research because of
   a)   subject/respondent problems.
   b)   design problems.

Problem 5

Frith *et al.* (2005) studied how the ideal of beauty is constructed across cultures. They analysed the content of advertisements from women's fashion and beauty magazines in Singapore, Taiwan, and the US to compare how beauty is encoded.

The study was guided by the following hypotheses:

H1: Caucasian models will be used more often across cultures than models of other ethnic groups in women's beauty and fashion magazine advertising.

H2: The beauty types used in women's magazine advertising will differ in the US, Singapore and Taiwan.

H3: The beauty types used for Caucasian models will differ from those used for Asian models.

H4: The types of products advertised in women's fashion and beauty magazines will differ across cultures.

Method

Advertisements from popular fashion and beauty women's magazines in Singapore, Taiwan, and the United States were content analysed. For comparability, the magazine types from each country were matched by format, audience demographics, local language and circulation figures. For circulation figures, they selected magazines that claimed that 80 percent or more of their readers were primarily local women between the ages of 20 and 35. The content for each magazine chosen was focused mainly on fashion and beauty. They also selected popular women's magazines that were published in the main local language, which was English in the US and Singapore and Mandarin in Taiwan. The women's magazines selected from Singapore were *Her World*, *Female*, and *Cleo*. *Glamour*, *Vogue* and *Elle* are among the most popular and influential magazines in the United States that focus primarily on fashion and beauty. They were selected as the reference for a comparison with the two sets of magazines from Singapore and Taiwan. Three of the most popular Taiwanese women's fashion and beauty magazines were chosen for this study: *Citta Bella*, *Jasmine* and *Vivi*. Three issues of each magazine were selected at random from within the 14-month period, March 2001 to April 2002. The unit of analysis was restricted to advertisements of one or more full pages containing at least one woman. The coding criteria for beauty types required that both the face and some part of the model's dress be shown in the ad. In advertisements where more than one woman was present, the largest or most dominant woman was coded. Advertisements with numerous representations of women of the same size or having no dominant main character were not included in the collection. Identical advertisements were included in the coding process because repetition is a strategy frequently used in advertising campaigns. As a result, a total of 1,236 advertisements were collected from the above-mentioned nine women's fashion and beauty magazines published in the three societies under study.

Content Categories

The coding categories were Classic, Sensual/Sex Kitten, Cute/Girl-Next-Door and Trendy. In addition to beauty types, the models in the ads were content analysed for race. Product categories were also analysed (such as alcoholic beverages, cleaning supplies and beauty products).

Coding

Two independent Singaporean coders, both of whom had previously lived in the US, carried out the coding. They were bilingual (speaking both English and Mandarin). Coders were trained using a preliminary subset of about 50 advertisements. The coders met to compare their results. When disagreements arose, coders discussed their interpretations and a final decision was made by consensus. This process continued until both coders were comfortable with the categories. Definitions and examples of the various categories were available at all times. To establish inter-coder reliability, the two coders coded the same 240 advertisements (approximately 20% of the total sample), with 80 from each country. The reliabilities were determined for race types ($k = 0.96$) [note: reliability coefficients close to 1.0 mean high reliability], beauty types ($k = 0.85$), and product types ($k = 0.94$).

Results

Caucasian female models were used most frequently in all three societies under study, with 91% appearing in the United States, 65% in Singapore and 47% in Taiwan. These findings are statistically significant ($\chi2 = 304.12$, df = 8, $p < 0.001$). Thus, H1 was supported.

The beauty types used in the magazine advertisements did differ ($\chi2 = 50.27$, df = 8, $p < 0.001$) among the US, Singapore and Taiwan ads.

Although Sexual/Sex Kitten was used more often in US ads (32%) than in Singapore (19%) and Taiwanese (22%) ads, Cute/Girl Next Door was portrayed most frequently in Taiwanese ads (27%). These statistically significant differences confirmed H2. There were significant differences in the beauty types for each race. The Classic beauty was used most frequently for both races. However, the Sensual/Sexy type was used more often (27%) with Caucasian models than with Chinese models (11%). The Cute/Girl-Next-Door type was more popular with Chinese models (25%) than with Caucasians (16%). In addition, the Trendy type was used more frequently with Caucasian models (9%) than with Chinese models (6%). These differences were statistically significant ($\chi^2 = 35.41$, df = 4, $p < 0.001$). Therefore, H3 predicting that beauty types are used differently for different races of models in women's magazine advertisements was confirmed. There was a significant difference in the product types advertised across cultures ($\chi^2 = 168.29$, df = 14, $p < 0.001$). The types of product advertised in women's magazines differed dramatically across cultures with beauty products occupying the greatest proportion in Singapore (40%) and Taiwan (49%), whereas clothing occupied the largest proportion of ads in the US (54%). Thus, H4 was supported.

   The authors conclude that beauty in the US may be constructed more in terms of 'the body', whereas in Singapore and Taiwan the defining factor is more related to a pretty face. They suggest that the sexual objectification of women in advertising may need to be considered within their historical, Western context of origin.

   (From: Frith, K., Shaw, P. and Cheng, H. (2005) The construction of beauty: a cross-cultural analysis of women's magazine advertising, *Journal of Communication* 55(1): 56–70.)

Exercise for Chapter 1

Is this a deductive or inductive research design? Explain your answer.

Exercises for Chapter 2

What is the unit of analysis (who or what was observed)?
Describe the sample (include as much information as you can from the above scenario). Decribe the sampling frame.
Do you know how the sample was selected and whether it is a probability sample? What is the population?
What type of data did the authors collect (Primary or secondary? Cross-sectional or longitudinal?)
Rewrite the hypotheses as mathematical formulas.

Exercises for Chapter 3

Explain how the hypothesis is causal.
    Name the dependent variable(s).
        Any operationalization (definition) available?
Explanatory variables:
    Name the independent variable(s) in the scenario.
        Any operationalization (definition) available?
Extraneous variables:
    Name any controlled variables.
    Name at least 4 uncontrolled variables (what could influence the
        dependent variables other than the independent variable and
        the controlled variables?)
Draw a diagram of the hypothesis using the boxes in Figure 7.1.

Exercises for Chapter 4

Briefly rewrite the method of the study to adhere to an inductive qualitative design.
Did this study use a qualitative orientation? If yes, how? If no, how would a qualitative approach contribute to a greater understanding of this topic?

Exercises for Chapter 5

This is a content analysis. Is it qualitative or quantitative?
Was the data collection process obtrusive or unobtrusive?
What is the 'text' studied for content?
Did the authors use manifest or latent coding?
How did they ensure reliability of the coding scheme?

Exercise for Chapter 6

Identify any limitations of the research because of
    a)   subject/respondent problems.
    b)   design problems.

Problem 6

Staller (2003) examined the social construction of 'runaway youth' in print media during 1960–78. Her research question was, 'How did running away emerge as a serious social problem in media discourse during the 1970s?' To answer that question she examined the framing of print news media stories on running away published in the New York Times between 1960 and 1978 (the earlier date was used to capture change in attitudes and values between the 50s and the 60s; the later date includes the passage of legislation on runaway and homeless youth in the 1970s).

Method

A total of 809 articles from the New York Times (NYT) were selected using an initial broad search of all articles that might relate to troubled, wandering or restless children under the large category of 'Children and Youth' and its subheadings, 'lost, missing and runaway children' and 'behavioural and training problems'. A preliminary analysis of these articles indicated the importance of a 'hippie discourse' of the late 1960s and a 'prostitution discourse' of the 1970s in the runaway discussions, resulting in two additional sampling procedures: 1) the NYT index was reexamined for articles on 'hippies' and 'prostitution' adding articles to the sample; and 2) articles that were outside the scope of the core runaway discourse were eliminated from the original sample (e.g. civil disobedience, student protest movements), yielding a sample of 573 articles. These 573 articles were examined again and pruned to include only articles implicitly or explicitly mentioning runaways; hippie articles that focused on New York City or San Francisco (attractive destination points for runaway youth), and prostitution articles on New York City's vice campaign of the mid-70s (New York City was a pipeline of Midwestern runaway girls who supplied the city's sex trade). The final sample included 284 articles, 71 hippie articles and 105 prostitution articles (only 4 of which appeared before 1967). In the total sample, 51% focused primarily on runaways, and of these 92 were gender specific, and of these 68% involved girls; 25% of the runaway girl articles after 1967 linked running away with prostitution; none of the runaway girl articles prior to 1967 made that connection. Of the boy-specific articles before 1967, all but one featured harmless adventures of returned runaways, while none fell into this category after 1967. Inter-rater reliability proportion of observed agreement in the coding scheme ranged from 89% to 96% (i.e. meaning the two raters had similar codes 89–96% of the time).

Findings

Three distinct patterns were found in the data (each of which had a cluster of themes, patterns, descriptions and story scripts that were different in tone and content from the other stages). The first stage was the *unconstructed runaway* (1960–66) in which running away was harmless adventures of children (primarily boys) never harmed and always reunited with their families. Stage two was *runaway panic* (1967) in which the 'hippie' discourse resulted in rewriting the basic runaway narrative to include luring children to counterculture neighbourhoods and counterculture communities providing crash pads, free food and other recourses, and the ineffectiveness of the authorities to control runaway behaviour. The third stage was the *constructed runaway problem* (1968–78), which featured teenage girl prostitutes who, at risk of exploitation and death, became the typical runaway, a version of the runaway story that had political currency because it generated public sympathy and moral outrage.

The author concludes that her study provides insight into the rhetorical processes used by the print media in public problem construction and the mechanics of how moral panic alters basic scripts in public problem narratives.

(From: Staller, K.M. (2003) Constructing the runaway youth problem: boy adventurers to girl prostitutes, 1960–1978, *Journal of Communication* 53(2): 330–46.)

Exercise for Chapter 1:

This study is a content analysis, like the prior problem, but it takes a different reasoning approach. In what way is this research different from Problem 5?

Exercises for Chapter 2

What is the unit of analysis (who or what was observed)?
Describe the sample (include as much information as you can from the above scenario).
What is the sampling frame? What is the population?
What type of data did the author collect (Primary or secondary? Cross-sectional or longitudinal?)

Exercises for Chapter 3

Name any controlled variables.
Name at least 4 uncontrolled variables.
Write the method of the study to adhere to a deductive quantitative design.

Exercise for Chapter 4

Did this study use an inductive, qualitative orientation? If yes, how and what are the advantages of using this approach? If no, how would a qualitative approach contribute to a greater understanding of this topic?

Exercises for Chapter 5

What is the 'text' studied for content?
Did the author use manifest or latent coding?
How did she ensure reliability of the coding scheme?
Was the data collection process obtrusive or unobtrusive?

Exercise for Chapter 6

Drawing on the design limitations and challenges involved in conducting social science research described in this chapter, what are some strategies the researcher could use to increase the quality of her study (e.g. increase the believability of the findings)?

Problem 7

Wilska (2003) conducted an empirical study of the connection between consumption patterns and mobile phone use among Finnish adolescents. The data were derived from a larger survey on the consumer cultures of young people that was carried out in Finnish schools in the spring of 2001 by the author and a colleague. The target group for the survey was young people aged 16–20 in upper secondary schools, vocational schools and other middle-level educational institutes throughout Finland in cities, small towns and the countryside, in both wealthy and deprived areas. The questionnaires were filled out during school lessons, under supervision. There were slightly more girls (55%) than boys (45%) in the final sample of 637 respondents.

Respondents were asked to evaluate themselves as consumers, on a five-point Likert scale, with respect to frugality, trend-consciousness, impulsiveness, individualism and environmental consciousness. The majority of the respondents placed themselves in the middle categories for most consumption styles. The means of the values for self-perception on the 1–5 Likert scale indicate that the respondents regarded themselves as prudent, thrifty, and environmentally conscious consumers slightly more often than they regarded themselves as squanderers, impulse shoppers or free-riders. The means of individualism and trend-consciousness also indicate that the respondents more often regarded themselves as trend-conscious and individualistic than as laggards and mass consumers.

The different ways of using a mobile phone were examined with a set of statements that measured attitudes and everyday practices related to the mobile phone. A Likert scale from 1 to 5 was used for measuring the attitudes (1 = strongly agree, 5 = strongly disagree). The data were then subjected to statistical analysis. For someone with a high score on an 'addictive use' factor, talking on the phone and sending and receiving text messages were important in themselves, even without a specific issue to talk about. If the phone was not at hand, one felt very uncomfortable. The 'addictive use' of the phone included frequent checking for calls and messages, talking over the phone even in public places, and having difficulties in paying the phone bills. The second type of use was termed 'trendy use.' For someone with a high score on the 'trendy use' factor, the mobile phone itself was an important gadget. It had to be new and 'posh,' use the latest technology, preferably be provided with an Internet connection. Moreover, the phone had to fit into its user's general image and clothing style. The operator and the connection type were important: they had to be particularly trendy. On the third use type, 'thrifty use,' statements such as: 'a basic phone is good enough' and 'price is the most important issue when choosing a phone' were significant. Advanced technology or new functions were not important. For someone with a high score on the 'thrifty use' factor, the use of the phone was restricted to the necessary minimum.

The results indicate that young people's relationship to the mobile phone is consistent with their general consumption styles. An 'addictive' use of the phone was related to 'trendy' and 'impulsive' consumption styles and prevalent among females. Technology enthusiasm and trend-consciousness was linked to impulsive consumption and 'hard' values and prevalent among males. A frugal mobile phone use was not related to gender but to environmentalism and thrifty consumption in general. The traditional gender division in mobile phone use styles that could be observed is interesting in the light of conjectures that genders are becoming more alike in their use of new technology. Technology enthusiasm, usually regarded as a 'typically male' thing, was also linked to 'female' consumption styles. This may reflect young men's changing relationship to consumption.

(From: Wilska, T.A. (2003) Mobile phone use as part of young people's consumption styles, *Journal of Consumer Policy* 26: 441–63.)

Exercise for Chapter 1

Is this a deductive or inductive research design? Explain your answer.

Exercises for Chapter 2

What is the unit of analysis (who or what was observed)?
Describe the sample (include as much information as you can from the above scenario).

Do you know how the sample was selected and whether it is a probability sample? What is the population?

What type of data did the author collect (Primary or secondary? Cross-sectional or longitudinal?)

State the hypothesis in words.

Exercises for Chapter 3

Explain how the hypothesis is causal.

Name the dependent variable(s).

>   Any operationalization (definition) available?

Explanatory variables:

>   Name the independent variable(s) in the scenario.

>>   Any operationalization (definition) available?

Extraneous variables:

>   Name any controlled variables.

>   Name at least four uncontrolled variables (what could influence the dependent variables other than the independent variable and the controlled variables?)

Draw a diagram of the hypothesis using the boxes in Figure 7.1.

Exercises for Chapter 4

Briefly rewrite the method of the study to adhere to an inductive qualitative design.

What would be the advantages of studying this research question with a qualitative lens?

Exercises for Chapter 5

This research used a survey design. Rewrite the study as one of the other deductive data collection strategies described in Chapter 5.

What are the advantages and disadvantages of using this method of data collection over the survey design?

Was the data collection obtrusive or unobtrusive?

Exercise for Chapter 6

Identify any limitations of the research because of

>   a)   subject/respondent problems.

>   b)   design problems.

Problem 8

There are occasions that call for people to reflect and give accounts of their lives, which are referred to as 'autobiographical occasions'. Examples include first dates, anniversaries and job interviews. Vinitzky-Seroussi (2000) used the autobiographical occasion of high school class reunions as a case study to demonstrate its use as an informal process of social control. Class reunions are a unique event in that all gathered come from the same area and were born at the same time and thus share equal life opportunities. This occasion pushes one to reflect on his or her identity, present her or his life story to others and make comparisons between peers. The goal of the study was to understand how reunions serve as a form of informal social control in society, since it serves to confirm people's place in the social order by having them construct their identity (drawing on the past and present) and publicly present themselves. To do this, 71 attendees at five class reunions were interviewed in 1990, and 11 class members who did not attend their reunions were also interviewed. The researcher attended all five reunions and conducted an additional 10 interviews with organizers or attendees of reunions not attended. The reunions were located in a mix of working, lower-middle class, and middle class US neighbourhoods and represented 10th, 20th and 25th reunions. The researcher argues that reunions provide the opportunity for individuals to present their life stories and to define and reaffirm their position in the social order. In some cases this is done formally through awards like longest marriage but often is done more informally through processes such as collective definitions of success (e.g. sorting out more prestigious professional statuses from lower statuses).

(From: Vinitzky-Seroussi, V. (2000) 'My God, What am I gonna say?' Class reunions as social control, *Qualitative Sociology*, 23: 57–75.)

Exercise for Chapter 1

Is this a deductive or inductive research design? Explain your answer.

Exercises for Chapter 2

What is the unit of analysis (who or what was observed)?
Describe the sample (include as much information as you can from the above scenario).
Do you know how the sample was selected and whether it is a probability sample? What is the population?
What type of data did the author collect (Primary or secondary? Cross-sectional or longitudinal?)

Exercise for Chapter 3

Briefly rewrite the study design to be quantitative.

Exercises for Chapter 4

Describe how this study uses an inductive approach.
What are the advantages of using a qualitative approach to studying this topic?

Exercises for Chapter 5

What technique(s) was used to collect the data in this study?
This research is a case study that draws on a triangulation of data sources. What do we mean by this and why do researchers triangulate their data sources?
Was the data collection process obtrusive or unobtrusive?
Was the observation direct or participant?

Exercise for Chapter 6

Identify the limitations of this study. What could the researcher do to minimize these limitations?

Problem 9

Social movements attacking restrictive abortion policies in Sweden and the US were successful in the 1970s in decriminalizing abortion in those nations. Linders (2004) compares the movements in Sweden and in the US because the post-repeal environment in the two nations took very different forms, while sharing the same goal of legal access to abortion. In comparison to Sweden, the environment in the US after decriminalization was more hostile as political conflicts ensued over a range of abortion-related issues, which generally made abortion more costly, cumbersome and subject to harassment. The researcher uses three categories of outcomes from the movements to identify differences between the nations: 1) institutional abortion movement (e.g. where abortions are performed, who performs them, who pays for them); 2) cultural environment (e.g. public opinion, terms of public discourse); and 3) sociopolitical environment (e.g. countermovement activities, legislative challenges). To understand the nature of these differing outcomes, the interplay between the politics of abortion and different institutional arrangements surrounding abortion as an issue are traced. It is argued that the institutional, cultural and sociopolitical situations surrounding abortion in Sweden and the US prior to the movements to legalize abortion beginning in the 1960s gave the movements different sets of opportunities and challenges, which impacted subsequent developments regarding abortion (e.g. the level of coordination between advocacy groups in the country; historical legislation and public views regarding abortion in the countries such as defining abortion a capital crime in Sweden until 1864).

(From: Linders, A. (2004) Victory and beyond: a historical comparative analysis of the outcomes of the abortion movements in Sweden and the United States, *Sociological Forum*, 19(3): 371–404.)

Exercise for Chapter 1

Can you determine if this is a deductive or inductive research design? Explain your answer.

Exercises for Chapter 2

What is the unit of analysis (who or what was observed)?
Describe the sample (include as much information as you can from the above scenario).
Do you know how the sample was selected and whether it is a probability sample? What is the population?
What type of data did the author collect (Primary or secondary? Cross-sectional or longitudinal?)

Exercise for Chapter 3

Briefly rewrite the study design to be quantitative.

Exercises for Chapter 4

Describe how this study takes a qualitative approach and the advantages of a qualitative design.
Does it seem that the researcher was able to obtain an emic perspective into the topic? What does this mean?

Exercises for Chapter 5

What technique(s) was used to collect the data in this study?
What are the advantages and disadvantages of this approach to studying this topic?
Was the data collection process obtrusive or unobtrusive?

Exercises for Chapter 6

Identify possible limitations of this study. What could the researcher do to minimize these limitations?

Problem 10

Fairweather and Swaffield (2001) conducted a study to identify visitor experiences of landscape in Kaikoura, New Zealand, to better understand the tourist experience, a growing part of New Zealand's economy. Kaikoura is the south island and has become a popular tourist destination due largely to its promotion of whale watching. Photographs representing different landscape experiences were Q sorted by a non-random sample of both overseas and New Zealand visitors. Views of landscape settings and land uses were taken from 'typical' viewing locations such as roadsides. For cultural features and activities, views were selected that captured the essential quality of the location or activity, but omitted peripheral land uses, etc. There were 30 photographs in the final selection.

The researchers wanted to obtain a diverse, non-random sample but they also wanted to be sure that the sample included both men and women and New Zealand and overseas visitors. A total of 66 visitors were interviewed. There were 41 visitors from New Zealand and 25 from overseas with 31 men and 35 women. Most of the overseas visitors were from Europe, with some from North America, Asia and Australia. Interviews were undertaken from February to April 1998.

Each subject completed a Q sort of the 30 photographs. The Q sort distribution consisted of nine piles of photographs with the number of photographs in each pile running in the following sequence, which approximates a normal distribution:

Number of photographs:	1	2	3	5	8	5	3	2	1
Score:		−4	−3	−2	−1	0	+1	+2	+3	+4

The right-hand end of the distribution contained photographs that people liked and they were given a positive score. The left-hand end contained photographs that people disliked and they received a negative score. The middle piles contained photographs neither strongly liked nor disliked. Subjects sorted the photographs according to what they liked or disliked for whatever reason. When they had completed their Q sort they were asked to explain their reasons for choosing the six top and the six bottom-ranked photographs.

The data were factor analysed to yield five groups each describing a distinct visitor experience, and the results were interpreted on the basis of the photographs most and least liked, and the comments made about them by the people interviewed. The eco-tourist experience is characterized by being close to marine mammals in a spectacular setting. The maritime recreational experience emphasizes boating and fishing. The coastal community experience emphasises quiet appreciation of a small community in a natural setting. The picturesque landscape experience is focused on passive appreciation of the scenery. The family coastal holiday experience is characterized by appreciation of marine mammals and enjoyment of the facilities of the town, in contrast to the other factors which tend to respond negatively to commercial settings. The study showed the varied ways in which Kaikoura is experienced as a tourist destination, and provides evidence of subtle but significant distinctions between the experiences sought and appreciated by different visitor groups.

(From: Fairweather, J.R. and Swaffield, S.R. (2001) Visitor experiences of Kaikoura, New Zealand: an interpretative study using photographs of landscapes and Q method, *Tourism Management* 22(3): 219–28.)

Exercise for Chapter 1

Is this a deductive or inductive research design? Explain your answer.

Exercises for Chapter 2

What is the unit of analysis (who or what was observed)?
Describe the sample (include as much information as you can from the above scenario).
Do you know how the sample was selected and whether it is a probability sample? What is the population?
What type of data did the author collect (Primary or secondary? Cross-sectional or longitudinal?)

Exercise for Chapter 3

Briefly describe the quantitative nature of this design.

Exercise for Chapter 4

Does this research move from data to theory? Explain.

Exercises for Chapter 5

This research is a multi-method Q study that uses both qualitative and quantitative data. What do we mean by this and what is the advantage of such an approach?
Was the data collection process obtrusive or unobtrusive?

Exercise for Chapter 6

Identify the limitations of this study. What could the researcher do to minimize these limitations?

Problem 11

Social scientists have endeavored to uncover ways to influence and change human behavior. One influence on behavior that has been consistently identified is social networks – family, friends, and others one associates with. Latkin *et al.* (1995) examined the structural and relationship characteristics of the social networks of injecting drug users. The characteristics of network members were assessed in relation to frequency of injecting heroin and cocaine, behaviors putting individuals at risk for HIV infection. The study sample was comprised of 293 inner city injecting drug users in Baltimore, Maryland. Respondents were recruited from a study of the natural history of HIV infection in injecting drug users in Baltimore. The primary means of recruitment for the study were community outreach and word-of-mouth. Eligible potential participants (at least 18 years old and had injected and shared drugs within the last 6 months) were administered a detailed interview on their background, HIV-related behaviours and personal social networks. The data for the study were collected between 1991–1992 prior to an AIDS preventive intervention.

The personal social network interview asked the participants to list (by giving the first name and first letter of the last name or pseudonyms) members of their social network who they had known for at least one month. Respondents were asked to list individuals who could provide them support with intimate interactions, material assistance, socializing, physical assistance, positive feedback and health information. Participants were also asked to list individuals who, in the last 6 months, were their sex partners and individuals with whom they had shared drugs. After the list was compiled, participants were asked to report their network member's age, gender and their relationship to the other network members listed.

Most participants (89%) reported at least one family member in their social network, and 44% listed their mother or stepmother in their network. Presence of family members in personal social networks was not related to patterns of drug use examined here; however, those who reported a partner in their personal social network injected significantly less often than those who did not report a partner. Network density and size of drug sub-networks were positively associated with frequency of drug injection. The results of this study suggest that social network analysis may be a useful tool for understanding the social context of HIV/AIDS risk behaviours.

(From: Latkin, C., Mandell, W., Oziemkowska, M., Celentano, D., Vlahov, D., Ensminger, M. and Knowlton, A. (1995) Using social network analysis to study patterns of drug use among urban drug users at high risk for HIV/AIDS, *Drug and Alcohol Dependence*, 38(1): 1–9.)

Exercise for Chapter 1

Is this a deductive or inductive research design? Explain your answer.

Exercises for Chapter 2

What is the unit of analysis (who or what was observed)?
Describe the sample (include as much information as you can from the above scenario).
Do you know how the sample was selected and whether it is a probability sample? What is the population?
What type of data did the author collect (primary or secondary? Cross-sectional or longitudinal?)

Exercise for Chapter 3

Provide an example of the quantitative nature of this study.

Exercise for Chapter 4

Does this research move from data to theory? Explain.

Exercises for Chapter 5

This research is a social network analysis. What is the advantage of such an approach?
Was the data collection process obtrusive or unobtrusive?

Exercise for Chapter 6

Identify any limitations of the research because of
- a) subject/respondent problems.
- b) design problems.

Glossary

Advocacy research   Research that is undertaken by a researcher who has a vested interest in the outcome of the study, such as being involved in a related social movement or being paid by an organization to carry out the research.

Aggregate   Unit of analysis that pools together groups of cases, for example, studying nations rather than individual citizens, studying companies rather than individual employees. When working with aggregate data, we must be careful not to make conclusions about individual units (see **ecological fallacy**).

Alternative explanation   For a theory to be scientific, it must be falsifiable, meaning it can be tested empirically and either supported or refuted. The explanation that refutes the theory is an alternative explanation.

Anonymity   Removal of all links between a research participant's data and their contact information to conceal individuals' identities.

Archival data   See **secondary data**.

Artificial response   Data, such as a response to a survey or an individual's behaviour, that result from being in a research situation rather than a true or natural 'response'.

Artificial setting   A setting designed specifically to carry out a research project, such as a laboratory.

Bar graph   A graph used to show the values for each case on a particular variable; the graph can also be used to show the frequency or percentage of data points falling into each category or value of a variable.

Bricoleur   Defined as a 'Jack of all trades or a kind of do-it-yourself person'; a scientist who uses a range of strategies and methods that are best suited to study a particular situation and is flexible in their scientific thinking.

Case   One unit in the sample (e.g. one individual, one country); also known as a data point.

Case study   An in-depth study of a single person, event, community or group.

Causal diagram   Visual tool used to show the hypothesized relationships (or relationships found in the data) between two or more variables; the diagrams depict how variables are related to each other – causally related or correlated, independent or dependent variables.

Closed-ended question   Survey question where respondents are asked to select a response(s) from a series of pre-designated choices (e.g. 'On a 1–5 scale, how severe is your knee pain?' – 1 'not at all severe', 2 'a little severe', 3 'somewhat severe', 4 'severe' and 5 'very severe').

Cluster sampling   Method of sampling based on selecting groups from a population and sampling from the groups rather than individual cases in the population. For example, if we want to study government workers, we could select a sample by first selecting government agencies and then selecting employees from the agencies rather than sampling from a list of all government employees.

Code   The name or designation used to label an idea, pattern or theme that is identified in the data.

Coding   The process of organizing and interpreting data; the set of categories (codes) that a researcher develops to summarize text and make theoretical statements.

Coding scheme   A well-defined set of rules on how to systematically characterize the text.

Confidentiality   Removal of all identifying information about individuals from research reports to protect the identity of research participants. When a researcher insures the *anonymity* of participants, no information exists to link back to specific participants. When a researcher insures the *confidentiality* of participants, information exists that could be linked to specific participants, but the researcher commits to using procedures that will prevent such identification from being available to anyone but the research team.

Confirmability   The degree to which others can confirm a study's results; in qualitative research confirmability can be increased by checking findings with other sources of data to provide additional support and by carefully documenting all aspects of the research process.

Confirmatory research   A deductive research design in which the goal is to test a theory with data and draw conclusions about whether the theory can be refuted or *confirmed*.

Constructionism   According to this perspective, the best way to understand the world is to examine how people see and define it. Constructionists believe that the social world is actively constructed through interactions and that symbols, like language, are key to interacting. The goal of research is to understand how people construct and make sense of others and of the world. This perspective contrasts positivism.

Content analysis   Technique used to analyse written, visual or spoken text; the goal is to systematically classify words, phrases and other units of text into meaningful categories.

Control group   In experimental research, this is the group of participants who do not receive the experimental 'manipulation'. The results of this group are compared to the experimental group who receive the treatment of interest; see also **experimental group**.

Controlled variable   A variable whose effects are being taken into account when examining the relationship between a variable of interest (the independent variable) and another variable (the dependent variable).

Controlling   Statistical technique allowing us to take into account the effect of some variables (control variables), while looking at the effects of the variable(s) of interest (a dependent variable).

Convenience sampling   Selecting sample members who are readily available; a non-random sample.

Covert observation   Data collection that is done with research participants who know they are part of a research project; also known as concealed observation.

Credibility   How accurately the data reflect reality.

Critical theory   Theory asserting that the goal of research is to expose social injustices and work to change the injustices; often the focus is on groups in society who are oppressed.

Critical thinking   The art of evaluating and analysing the claims of others.

Cross-cultural data   Comparisons made across countries or cultures.

Cross-sectional data   Collection of data/observations at one point in time.

Crystallization   Metaphor sometimes used to describe the research process in response to the notion of triangulation. The triangulation metaphor implies there are only three sides or vantage points from which social phenomena can be approached. The shape of a crystal suggests the use of multiple angles and dimensions to address research questions.

Data point   See **case.**

Data source   The source of information a researcher uses to understand the world (e.g. self-report survey, researcher's observations, government statistics).

Deductive   Approach to research in which the data are derived out of a theory.

Delphi Survey Technique   Data collection technique combining questionnaires and group feedback. Typically several rounds of surveys and group feedback occur where individuals give their opinion in a survey and then they are provided anonymous feedback on how other participants responded. Respondents are then invited to revise their previous answers. The goal of this technique is to encourage the exchange of ideas between individuals and sometimes to achieve consensus about an issue among participants while avoiding the costs and some of the adverse effects of face-to-face meetings (e.g. group think, dominance by one or a few individuals).

Dependability   Criteria used to assess qualitative research; reflects how truthful the researcher is and how truthful the research is; similar to the quantitative emphasis on reliability in research.

Dependent variable   The variable that we are trying to predict/explain; often labelled as Y in statistical equations.

Deterrence theory   Theory in criminology stating that the fear of punishment will prevent some people from committing crime.

Diagram   A visual display used to organize and systematically present data, such as a table or chart.

Direct observation   Observational data collection technique where the researcher watches people but does not become a participant in the setting and tries to intrude in the setting as little as possible. Sometimes a video camera is used to make direct observations or observations are made behind a one-way mirror.

Distorted memory   See selective memory.

Ecological fallacy   Studying one kind of thing (i.e. unit of analysis) and (inappropriately) making conclusions about another unit of analysis.

Ecological modernization theory   Theory in sociology proposing that as countries become very affluent, their impact on the environment decreases.

Emergent methods   State of the art research designs that cross disciplines and address the gap between theory and methods; social network analysis is an emergent method.

Emic perspective   Goal is to gain an understanding of a given subject matter or group from the individuals' perspectives themselves; also known as gaining an 'insider's' perspective. This can be done by spending a considerable amount of time with individuals through ethnographic research and/or conducting in-depth individuals with them.

Empirical   Information based on data through observations or other data sources.

Epistemology   The theory of what we can know. Epistemology ranges from the belief that we can conduct objective, unbiased observations and that is how we can understand the world accurately. At the other end of the spectrum is the view that all observations of the world are our own social constructions rather than an objective, external world.

Ethics   Rules and definitions about what is and is not permissible to do when conducting research.

Ethnography   Data collection technique in which the researcher goes into a setting of interest and observes individuals and their behaviours, interactions and communications. This data collection strategy tends to take longer to carry out than others because researchers sometimes spend months to years making observations. This technique is sensitive to a researcher's observations and interpretations, so careful notetaking and documentation of observations is critical to obtaining high quality data. Also known as field research, fieldwork, participant observation and naturalistic observation.

Experiment   A research design in which subjects are divided (typically randomly) into two or more groups: experimental/treatment group and control group. All groups receive the same experience except for the factor being studied (the experimental manipulation), which is varied systematically across the groups; see also **experimental group** and **control group**.

Experimental group   In experimental research, this is the group of participants who receive the experimental 'manipulation' – the thing that the researcher is interested in seeing its effects; also called the treatment group; see also **control group**.

Explanatory variable   Another name for the independent variables in a study.

Exploratory research   Research aimed at exploring a topic without a preexisting theory either because one does not exist or because the researcher wishes to build insights from the data directly without imposing preexisting ideas; often done with an inductive design.

External validity   The extent to which the results from a sample can be used to make statements (i.e. generalize) about the population; see **generalizability**.

Extraneous variable   A variable that may have an impact on the dependent variable but is not the focus of the study; extraneous variables can be controlled or uncontrolled. If controlled, its possible effects on the dependent variable are being taken into account. If uncontrolled, its possible effects on the dependent variable are not being taken into account.

Extreme case sample   Selection of a sample of unusual cases or cases that fall outside the general pattern; a non-random sample.

Face-to-face interview   See **in-person interview**.

Field research   Data collection strategy where the researcher goes into a setting (going into the 'field') and makes observations; see **ethnography**.

Fieldwork   See **ethnography** and **field research**.

Focus group   Group interview designed to explore what a specific group of people think about a topic; the advantage of these small group discussions is that the brainstorming and discussion among group members leads to different ideas than would be generated by any one individual him or herself.

Gatekeeper   The person a researcher must contact and negotiate with to gain access to a setting and its members to carry out a participant observation/ethnographic study.

Generalizability   How well the sample accurately reflects the population. When a sample has high generalizability, the information generated from the sample can be used to make statements about the larger population. Also called **external validity**.

Going native   When an ethnographic researcher becomes an active, complete participant in a research setting, this is called 'going native'; see also **ethnography**.

Grounded theory   An inductive approach typically used to study qualitative-oriented research questions, which is based on rigorous techniques for generating theoretical ideas from empirical data. This approach calls for an iterative process involving simultaneous data collection and data analysis and interpretation. The term reflects the fact that the theory is rooted in or 'grounded' in the data.

Guiding question   A question that helps direct the course of data collection and analysis.

Historical-comparative   Comparison and analysis of macro-level phenomena, such as nations, a particular period of time in-depth, and/or societal changes over time.

Hypothesis   A proposed statement about what should happen if a particular condition exists; often takes the form of an 'if, then' statement (if something is true/occurs, then something else is true/will occur).

Independent variable   A variable that is used to try to explain/predict a dependent variable; usually known as X in statistical equations.

In-depth interview   A series of mostly open-ended questions used to obtain detailed or descriptive information from study participants. In-depth interviews are used to learn about a topic in detail and from individuals' own perspectives.

Inductive   Approach to research where theoretical insights are derived out of the data; in other words a researcher collects data and then identifies patterns and theory from the data.

Informed consent   When asked to participate in a research project, potential subjects should be told what they are being asked to do so they can make an informed decision about whether to participate.

In-person interview   An interview that is completed by an interviewer and interviewee who meet in person in an agreed-upon location. This type of interview allows for the interviewer and respondent to build rapport and to utilize visual aids in some cases, although this type of interview is typically more time consuming than other types of interviews (e.g. telephone); also called a face-to-face interview.

Insider   An individual who is knowledgeable about a research setting and can help an ethnographic researcher gain information about the setting and group and in some cases enhance access to and communications with other group members; also called key informant.

Insider perspective   See **emic perspective**.

Inter-coder reliability   Two (or more) researchers independently review data and code the text using the established codebook. After the coding is completed by the team, the researchers compare their codes and try to reconcile any differences that they find in their coding. When there is high agreement between the independent coders, the inter-coder reliability is said to be high.

Internal validity   The extent to which the researcher makes appropriate conclusions from the data; poor internal validity can result from not measuring what one intends to measure (having invalid operational definitions) or making incorrect conclusions about relationships between variables.

Interpretive approach   Theoretical perspective used to describe the lived experiences of individuals from their own viewpoints and to understand how people make sense of ('interpret') their experiences; qualitative methods are typically used to investigate questions from an interpretive perspective.

Interview   A series of questions are read to an individual (interviewee) by an interviewer; interviews are administered in person or over the telephone.

Interviewee   Member of a sample who participates in an interview.

Interviewer   The person who administers a survey interview to study participants.

Interview guide   The set of questions and/or topics that an interviewer uses in conducting interviews.

Key informant   See **insider**.

Latent coding   While manifest coding deals with the visible aspects of text (e.g. counts of the frequency a term is mentioned in the text), latent coding involves the analysis of the more implicit meaning of text; see also **manifest coding**.

Longitudinal data   Collection of data over multiple time points.

Macro level phenomena   Phenomena occurring at a large scale, meaning patterns that characterize a society or groups; see also **micro level phenomena**.

Mail survey   Survey that is sent to and returned by sample members by mail, typically to their homes. A mail survey allows participants to complete it at their convenience and in private, although response rates to mail surveys tend to be lower than other survey modalities.

Manifest coding   Analysis of the visible aspects of text, such as counts of the occurrence of an idea, without considering the connotation or meaning of the text; see also **latent coding**.

Member checking   Technique used in qualitative research to ensure the credibility of the findings and conclusions made; the researcher asks study participants to review their notes or preliminary conclusions to see if they agree or can elaborate on that information.

Memo   A special type of research note; the researcher writes out their thoughts and ideas throughout the research process, which helps in the development of themes and concepts. Often memos start very broad and then are refined during the research process. Memos are sometimes thought of as extensive marginal notetaking.

Meta data   Careful documentation of how the sample was selected, how data were collected, and how variables were coded.

Methodological pluralism   The use of both qualitative and quantitative perspectives to explore an aspect of the world; see also **triangulation**.

Methods   The rules that the scientific community has agreed upon to determine how well theories fit with observations that are made about the world.

Micro level phenomena   Phenomena occurring at a small scale – at the level of individuals (e.g. individuals' attitudes); see also **macro level phenomena**.

Missing data   See **non-response**.

Mixed methods   The use of both qualitative and quantitative approaches to understand a research topic.

Multiple regression   A statistical technique that estimates the effects of each independent variable on the dependent variable, taking into account the effects of all the other explanatory/independent variables.

Naturalistic observation   Studying people, groups or a topic in their natural setting as opposed to a laboratory setting; see also **ethnography** and **natural setting**.

Natural setting   A place where individuals regularly interact; research conducted in natural settings allows a researcher to make observations in individuals' regular environments.

Negative case analysis   To increase the credibility of the findings of qualitative research, a researcher may look for instances/cases that run counter to the conclusions made to understand how and why these cases differ from the majority of cases.

Nominal Group Technique   A small group discussion that is structured to maximize each group member's participation. Each group member is first asked to silently write down their thoughts about a question or topic and then group members go around one by one sharing their thoughts. This structure helps avoid the dominance of any group member and minimizes conflict among members, which are some of the drawbacks of more traditional small group discussions (e.g. focus groups).

Non-response   When a research participant does not answer a question, the data for that case is missing on that question/variable; also called **missing data**.

Non-probability sampling   Sample selection is not done randomly from a population; see also **convenience**, **extreme case**, **purposive**, **quota**, **snowball** and **theoretical sampling**.

Non-random sample   See **non-probability sampling**.

Non-representative sample   A non-probability, non-random sample. There is no way to know the probability that a case will be selected for the sample nor how representative the sample is of the population.

Notetaking   In observational research, the researcher takes careful notes about the research site and all observations, which become the primary source of data. Notetaking should be done systematically and in great detail, with the goal being to give an accurate and rich description of observations to maximize recall later.

Observation   See **naturalistic observation; ethnography; participant observation; direct observation**.

Obtrusive   The researcher's presence and involvement in the research process may have an impact on the data; experiments and surveys are examples of obtrusive research.

On-stage effects   When research participants know they are being observed, they may 'act' or perform for the researcher; they may behave or respond in ways they think the researcher wants them to or may try to look 'good' for the researcher; see also **social desirability**.

Ontology   A theory of what exists. There are two general beliefs about ontology: **realism** and **phenomenology** (see definitions).

Open-ended question   A question asking individuals to provide an answer in their own words; there is no pre-existing set of responses for individuals to choose from (e.g. 'What is your earliest childhood memory?'); see also **closed-ended question**.

Operationalization   Taking theoretical concepts and designing ways to measure the concepts empirically (e.g. operationalizing deterrence theory into homicide rate in a state and whether the state has the death penalty or not).

Opportunity costs theory   Theory in demography suggesting that people, particularly women, face a tradeoff between pursuing education and a career on the one hand and having children on the other.

Outlier   A case (data point) that diverges considerably from the majority of other cases.

Overt observation   Data collection that is conducted with research subjects knowing they are participating in a research project.

Participant   An individual who participates in a research study; also known as research subject and respondent.

Participant observation   Observational data collection technique where the researcher immerses her or himself into the research setting to make observations; see also **ethnography**.

Peer debriefing   To increase the credibility of conclusions made in a qualitative study, the researcher may discuss her research with a colleague at all stages of the process. These deliberations give the researcher another perspective and can help the researcher identify what she may be missing.

Phenomenology   Ontological perspective that contrasts realism; individuals' interpretations of the world are what are important (see also **ontology** and **realism**).

Pilot testing   Before administering a survey or carrying out an experiment, researchers can test ('pilot') how well their survey questions or experimental conditions work to help ensure they will obtain the information they are seeking; also called **pre-testing**.

Population   All the possible units being studied; a collection of people, objects, countries, etc., that share a common characteristic of interest (e.g. all countries, all residents of a designated city in a given year); see also **sample**.

Positivism   The view that there is an objective world independent of our observations and that science can lead us to an understanding of the world that is free of social, political and cultural influences; rooted in epistemological and ontological realism; stands in contrast to **constructionism**.

Practical question   Questions used to determine the particularities of a research design (e.g. what is the best way to select a sampling frame that best encapsulates the population?).

Primary data   Data collection based on first-hand observations; the researcher collects her own data; see also **secondary data**.

Private documents   Data taken from individuals' personal documents, such as diaries and letters.

Probability sample   A sample that is representative of the population being studied; see also **random sample**.

Probability value   Statistic used in quantitative research to determine whether the result found was due to chance or due to a true relationship or difference in groups; in the language of statistics, the probability value tells us whether a result is 'statistically significant'; also known as p **value**.

Purposive sampling   See theoretical sampling.

Q methodology   A technique for investigating individuals' subjective attitudes and beliefs on a topic for the purpose of identify differing perspectives; can be used to identify both what discourses exist within a community and who subscribes to or rejects these discourses.

Qualitative research   Methods used to understand the meanings people assign to things and to gain detailed understandings of processes in the social world; these methods emphasize how and why people do what they do and think what they think; rather than investigating questions with numbers and statistical tools (see **quantitative tools**), qualitative investigations rely on researchers' observations and analysis of words and sometimes symbols.

Quantification   The use of numbers in science and research to understand the world.

Quantitative research   Methods used to understand variation in things, test causal relationships, and identify the prevalence or distribution of phenomena; also the use of statistical tools to interpret data.

Quasi-experiment   A research design in which an independent variable is manipulated (i.e. the level of the variable is changed between groups) like in an experiment, but the control and experimental groups are not equivalent (i.e. no random assignment occurs into the two groups).

Questionnaire   A series of survey questions that respondents read themselves and answer; an interview, in contrast, is a series of survey questions that is read to an individual by an interviewer.

Quota sampling   A non-random sample in which the number of cases in particular categories of interest to the researcher (e.g. age groups) is predetermined.

Random   Something that occurs that is not related to any of the things we study and that occurs by chance.

Random assignment   See randomization.

Randomization   In experimental research, this is the process of randomly assigning participants to the control or experimental groups. Through randomization, the two groups should be equivalent in characteristics, so any differences found between the two groups will be due to the experimental 'manipulation'.

Random sample   Every member of a population has an equal chance of being included in the sample.

Realism   The ontological belief that there is a real world outside of individuals' interpretations of the world; in other words, there is an external reality that exists independent of our perceptions of it; see also **ontology** and **phenomenology**.

Reliability   The extent to which the results found can be replicated with repeated tests; reliability can also be thought of as the consistency of the results. In survey research efforts to increase reliability include asking multiple questions to measure the same topic and combining the responses into an overall score.

Representative sample   A sample in which every member of the population has an equal chance of being elected; see also **probability sample**.

Research methods   See **methods**.

Researcher bias   When a researcher's own expectations about and interests in the study affect the research design and/or conclusions drawn.

Respondent   An individual who participates in a research study; also known as a research subject or participant.

Role theory   A theory in sociology proposing that boys and girls learn at young ages certain social expectations for gender roles, such as boys should be good at mathematics and science and girls should not be as good in these subjects.

Sample   A subset of a population that is studied.

Sampling bias The extent to which a sample does not accurately reflect the population of interest; generating a random probability sample reduces sampling bias.

Sampling error The degree a sample does not reflect the population due to differences between the population and the sample generated by a random selection of cases.

Sampling frame The set of cases in the population from which the sample will be chosen.

Scatterplot A visual tool used to show the relationship between two variables.

Science The process that occurs or dialogue that takes place among scientists with the goal of understanding aspects of the world.

Scientific explanation A theory must be testable and falsifiable to be considered a scientific theory; a proposition/theory that can be tested using the scientific method is called a scientific explanation.

Scientific method The procedures used to test theoretical assertions about the world with data to determine whether the theories do or do not match the data and how they should be changed to better reflect the data.

Secondary data The use of data or records that have already been collected, such as previously collected survey information or government statistics; also known as archival data; see also **primary data**.

Selective memory When study participants are asked to recall situations that happened in the past or are painful and therefore are difficult to remember and accurately recall; also referred to as distorted memory.

Self-report Individuals provide their own accounts or responses to questions.

Sensitizing question A question to help the researcher determine what the data indicate.

Small group research See **focus group, Delphi survey technique** and **Nominal Group Technique**.

Snowball sampling People in a group of interest inform the researcher about other cases in that population who could also fit the criteria for inclusion in a study; a non-random sample.

Social constructionism See **constructionism**.

Social desirability   Study participants try to present a positive image of themselves to the researcher by acting in ways they think the researcher wants or answering questions as they think the researcher wants.

Social network analysis   Approach that explores the structure of group relationships to identify relationships and connections between individuals.

Source of data   See **data source**.

Statistics   The set of methods used to make sense of the numbers used in research.

Strata   Groupings of a population of interest (e.g. age categories, religious groups).

Stratified sample   Generating a sample from a population by selecting from strata or groupings of the population that are of interest to the researcher; see also **strata**.

Structured survey   A survey with a predetermined set of questions that are administered in a designated order. The goal of a structured survey is to achieve standardization in data collection across study participants so results can be compared across cases.

Subject   An individual who participates in a research study; also known as a research participant or respondent.

Summary statistic   A number that is used to give a good summary measure of a variable, such as the average score on a variable (called the 'mean' in statistics) or most frequently occurring value on a variable (called the 'mode').

Survey   A series of questions that individuals answer about a topic(s) of interest. Surveys are the most common method of data collection in the social sciences since they can be used to explore a wide array of topics, can be used to study many different populations, and are used for both qualitative and quantitative designs; see also **unstructured survey**; **structured survey**; **interview**; **telephone survey**; **web survey**; **mail survey**; **in-depth interview**.

Systematic sampling   Generating a sample by selecting every nth person from a list to be included in a sample.

Telephone survey   An interview that is conducted between an interviewer and interviewee over the telephone. This survey modality is beneficial because most people have telephone access and a wide range of questions and topics can be asked, although telephone interviews tend to be short or participants will lose interest.

Text Data in the form of words, such as archival documents, interview transcripts and a researcher's observational notes; text can also be other forms of communication such as photographs, poems and paintings.

Theme A name or label that reflects a substantive concept found in the data.

Theoretical question A question used to identify patterns in the data and understand whether and why differences between cases are found.

Theoretical sampling A non-random sample which is generated as theoretical insights and questions emerge from information gathered from other cases; also known as **purposive sampling**. The sample is therefore formed as data are being collected and initial analyses suggest the value of searching for cases with particular characteristics.

Theory An idea about how some part of the world works, often taking the form of causal statements. A theory must be testable and falsifiable to be considered scientific.

Transferability The extent that results from one research location can be applied to other settings or situations; this is the alternative version of generalizability (more applicable to quantitative research) that is more applicable to qualitative research.

Treatment group See **experimental group**.

Triangulation A multi-faceted approach to studying a topic. Triangulation can involve the use of multiple data sources, multiple theories and/or multiple methods to provide a more well-rounded understanding of a topic.

Unit of analysis The thing being studied, for instance countries, individuals or organizations.

Unobtrusive The researcher does not have an impact on the data that are collected; analysis of secondary data (e.g. archival documents, content analysis) and making observations in a natural setting by the use of a video recorder are examples of unobtrusive data collection strategies.

Unstructured survey A questionnaire designed to explore a topic broadly, so there is no formal survey instrument. Typically there is a set of initial questions and/or topics to ask study participants but the interview and set of questions that are asked by the interviewer vary across individuals and depend on the comments made by each interviewee and each interviewer's decisions.

Unusual case   See **outlier**.

Validity   A 'goodness of fit' between the details of the research, the evidence, and the conclusions drawn by the researchers; see also **external validity** and **internal validity**.

Value-free science   The researcher does not introduce their interests or biases into the decisions regarding what to study and how to carry out the study.

Value-engaged science   The choice of the research topic is largely driven by the interests that the researcher supports.

Variable   A measured/observed item or characteristic (e.g. respondent's gender; a country's gross domestic product).

Variance   The extent to which something (values on a variable) varies/differs across cases.

Web survey   A survey that participants take on an Internet website. This survey modality has the advantages of using images and sounds in the survey, allowing for an interactive mechanism between respondents or respondents and the researcher, confidentiality for respondents' answers and quick receipt and compilation of data for a researcher's use. A major disadvantage though is that not everyone has access to or knows how to use the Internet.

References

Addams, H. (2000) Q methodology, in H. Addams and J. Proops (eds), *Social Discourse and Environmental Policy: An Application of Q Methodology*. Cheltenham: Edward Elgar.

Agyei, W.K.A., Biritwum, R.B., Ashitey, A.G. and Hill, R.B. (2000) Sexual behaviour and contraception among unmarried adolescents and young adults in greater Accra and eastern regions of Ghana, *Journal of Biosocial Science*, 32(4): 495–512.

Alba, R.D. and Moore, G. (1983) Elite social circles, in R. Burt and M. Minor (eds) *Applied Network Analysis: a Methodological Introduction*. Beverly Hills, CA: Sage.

Bainbridge, W.S. (2007) The scientific research potential of virtual worlds, *Science*, 317: 474–6.

Baron, L. and Straus, M.A. (1988) Cultural and economic sources of homicide in the United States, *The Sociological Quarterly*, 29: 37–9.

Becker, H.S. (1998) *Tricks of the Trade: How to Think About Your Research While You're doing It*. Chicago: University of Chicago Press.

Berg, B. (1998) *Qualitative Research Methods for the Social Sciences* (3rd edn). Boston: Allyn and Bacon.

Berger, P.L. and Luckmann, T. (1966) *The Social Construction of Reality: A Treatise in the Sociology of Knowledge*. New York: Anchor.

Bhaskar, R. (1975/1997) *A Realist Theory of Science*. London: Verso.

Bluebond-Langner, M. (1978) *The Private Worlds of Dying Children*. Princeton, NJ: Princeton University Press.

Bourgois, P. (1989) Crack in Spanish Harlem: Culture and economy in the inner city, *Anthropology Today*, 5(4): 6–11.

Bourgois, P. (2000) Disciplining addictions: the biopolitics of methadone and heroin in the United States, *Culture, Medicine, and Psychiatry*, 24(2): 165–95.

Brady, H.E. and Collier, D. (eds) (2004) *Rethinking Social Inquiry: Diverse Tools, Shared Standards*. Oxford: Rowman & Littlefield.

Brown, S.R. *The History and Principles of Q Methodology in Psychology and the Social Sciences*. http://facstaff.uww.edu/cottlec/QArchive/Bps.htm

Calasanti, T.M. (1996) Gender and life satisfaction in retirement: an assessment of the male model. *Journal of Gerontology: Social Sciences,* 51B(1): S18–S29.

Campbell, D.T. (1969) Reforms as experiments, *American Psychologist* 24: 409–29.

Campbell, D.T. and Fiske, D. (1959) Convergent and discriminant validation by the multitrait-multimethod matrix, *Psychological Bulletin,* 56: 86–105.

Canadian Census. (2001) *Selected ethnic origins, for Canada, Provinces and Territories.* (http://www12.statcan.ca/english/census01/products/ highlight/ETO/Table1.cfm?Lang=E&T=501&GV=1&GID=0).

Carlson, J.M. and Trichtinger, R. (2001) Perspectives on entertainment television's portrayal of a racial incident: an intensive analysis, *Communication Review* 4: 253–78.

Cohen, C.I., Teresi, J., Holmes, D. and Roth, E. (1988) Survival strategies of older homeless men, *The Gerontologist,* 28(1): 58–65.

Cook, T.D. and Campbell, D.T. (1979) *Quasi-experimentation: Design and Analysis for Field Settings.* Chicago: Rand McNally.

Cook, T.D., Campbell, D.T. and Shadish, W.R. (2002) *Experimental and Quasi Experimental Designs for Generalized Causal Inference.* New York: Houghton Mifflin.

Day, J.C., Janus, A. and Davis, J. (2005) Computer and Internet use in the United States: 2003. *Current Population Reports.* Washington, DC: US Census Bureau.

Dayton, B. (2000) Policy frames, policy making and the global climate change discourse, in H. Addams and J. Proops (eds), *Social Discourse and Environmental Policy: An Application of Q Methodology.* Cheltenham: Edward Elgar.

Declaration of Helsinki (1964). *Ethical Principles for Medical Research Involving Human Subjects.* (http://www.wma.net/e/policy/b3.htm).

Delbecq, A.L., Van de Ven, A.H. and Gustafson, D.H. (1975) *Group Techniques for Program Planning: A Guide to the Nominal Group and Delphi Process.* Glenview, IL: Scott-Foresman.

Denzin, N.K. and Lincoln, Y.S. (2000) The discipline and practice of qualitative research, in N.K. Denzin and Y.S. Lincoln (eds), *Handbook of Qualitative Research.* (2nd edn). Thousand Oaks, CA: Sage Publications, Inc.

Dietz, T., Stern, P.C., and Rycroft, R.W. (1989) Definitions of conflict and the legitimation of resources: the case of environmental risk, *Sociological Forum* 4: 47–70.

Dillman, D.A. (1978) *Mail and Telephone Surveys: The Total Design Method.* New York: John Wiley and Sons, Inc.

Dillman, D.A. (2000) *Mail and Internet Surveys. The Tailored Design Method.* New York: John Wiley and Sons, Inc.

Dillman, D.A., Christenson, J.A., Carpenter, E.H. and Brooks, R.M. (1974) Increasing mail questionnaire response: a four state comparison, *American Sociological Review*, 39(5): 744–56.

Dornenburg, M. and Page, K. (1998) *Dining Out: Secrets from America's Leading Critics, Chefs and Restaurateurs.* New York: John Wiley & Sons.

Dornenburg, M. and Page, K. (2003) *Becoming a Chef.* New York: John Wiley & Sons.

Druckman, D. (2005) *Doing Research: Methods of Inquiry for Conflict Analysis.* Thousand Oaks: Sage Publications.

Dryzek, J.S. and Braithwaite, V. (2000) On the prospects for democratic deliberation: values analysis applied to Australian politics, *Political Psychology*, 21(2): 241–66.

Durkheim, E. (1951/1897) *Suicide. A Study in Sociology* (translated by J.A. Spaulding and G. Simpson). New York: The Free Press.

Ehrenreich, B. (2005) *Bait and Switch: The (Futile) Pursuit of the American Dream.* New York: Henry Holt.

Ehrenreich, B., Hochschild, A. and Kay, S. (2002) *Nickel and Dimed: On (Not) Getting by in America.* New York: Henry Holt.

Ehrlich, K. and Carboni, I. *Inside Social Network Analysis.* (http://domino.watson.ibm.com/cambridge/research.nsf/c9ef590d6d00291a85257141004a5c19/3f23b2d424be0da6852570a500709975/$FILE/TR_2005-10.pdf)

Elder, L. and Paul, R. Universal intellectual standards. The critical thinking community (http://www.criticalthinking.org/articles/universal-intellectual-standards.cfm).

Ellis, C. (1986) *Fisher Folk, Two Communities on Chesapeake Bay.* Lexington, KY: University of Kentucky Press.

Fairweather, J.R. and Swaffield, S.R. (2001) Visitor experiences of Kaikoura, New Zealand: an interpretative study using photographs of landscapes and Q method, *Tourism Management*, 22(3): 219–28.

Feldman, R. and Maposhere, C. (2003) Safer sex and reproductive choice: findings from 'Positive Women: Voices and Choices' in Zimbabwe, *Reproductive Health Matters*, 11(22): 162–73.

Fine, G. (1996) *Kitchens: The Culture of Restaurant Work.* Berkeley, CA: University of California Press.

Fine, G. (1987) *With the Boys: Little League Baseball and Preadolescent Culture.* Chicago: University of Chicago Press.

Freyhofer, H.H. (2004) *The Nuremberg Medical Trial: The Holocaust and the Origin of the Nuremberg Medical Code.* New York: Peter Lang Publishing.

Frith, K., Shaw, P. and Cheng, H. (2005) The construction of beauty: a cross-cultural analysis of women's magazine advertising, *Journal of Communication*, 55(1): 56–70.

Gallivan, J. (1994) Subjectivity and the psychology of gender: Q as a feminist methodology, in J. Gallivan, S.D. Crozier and V.M. Lalande (eds), *Women, Girls, and Achievement*. Toronto: Captus University Publications.

George, A.L. and Bennett, A. (2004) *Case Studies and Theory Development in the Social Sciences*. Cambridge, Massachusetts: The MIT Press.

Geuss, R. (1971) *The Idea of a Critical Theory*. Cambridge: Cambridge University Press.

Gimlin, D. (2000) Cosmetic surgery: beauty as commodity, *Qualitative Sociology*, 23(1): 77–98.

Glaser, B.G. and Strauss, A.L. (1967) *The Discovery of Grounded Theory*. Chicago: Aldine.

Gould, S.J. (1981/1996) *The Mismeasure of Man*. New York: Norton.

Gray, F.D. (2002) *The Tuskegee Syphilis Study: The Real Story and Beyond*. Montgomery, AL: NewSouth Inc.

Greenberg, D.S. (2001) *Science, Money and Politics: Political Triumph and Ethical Erosion*. Chicago: University of Chicago Press.

Greenberg, D.S. (2007) *Science for Sale: The Perils, Rewards, and Delusions of Campus Capitalism*. Chicago: University of Chicago Press.

Guba, E.G. and Lincoln, Y.S. (1989) *Fourth Generation Evaluation*. Newbury Park, CA: Sage.

Habermas, J. (1984) *The Theory of Communicative Action*. Boston: Beacon Press.

Hayles, N.K. (1995) Searching for common ground, in M.E. Soulé and G. Lease (eds), *Reinventing Nature? Responses to Postmodern Deconstruction*, 47–63. Washington, DC: Island Press.

Heine, B. (1985) The mountain people: some notes on the Ik of north-eastern Uganda, *Africa: Journal of the International African Institute*, 55(1): 3–16.

Hesse-Biber, S.N. and Leavy, P.L. (2006) *Emergent Methods in Social Research*. Thousand Oaks, CA: Sage Publications.

Hinton, W.L. and Levkoff, S. (1999) Constructing Alzheimer's: narratives of lost identities, confusion and loneliness in old age. *Culture, Medicine, and Psychiatry*, 23: 453–75.

Hodgson, L.G. and Cutler, S. (1997) Anticipatory dementia and well-being, *American Journal of Alzheimer's Disease and Other Dementias*, 12(2): 62–6.

Humphreys, L. (1975) *Tearoom Trade: Impersonal Sex in Public Places*. Chicago: Aldine.

International Sociological Association (2001) *Code of Ethics*. (http://www.isa-sociology.org/about/isa_code_of_ethics.htm).

Jacobs, J. (1974) *Fun City: An Ethnographic Study of a Retirement Community*. New York: Holt, Rinehart and Winston.

Kalof, L. (1993) Dilemmas of femininity: gender and the social construction of sexual imagery, *The Sociological Quarterly*, 34(4): 639–51.

Kalof, L. (1999) The effects of gender and music video imagery on sexual attitudes, *The Journal of Social Psychology*, 139(3): 378–85.

King, G., Keohane, R.O. and Verba, S. (1994) *Designing Social Inquiry: Scientific Inference in Qualitative Research*. Princeton NJ: Princeton University Press.

King, G. (1997) *A Solution to the Ecological Inference Problem. Reconstructing Individual Behavior from Aggregate Data*. Princeton, NJ: Princeton University Press.

Kitzinger, C. (1986) Introducing and developing Q as a feminist methodology: a study of accounts of lesbianism, in S. Wilkinson (eds), *Feminist Social Psychology: Developing Theory and Practice*. Philadelphia: Open University Press.

Koegel, P., Burman, M.A. and Morton, S.C. (1996) Enumerating homeless people. *Evaluation Review*, 20: 378–403.

Krimsky, S. (2003) *Science in the Private Interest: Has the Lure of Profits Corrupted Biomedical Research?* Lanham: Rowman & Littlefield Publishers.

Krueger, R.A. (1988) *Focus Groups: A Practical Guide for Applied Research*. London: Sage.

Kulik, L. (2007) Equality in the division of household labor: a comparative study of Jewish women and Arab Muslim women in Israel, *The Journal of Social Psychology*, 147(4): 423–40.

Latkin, C., Mandell, W., Oziemkowska, M., Celentano, D., Vlahov, D., Ensminger, M. and Knowlton, A. (1995) Using social network analysis to study patterns of drug use among urban drug users at high risk for HIV/AIDS, *Drug and Alcohol Dependence*, 38(1): 1–9.

Latour, B. Prologue. (http://www.ensmp.fr/~latour/articles/article/090.html).

Lévi-Strauss, C. (1966) *The Savage Mind*. London: Weidenfeld & Nicolson.

Lincoln, Y.S. and Guba, E.G. (1985) *Naturalistic Inquiry*. Newbury Park, CA: Sage.

Linders, A. (2004) Victory and beyond: a historical comparative analysis of the outcomes of the abortion movements in Sweden and the United States, *Sociological Forum*, 19(3): 371–404.

Linstone, H.A. and Turoff, M. (1975) *The Delphi Method. Techniques and Applications*. Reading, MA: Addison-Wesley Publishing Co, Inc.

Lofland, L.H. (1972) Self management in public settings: Parts I and II, *Urban Life*, 1: 93–108, 217–31.

MacDonald, C.J. (1974) The contribution of the Tuskegee Study to medical knowledge, *Journal of the National Medical Association*, 66(1): 1–7.

Mangione, T.W. (1995) *Mail Surveys. Improving the Quality*. Thousand Oaks, CA: Sage Publications.

Mangione, T.W. (1998) Mail survey, in L. Bickman and D. Rog (eds), *Handbook of Applied Social Research Methods*. Thousand Oaks, CA: Sage Publications.

Marcum, C.D. (2007) Interpreting the intentions of Internet predators: an examination of online predatory behavior. *Journal of Child Sexual Abuse*, 16(4: 99–114.

Martínez, A., Dimitriadis, Y., Rubia, B., Gómez, E. and de la Fuente, P. (2003) Combining qualitative evaluation and social network analysis for the study of classroom social interactions, *Computers & Education*, 41(4): 353–68.

Marx, K. (1867/1999) *Das Kapital* [Gateway editions (English translation)]. Washington DC: Regnery Publishing, Inc.

Mason, J. (1998) *Qualitative Researching*. London: Sage Publications.

McCarthy, T. and Hoy, D. (1994) *Critical Theory*. London: Basil Blackwell.

McGarva, A.R., Ramsey, M. and Shear, S.A. (2006) Effects of driver cell-phone use on driver aggression, *The Journal of Social Psychology*, 146(2): 133–46.

McLaughlin, P. (1996) Resource mobilization and density dependence in cooperative purchasing associations in Saskatchewan, Canada, *Rural Sociology*, 61(2): 326–48.

McMillan, S., Duska, R., Hamilton, R. and Casey, D. (2006) The ethical dilemma of research and development openness versus secrecy, *Journal of Business Ethics*, 65(3): 279–85.

Menne, H.L., Kinney, J.M., and Morhardt, D.J. (2002) 'Trying to continue to do as much as they can do.' Theoretical insights regarding continuity and meaning making in the face of dementia, *Dementia*, 1(3): 367–82.

Miles, M.B. and Huberman, A.M. (1994) *Qualitative Data Analysis: An Expanded Sourcebook*, 2nd edn. Thousand Oaks, CA: Sage.

Mooney, C. (2007) *Storm World: Hurricanes, Politics and the Battle over Global Warming*. New York: Harcourt.

Morgan, D.L. (1997) *Focus Groups as Qualitative Research*, 2nd edn. London: Sage.

Newburger, E.C. (2001) Home computers and Internet use in the United States: August 2000 *Current Population Reports* (September). Washington, DC: US Census Bureau.

Ogburn, W.F. and Goltra, I. (1919) How women vote, *Political Science Quarterly*, 34(3): 413–33.

Oliver, M. (1988) The urban black community as network: toward a social network perspective, *Sociological Quarterly*, 29: 623–45.

Osgood, C.E., Suci, G.J. and Tannenbaum, P.H. (1957) *The Measurement of Meaning*. Champaign: University of Illinois Press.

Paul, R. and Elder, L. (2006) *The Miniature Guide to Critical Thinking Concepts and Tools* (http://www.criticalthinking.org/files/Concepts_ Tools.pdf).

Persico, J.E. (1995) *Nuremberg: Infamy on Trial*. London: Penguin Books.

Popovich, K. and Popovich, M. (2000) Use of Q methodology for hospital strategic planning: a case study, *Journal of Healthcare Management*, 45(6): 405–14.

Radloff, L.S. (1977) The CES-D scale: a self-report depression scale for research in the general population, *Applied Psychological Measurement*, 1: 385–401.

Ragin, C. and Becker, H.S. (eds) (1992) *What is a Case? Exploring the Foundations of Social Inquiry*. Cambridge: Cambridge University Press.

Richardson, L. (1992) The consequences of poetic representation. Writing the other, rewriting the self, in C. Ellis and M.G. Flaherty (eds), *Investigating Subjectivity: Research on Lived Experience*. Newbury Park, CA: Sage.

Richardson, L. (1994) Writing: a method of inquiry, in Y. Lincoln and N. Denzin (eds), *Handbook of Qualitative Research*. Thousand Oaks, CA: Sage.

Robyn, R. (2000) A methodological approach to national identity in Europe, *Politique Europeenne*, 1: 84–107.

Rosa, E. (1998) Metatheoretical foundations for post-normal risk, *Journal of Risk Research*, 1: 15–44.

Rossi, P.H., Wright, J.D., Fisher G.A. and Willis, G. (1987) The urban homeless: estimating composition and size, *Science*, 235: 1336–41.

Rothenberg, R.B., Potterat, J.J., Woodhouse, D.E., Muth, S.Q., Darrow, W.W. and Klovdahl, A.S. (1998) Social network dynamics and HIV transmission, *AIDS*, 12(12): 1529–36.

Roudi-Fahimi, F. and Moghadam, V. (2003) *Empowering Women, Developing Society: Female Education in the Middle East and North Africa*. Washington, DC: Population Reference Bureau.

Scarce, R. (2005) *Contempt of Court: A Scholar's Battle for Free Speech from Behind Bars*, Crossroads in Qualitative Inquiry, vol. 6. Walnut Creek: CA: AltaMira Press.

Shrader-Frechette, K. (1991) *Risk and Rationality: Philosophical Foundations*. Berkeley and Los Angeles: University of California Press.

Spencer, S.J., Steele, C.M. and Quinn, D.M. (1999) Stereotype threat and women's math performance, *Journal of Experimental Social Psychology*, 35: 4–28.

Staller, K.M. (2003) Constructing the runaway youth problem: boy adventurers to girl prostitutes, 1960–1978, *Journal of Communication*, 53(2): 330–46.

Stark, R. and Bainbridge, W.S. (1980) Networks of faith: interpersonal bonds and recruitment to cults and sects, *American Journal of Sociology*, 85: 1376–95.

Stenner, P. and Rogers, R.S. (1998) Jealousy as a manifold of divergent understandings: a Q methodological investigation, *European Journal of Social Psychology*, 28: 71–94.

Stern, P.C., and Fineberg, H. (eds) (1996) *Understanding Risk: Informing Decisions in a Democratic Society*. Washington, DC: National Academy Press.

Strauss, A. (1987) *Qualitative Analysis for Social Scientists*. New York: Cambridge University Press.

Strauss, A. and Corbin, J. (1990) *Basics of Qualitative Research: Grounded Theory Procedures and Techniques*. London: Sage.

Tashakkori, A. and Teddlie, C. (eds) (2003) *Handbook of Mixed Methods in the Social and Behavioral Science*. Thousand Oaks, CA: Sage.

Thomson, W. (1891) *Popular Lectures and Addresses, Volume 1: Constitution of Matter*. London and New York: Macmillan and Company.

Trials of War Criminals before the Nuremberg Military Tribunals under Control Council Law No. 10. Nuremberg, October 1946–April 1949. Washington, DC: US GPO, 1949–1953. (http://www.ushmm.org/research/doctors/Nuremberg_Code.htm).

Turnbull, C.M. (1972) *The Mountain People*. New York: Simon & Schuster, Inc.

Uebel, T. (2006) Vienna Circle. *The Stanford Encyclopedia of Philosophy*. (http://plato.stanford.edu/entries/vienna-circle/).

UNAIDS/WHO (2004) *India. Epidemiological Fact Sheets on HIV/AIDS and Sexually Transmitted Infections*. Report available at: http://www.unaids.org/en/geographical+area/by+country/india.asp

Uniform Crime Reports (2006) *Table 4: Crime in the United States by Region, Geographic Division, and State, 2004–2005*. Downloaded from: http://www.fbi.gov/ucr/05cius/offenses/standard_links/state.html United States. *Sociological Quarterly*, 29: 371–90.

US Census Bureau. Tables of state statistics. (http://www.census.gov/compendia/statab/).

Vinitzky-Seroussi, V. (2000) 'My God, What am I gonna say?' Class reunions as social control, *Qualitative Sociology*, 23: 57–75.

Walker, A.J. (1996) Couples watching television: gender, power, and the remote control, *Journal of Marriage and the Family*, 58(4): 813–23.

Webler, T. and Tuler, S. (2001) Public participation in watershed management planning: views on process from people in the field? *Human Ecology Review*, 8(2): 29–39.

Wiggershaus, R. (1994) *The Frankfurt School*. Cambridge, MA: MIT Press.

Wilska, T.A. (2003) Mobile phone use as part of young people's consumption styles, *Journal of Consumer Policy*, 26: 441–63.

Yodanis, C.L. (2000) Constructing gender and occupational segregation: a study of women and work in fishing communities, *Qualitative Sociology*, 23(3): 267–90.

Index